Prentice Hall

LITERATURE

PENGUIN EDITION

Unit Four Resources

Grade Eight

PEARSON

Upper Saddle River, New Jersey
Boston, Massachusetts
Chandler, Arizona
Glenview, Illinois

BQ Tunes Credits
Keith London, Defined Mind, Inc., Executive Producer
Mike Pandolfo, Wonderful, Producer
All songs mixed and mastered by Mike Pandolfo, Wonderful
Vlad Gutkovich, Wonderful, Assistant Engineer
Recorded November 2007 – February 2008 in SoHo, New York City, at Wonderful, 594 Broadway

ISBN–13: 978-0-13-366446-1
ISBN–10: 0-13-366446-5

PEARSON

3 4 5 6 7 8 9 10 12 11 10 09

CONTENTS

For information about the Unit Resources, assessing fluency, and teaching with BQ Tunes, see the opening pages of your Unit One Resources.

Before You Speak, performed by The Dave Pittenger Band

Something said that's **meaningful** always has importance for those who hear
Express ideas to make them clear maybe they'll **benefit** and help
A friend was down, her **experience** was a frightful incident
She **informed** me of her latest scare and told me how it all went down

Please don't misunderstand don't get the wrong idea
What I'm about to say is **relevant**—I know you can relate

She told me the significance, the importance of what she'd done wrong
I thought about my response the feedback I'd like to share
But everyone is different the beauty of the world is **individuality**
So what is true for some of us might not be **valid** for the rest

The things you've read and heard in the media are wrong
Life isn't always so bad
We all make mistakes
We've all done something wrong

I know our bond is strong
The connection will last in spite of what you've done
The secret is knowing what to say
By thinking before you speak

Explain it in a way that's clear, that's **sensory**—you can almost see and touch and feel it
The way we live, our cultural responsibility is to help those around us
Ooo, sometimes our words reprove and sometimes they console and sometimes they forgive
The secret is knowing what to say by thinking before you speak

---

Song Title: **Before You Speak**
Artist / Performed by The Dave Pittenger Band
Vocals & Guitar: Dave Pittenger
Bass Guitar: Jon Price
Drums: Josh Dion
Lyrics by Dave Pittenger
Music composed by Dave Pittenger
Produced by Mike Pandolfo, Wonderful
Executive Producer: Keith London, Defined Mind

Name ____________________ Date ____________

Unit 4: Poetry
Big Question Vocabulary—1

The Big Question: What is the secret to reaching someone with words?

Thematic Vocabulary

benefit: *n.* an advantage, an improvement, or a type of help that something offers
v. to offer an advantage, an improvement, or a type of help; other forms: *beneficial, beneficiary*

cultural: *adj.* belonging or relating to a particular society and its way of life; other form: *culture*

feedback: *n.* advice, praise, or criticism about how successful or useful something is

meaningful: *adj.* serious, important, useful, and valuable; other forms: *mean, meaning*

misunderstand: *v.* to understand someone or something incorrectly; other forms: *understand, misunderstanding*

A. DIRECTIONS: *Write the Thematic Vocabulary word that best completes each group of related words.*

1. comment, observation, ____________________
2. ethnic, traditional, ____________________
3. worthwhile, significant, ____________________
4. confuse, mistake, ____________________
5. aid, asset, ____________________

B. DIRECTIONS: *Complete each sentence by writing the correct Thematic Vocabulary word on the line.*

1. It is a ____________________ tradition to celebrate the Fourth of July in the United States.
2. Was the television program ____________________, or was it silly?
3. The teacher was careful to give each student helpful ____________________ regarding their reports.
4. Daily exercise will definitely ____________________ your health.
5. Listen carefully so that you don't ____________________ the directions.

Name ______________________________ Date ______________

Unit 4 Poetry
Big Question Vocabulary—2

The Big Question: What is the secret to reaching someone with words?

Thematic Vocabulary

connection: *n.* a joining together based on common thoughts or interests; other forms: *connect, connecting, connected*

experience: *n.* the act of living through an event

v. to be involved in an event; other forms: *experiencing, experienced*

express: *v.* to use actions or words to share thoughts and feelings; other forms: *expression, expressing, expressed*

relevant: *adj.* related directly to the subject being discussed; other form: *relevance*

sensory: *adj.* related to or affecting any of the five senses; other forms: *sense, sensing*

Gail's grandmother's birthday was coming up, and Gail wanted to write a poem for her. She asked some friends for advice.

DIRECTIONS: *Use the words and phrases in parentheses to write the dialogue she had with her friends. Use what you have learned about poetry and sensory details.*

Please help me. **(express, connection)**

Gail

(relevant, experience)

Hannah

(sensory details)

Maria

Name ______________________________ Date ______________

Unit 4 Poetry
Big Question Vocabulary—3

The Big Question: What is the secret to reaching someone with words?

Thematic Vocabulary

individuality: *n.* the sum of personal traits that makes a person unique; other form: *individual*

inform: *v.* to tell, share, or teach facts related to a subject; other forms: *information, informed*

media: *n.* institutions or items that present news and other information, such as newspapers, magazines, television programs, and Internet sources; other form: *medium*

significance: *n.* the meaning or importance of something; other forms: *significant, significantly*

valid: *adj.* believable and reasonable; other forms: *validity, validation*

DIRECTIONS: *For each Thematic Vocabulary word, list three items as instructed. Then, use the vocabulary word in a sentence about one of the things or reasons.*

> **Example:** List three *sensory* details about pizza.
>
> spicy smell   red and yellow color   hot from the oven
>
> **Sentence:** *I love the spicy smell of a pizza cooking in the oven.*

1. List three specific forms of the *media*.

   ______________ ______________ ______________

   Sentence: ______________________________

2. List three things about you that show your *individuality*.

   ______________ ______________ ______________

   Sentence: ______________________________

3. List three *valid* facts about the state in which you live.

   ______________ ______________ ______________

   Sentence: ______________________________

4. List three facts that illustrate the *significance* of good nutrition.

   ______________ ______________ ______________

   Sentence: ______________________________

5. List three facts that you would use to *inform* someone about one of your hobbies or interests.

   ______________ ______________ ______________

   Sentence: ______________________________

Name ______________________________ Date ______________

Unit 4: Poetry
Applying the Big Question

What is the secret to reaching someone with words?

DIRECTIONS: *Complete the chart below to apply what you have learned about the secret to reaching others with words. One row has been completed for you.*

Example	Type of communication	Goal of writer or speaker	Effect on reader or listener	How the goal was achieved
From Literature	Poem "Cat!" by Eleanor Farjeon	Share experience of her stubborn cat in an entertaining way	I could see and hear the cat and its owner throughout the action	Alliteration, onomatopoeia, rhyme, choppy rhythm
From Literature				
From Science				
From Social Studies				
From Real Life				

Name ______________________ Starting Date ____________ Ending Date ____________

Unit 4: Poetry Skills Concept Map—1

What is the secret to reaching someone with words?

Words you can use to discuss the Big Question

____
____
____
____
____
____
____
____

Literary Analysis: Poetry

Basic Elements of Poetry

- Sensory Language
- Figurative Language
- Sound Devices

Forms of Poetry

- Lyric
- Narrative
- Ballads
- Free Verse
- Haiku
- Rhyming Couplets
- Limericks

Poetry has **sound devices** (demonstrated in this selection) Selection name:

and **figurative language** (demonstrated in this selection) Selection name:

Reading Skills and Strategies: Context

You can **understand context** by **previewing the lines of verse to identify unfamiliar words** (demonstrated in this selection) Selection name:

and by rereading and reading ahead (demonstrated in this selection) Selection name:

Comparing Literary Works: Imagery (demonstrated in these selections)

Selection names:

1.

2.

is poetic language that uses words that appeal to **sight, hearing, touch** / **taste, smell**

Informational Text: Recipe (demonstrated in this selection) Selection name:

Note the different types of information in consumer texts by **comparing and contrasting features of consumer materials**

Student Log

Complete this chart to track your assignments.

Writing	**Extend Your Learning**	**Writing Workshop**	**Other Assignments**

Vocabulary Warm-up Word Lists

Study these words from the poetry of Jacqueline Woodson. Then, apply your knowledge to the activities that follow.

Word List A

awhile [uh WYL] *adv.* for a short time
I stayed awhile at the library, reading the newspapers.

dabbing [DAB ing] *v.* gently touching something, usually with a cloth
Dad kept dabbing his chin where he cut himself shaving.

grins [GRINZ] *v.* smiles with a very big smile
The toddler next door always grins and waves when she sees me.

regular [REG yuh luhr] *adj.* usual; not different or special
On a regular school day, not during exams, I have about two hours of homework to do.

squints [SKWINTS] *v.* looks at something with eyes partly closed
The boat captain squints into the sun as he steers us toward the dock.

upstate [UHP stayt] *adv.* in or toward the northern part of a state
The winter weather is quite cold upstate, but the summers are balmy.

Word List B

lava [LAH vuh] *n.* hot melted rock
In the pictures I have seen, lava looks like a boiling, red river.

maple [MAY puhl] *n.* a hardwood tree in northern areas that has sweet sap
Every year we get sap from the maple in our yard and make syrup.

moment [MOH muhnt] *n.* a particular point in time
My sixteenth birthday was an important moment in my life.

preacher [PREECH er] *n.* Minister; one who speaks about religion
A preacher prepares a sermon for the weekly service.

superheroes [SOO puhr heer ohz] *n.* fictional characters with super powers
As a child, I liked the superheroes who could fly through the air.

volcano [vahl KAY noh] *n.* a mountain that can erupt lava, rocks, gas, and ash
Some scientists get very close to a volcano even when it is active.

Name ______________________________ Date ______________

Poetry by Jacqueline Woodson

Vocabulary Warm-up Exercises

Exercise A *Fill in each blank in the paragraph below with an appropriate word from Word List A. Use each word only once.*

My grandmother lives [1] ________________, alone on a big farm. Last year, I got to ride the bus up there by myself. It was a long trip! I would read [2] ________________, then sleep, then listen to music. A few times I looked around at the other passengers. One man seemed sad, and he kept [3] ________________ his eyes with a tissue. I spotted plenty of young people and older folks, too. A few riders were dressed in strange outfits, but most of them wore [4] ________________ clothes. Have you ever noticed how sometimes a person our parents' age [5] ________________ while reading? Does closing your eyes part way really help you to see better? Anyway, my grandmother always [6] ________________ when she sees me. When I finally got off that bus, I don't know whose smile was bigger!

Exercise B *Revise the sentences so the underlined vocabulary words are used in logical ways. Be sure to keep each vocabulary word in your revisions.*

1. When lava and ash shoot out of a volcano, tourists are urged to get very close to take good pictures of the unusual sight.

   ____

2. Planting a maple in the front yard of a house in south Florida is a wise choice.

   ____

3. The preacher addresses his congregation each Sunday to talk about fire prevention.

   ____

4. When creating superheroes, the artists try to make them seem just like ordinary people.

   ____

5. The most amazing moment of the year was the month of July when I went to camp.

   ____

Name ______________________________ Date ______________

Poetry by Jacqueline Woodson

Reading Warm-up A

Read the following passage. Pay special attention to the underlined words. Then, read it again, and complete the activities. Use a separate sheet of paper for your written answers.

When life gets too hectic, it is soothing simply to enjoy nature. This is true for young people and adults alike. We all have many stresses during our regular, everyday lives. School, work, relationships, and responsibilities can sometimes weigh heavily on all of us. Taking awhile away from it all and, for a brief time, enjoying the beauty of nature can be very helpful.

Whether you are upstate among the lakes and mountains of the northern country, or farther south, or closer to a city, natural wonders are everywhere. Even a small park in the middle of town can be home to many plants and animals. If you are nowhere near a park of any kind, just look up at the sky! Clouds and their endless shapes are fun to watch during the day. Stars are lovely to see twinkling at night. In between are the amazing "light shows" of sunrise and sunset! Imagine how an artist squints at his painting, peering as he reaches for the perfect shading; the morning and evening skies seem to achieve this harmony with no effort at all.

Many people find that shifting their focus away from their worries and on to something bigger—like the natural world—can help to turn frowns into smiles, and even grins. This can happen more quickly than they might expect. Someone who might have been sadly dabbing a tear away might suddenly feel peaceful. Sometimes it is good to remind ourselves that we are only a very small part of a big world.

A hike on a shady woodland trail can be inspirational. The view of the nighttime sky from a city rooftop can be awe-inspiring. Even the sights right outside our windows can surprise us sometimes. Nature's gifts are everywhere.

1. Circle the word that means the same as regular. What is your ***regular*** morning routine?
2. Underline the words that describe what awhile is. Tell about something that you did ***awhile*** today or yesterday.
3. Circle the words that describe the opposite of upstate. Tell what ***upstate*** means.
4. Circle the word that is the opposite of grins. Then, underline the word that means the same as ***grins***.
5. Underline the words naming what someone might be dabbing. What else might someone be ***dabbing***?
6. Underline the word that tells what squints means. When someone ***squints***, what are they doing?

Name ______________________ Date ____________

Poetry by Jacqueline Woodson

Reading Warm-up B

Read the following passage. Pay special attention to the underlined words. Then, read it again, and complete the activities. Use a separate sheet of paper for your written answers.

When Tonya heard her family was moving to Hawaii, it was the most confusing day of her life. On one hand, she thought about how incredible it would be to live on a beach in one of the most beautiful places on earth. On the other hand, she could hardly stand to leave her friends in Chicago. That would the most horrible moment of her life. She blinked back the tears as she stared into the only backyard she had ever known. Her favorite climbing tree, the maple, was like an old friend, too. You could not climb a palm tree, could you?

Tonya's little brothers did not have mixed feelings because for them moving to Hawaii was an exciting new adventure. Her ten-year-old brother sounded like the family preacher when he said, over and over, "It is gonna be paradise!" Tonya's eight-year-old brother, who was currently very interested in seeing a real volcano, could not believe his good luck in going to an island where he might actually see lava flowing.

In the face of so much confidence about the move, Tonya fled to her room with her seesawing emotions. She wished she were eight or ten years old instead of thirteen. Back then, she still believed in superheroes, fairy-tale endings, and the ease of change. Now, practically a grown-up, she knew a move across the ocean to a strange place would not be magically easy. How would she make friends when she could not even surf? Wasn't that a requirement in Hawaii?

Tonya felt like throwing herself on the bed and crying. Then, she remembered that she was thirteen, practically a grown-up, and she should choose a more mature course of action. She took a deep breath, picked up the phone, and called her best friend Julia to discuss the news.

1. According to the passage, what would be the most horrible moment for Tonya? Explain what a *moment* is.
2. Underline the words giving more information about the maple. Then, describe a *maple* in your own words.
3. Circle the words identifying the person who sounded like a preacher. Then, explain why a *preacher* might talk about paradise.
4. Underline the words in the sentence that name the place where a volcano and lava can be seen. Then, write a sentence that explains the meanings of both *volcano* and *lava*.
5. Circle the words naming two other things Tonya believed in besides superheroes. Then, write a description of one of your favorite *superheroes*.

Name ______________________________ Date ______________

Jacqueline Woodson
Listening and Viewing

Segment 1: Meet Jacqueline Woodson

- How did Jacqueline Woodson's fascination with the "power of words" spark her interest in writing? Jacqueline Woodson tries to keep her writing "real and honest." What do you think that phrase means, and why is "real and honest" important?

____

____

____

____

Segment 2: Poetry

- Why does Jacqueline Woodson believe that the white space surrounding a poem on its page is important? How do you think poetry can give readers "room for free space" in their lives?

____

____

____

____

Segment 3: The Writing Process

- Why does Jacqueline Woodson call her writing "character driven"? Which one of Jacqueline Woodson's writing strategies would you use and why?

____

____

____

____

Segment 4: The Rewards of Writing

- In what way is writing rewarding to Jacqueline Woodson? Jacqueline Woodson thinks a writer must be brave and should welcome any reaction to his or her work. Do you agree or disagree with her? Why?

____

____

____

____

Name ______________________ Date ______________

Learning About Poetry

Poets put words together to create a musical quality and highly charged meaning. A poem combines verbal music and meaning to create a fresh outlook on a subject.

Figurative language is imaginative writing or speech that is not meant to be taken literally. Here are some common figures of speech:

- A **simile** uses a word such as *like* or *as* to compare two apparently unlike things: *Her eyes were like beacons of light.*
- A **metaphor** compares two apparently unlike things but does not use *like* or *as: The grass was a carpet of green.*
- **Personification** gives human qualities to nonhuman or inanimate things: *The waves danced in glee.*

Poets use **images**—descriptive, sensory language appealing to the senses: sight, sound, touch, taste, and smell. Poets also use various sound devices:

- **Rhyme** is the repetition of sounds at the ends of words.
- **Meter** is the rhythmical pattern—or the arrangement and number of stressed and unstressed syllables—in a poem.
- **Alliteration** is the repetition of consonant sounds in the beginning of words, as in *fearsome foe.*
- **Assonance** is the repetition of similar vowel sounds in stressed syllables that end in different consonant sounds, as in *made* and *rail.*
- **Consonance** is the repetition of final consonant sounds after different vowel sounds in stressed syllables, as in *lend* and *hand.*
- **Onomatopoeia** is the use of words that imitate sounds, as in *rap, swish,* and *flutter.*
- **Repetition** is the use of any element of language—a sound, word, phrase, clause, or sentence—more than once.

DIRECTIONS: *Circle the letter of the answer that best matches each numbered item.*

1. comparison using *like* or *as*
   A. metaphor B. personification C. simile
2. *the snow kissed her nose.*
   A. assonance B. personification C. limerick
3. sensory language
   A. consonance B. imagery C. alliteration
4. pattern of stressed and unstressed syllables
   A. free verse B. meter C. consonance
5. a line of poetry that says, "Their words are trumpet blasts."
   A. simile B. metaphor C. personification
6. *buzz, clink, toll, hiss*
   A. personification B. assonance C. onomatopoeia

Name ______________________________ Date ______________

The Poetry of Jacqueline Woodson

Model Selection: Poetry

Two basic elements of poetry are sound and meaning. Poets use **sound devices**—such as rhyme, meter, alliteration, assonance, and onomatopoeia—to create musical effects with words. Poets use **figurative language**—such as simile, metaphor, and personification—to go beyond the ordinary meanings of words to express ideas or feelings in a striking way. Meaning also becomes vivid and memorable when it is conveyed through **imagery,** or words appealing to the senses: sight, sound, smell, taste, and touch.

Directions: *Read the following passages from "Describe Somebody" and "Almost a Summer Sky." Then, use the space below each passage to answer the questions.*

I wrote, Ms. Marcus is tall and a little bit skinny. (from "Describe Somebody")

1. Name two sound effects in the preceding line. Which words are involved in each sound effect?

____

Eric's voice was like something
that didn't seem like it should belong
to Eric.
Seemed like it should be coming out of an angel. (from "Describe Somebody")

2. What figure of speech do the preceding lines contain? What is being compared with what?

____

____

You know what I love about trees, Rodney says.
It's like . . . It's like their leaves are hands reaching
out to you. Saying Come on over here, Brother.
Let me just . . . Let me just . . .
Rodney looks down at me and grins.
Let me just give you some shade for a while. (from "Almost a Summer Sky")

3. What figure of speech is most prominent in the preceding passage?

____

4. In the second line of the preceding passage from "Almost a Summer Sky," which two words create the sound effect called assonance? Which words create alliteration?

____

Name ______________________________ Date ______________

The Poetry of Jacqueline Woodson

Open-Book Test

Short Answer *Write your responses to the questions in this section on the lines provided.*

1. Poets often use sensory language in their work. How can sensory language make a poem more vivid?

2. A poet might use a word such as *popped, crackled, clanged,* or *murmured.* What is this kind of sound device called, and what does it do?

3. Similes and metaphors are both types of figurative language. How are they alike? How are they different?

4. There are several different forms of poetry. How would you define free verse in terms of its meter and rhyme?

5. The speaker talks about Eric in "Describe Somebody." What would you say his attitude is toward Eric? Explain using details from the poem.

6. In "Describe Somebody," the speaker says that Eric's voice "Seemed like it should be coming out of an angel." What figure of speech is used in this line? Explain.

Name ______________________ Date ______________

7. In "Almost a Summer Sky," Ms. Marcus tells the speaker that he has "a poet's heart." How does the speaker feel about this comment? Support your answer with details from the poem.

____

____

____

8. In "Almost a Summer Sky," the speaker talks about his foster family. What is his overall feeling about being part of this family? Explain your answer using details from the poem.

____

____

____

____

9. The poet uses figurative language when Rodney says about trees, "It's like their leaves are hands reaching/out to you. Saying Come on over here, Brother." What kind of figurative language is she using? Explain your answer using details from the poem.

____

____

____

____

10. "Describe Somebody" and "Almost a Summer Sky" have several similarities. Explain two of these similarities.

____

____

____

Essay

Write an extended response to the question of your choice or to the question or questions your teacher assigns you.

11. In both "Describe Somebody" and "Almost a Summer Sky," the speaker is a boy named Lonnie. In an essay, describe Lonnie in your own words. Then, state whether you would like to know him personally, and explain why or why not. Support your response with examples from the poems.

Name ______________________ Date ______________

12. Select one of the poems—"Describe Somebody" or "Almost a Summer Sky"—and explain why it can be classified as a lyric poem. Then, for the poem you have selected, give at least two examples of its figurative language, sensory language, or sound devices. Use the organizer to gather examples for your essay.

Poem:		
Figurative Language	Sensory Language	Sound Devices

13. In "Describe Somebody" and "Almost a Summer Sky," Jacqueline Woodson uses details to create a certain mood, or feeling. Choose one of the poems. In an essay, identify three details that you think help create the poem's mood. Finally, discuss how the details and the mood help communicate the poem's central message.

14. **Thinking About the Big Question: What is the secret to reaching someone with words?** In the poems "Describe Somebody" and "Almost a Summer Sky," Lonnie realizes that words can reach people powerfully. Choose one of the poems and explain what Lonnie learns about reaching someone with words. Use details from the poem to support your response.

Oral Response

15. Go back to question 7, 9, or 10 or to the question your teacher assigns you. Take a few minutes to expand your answer and prepare an oral response. Find additional details in "Describe Somebody" and "Almost a Summer Sky" that will support your points. If necessary, make notes to guide your response.

Name ______________________________ Date ______________

The Poetry of Jacqueline Woodson

Selection Test A

Learning About Poetry *Identify the letter of the choice that best answers the question.*

____ 1. Which word or phrase best explains what an *image* in poetry is?
A. sensory language
B. musical sound effect
C. repetition
D. simile

____ 2. Which of the following types of poetry tells a story?
A. lyric
B. haiku
C. couplet
D. narrative

____ 3. What is the name for poetry with no regular meter, no intentional rhyme, and no fixed line length?
A. lyric
B. ballad
C. free verse
D. haiku

____ 4. What is the general term for the words *popped, crackled, clanged,* and *murmured*?
A. alliteration
B. assonance
C. consonance
D. onomatopoeia

____ 5. What is the term for a figure of speech that uses *like* or *as* to compare two apparently unlike things?
A. metaphor
B. personification
C. couplet
D. simile

Critical Reading

____ 6. Who is Ms. Marcus in "Describe Somebody"?
A. the speaker's foster mother
B. Eric's mother
C. Angel's sister
D. the teacher

Name ______________________ Date ____________

___ 7. Who has talent in science, according to the speaker in "Describe Somebody"?
A. Eric
B. Lamont
C. Angel
D. Miss Edna

___ 8. What can you conclude about Eric from the speaker's description of him in "Describe Somebody"?
A. Eric's singing had very little impact on the listeners.
B. Eric had chosen a piece that was too difficult for him.
C. Eric fears being teased for singing in a church choir.
D. Eric was preparing to resign from the choir.

___ 9. In the final lines of "Describe Somebody," why does the speaker say, "Now I gotta write a whole new poem"?
A. His first draft doesn't rhyme, but it should.
B. He knows that Ms. Marcus will not like his first draft.
C. He knows not to tell classmates about Eric's singing and choir robe.
D. He feels he hasn't praised Eric enough.

___ 10. In "Describe Somebody," what makes Miss Edna dab at her eyes during Eric's solo?
A. She is upset that he is ruining a favorite song of hers.
B. She is emotionally moved by the beauty of his voice.
C. She wishes Lonnie had gotten the solo part.
D. She is reacting to the preacher's earlier sermon.

___ 11. In "Almost a Summer Sky," what detail about life upstate made the biggest impression on Rodney?
A. the constant rain
B. the farm animals
C. the trees
D. the late-night whistle of a train

___ 12. Which of the following describes the relationship between Rodney and Lonnie in "Almost a Summer Sky"?
A. foster brothers
B. classmates
C. distant acquaintances
D. uncle and nephew

Name ______________________________ Date ______________

____ 13. Name the figure of speech in the following lines from "Almost a Summer Sky."

No, upstate they got maple and catalpa and scotch pine,
all kinds of trees just standing.
Hundred-year-old trees big as three men.

What figure of speech do these lines contain?

A. metaphor
B. simile
C. personification
D. alliteration

____ 14. In "Almost a Summer Sky," what does the speaker say he "can't even imagine"?

A. how big the trees are upstate
B. why Rodney keeps talking about the trees
C. moving away and living anywhere else but home
D. why Ms. Marcus told him he had a poet's heart

____ 15. The *tone* of a poem is the author's attitude toward the characters, the subject matter, or the audience. Which of the following best describes the tone in "Almost a Summer Sky"?

A. hostile
B. sad
C. affectionate
D. indifferent

Essay

16. In both "Describe Somebody" and "Almost a Summer Sky," the speaker is Lonnie C. Motion. In an essay, first describe Lonnie in your own words. Then, state whether or not you would like to know him personally, and explain why.

17. The *theme* of a literary work is its central insight or overall message about human life or behavior. Authors sometimes state the theme of their works directly. More often, however, they invite readers to find clues in the work in order to figure out the theme themselves. In an essay, state what you think is the overall message of either "Describe Somebody" or "Almost a Summer Sky." Then, support your conclusion about the theme by mentioning specific details from the poem.

18. **Thinking About the Big Question: What is the secret to reaching someone with words?** In the poems "Describe Somebody" and "Almost a Summer Sky," Lonnie realizes that words can reach people in a powerful way. Choose one of the poems, and then write a brief essay about what Lonnie learns about reaching someone with words. Use details from the poem to support your response.

Name ______________________________ Date ______________

The Poetry of Jacqueline Woodson

Selection Test B

Learning About Poetry *Identify the letter of the choice that best completes the statement or answers the question.*

____ 1. Which of the following poetic devices describes one thing as if it were something else but does not use *like* or *as*?
- A. simile
- B. metaphor
- C. onomatopoeia
- D. assonance

____ 2. In a poem, the rhythmical pattern, or the arrangement and number of stressed and unstressed syllables, is known as
- A. consonance.
- B. personification.
- C. symbolism.
- D. meter.

____ 3. Sensory language in a poem creates
- A. repetitions.
- B. rhymes.
- C. images.
- D. lyrics.

____ 4. The words *sizzle, hiss,* and *clink* are examples of
- A. alliteration.
- B. assonance.
- C. onomatopoeia.
- D. consonance.

____ 5. The type of poetry that expresses the thoughts and feelings of a single speaker in musical verse is called
- A. narrative.
- B. dramatic.
- C. ballad.
- D. lyric.

____ 6. How many lines does a haiku contain?
- A. 3
- B. 5
- C. 7
- D. 17

____ 7. Humorous five-line poems with a specific rhythmical pattern and rhyme scheme are called
- A. lyrics.
- B. sonnets.
- C. ballads.
- D. limericks.

Name ______________________________ Date ______________

Critical Reading

____ 8. In "Describe Somebody," what is it about Ms. Marcus that makes the speaker "feel all good inside"?
A. her pretty clothes
B. her smile
C. her promptness
D. the high grades she gives the speaker

____ 9. In "Describe Somebody," Angel and Lamont are good at
A. reading and math.
B. science and drawing.
C. history and civics.
D. music and art.

____ 10. In "Describe Somebody," the speaker has an unexpected insight about Eric
A. on the football field.
B. at a concert.
C. in a church.
D. at a meeting of the debate club.

____ 11. What figure of speech does the poet use in the following lines from "Describe Somebody"?

Eric's voice was like something
that didn't seem like it should belong
to Eric.
Seemed like it should be coming out of an angel.

A. simile
B. metaphor
C. personification
D. onomatopoeia

____ 12. Which of the following words or phrases best expresses the speaker's attitude toward Eric in "Describe Somebody"?
A. admiring but a little fearful
B. mocking
C. indifferent
D. critical but compassionate

____ 13. Based on the portrayal of Eric in "Describe Somebody," why do you think Eric gives the speaker a "mean look"?
A. Eric has always disliked the speaker.
B. Eric will be embarrassed if the speaker tells the class that Eric sings in the choir.
C. Eric is coming down with the flu and feels uncomfortable.
D. Eric feels that the speaker is making fun of him.

____ 14. In "Almost a Summer Sky," where are Rodney and the speaker going?
A. to the grocery store
B. to the movies
C. to a park
D. upstate

Name ______________________________ Date ______________

____ 15. Based on his words in "Almost a Summer Sky," what can you conclude about Rodney?
A. He is bored living in the city.
B. He has a deep love and appreciation for nature.
C. He is not doing well in school.
D. He often becomes impatient with Lonnie, the poem's speaker.

____ 16. What poetic device appears in the following lines from "Almost a Summer Sky"?

You know what I love about trees, Rodney says.
It's like . . . It's like their leaves are hands reaching
out for you. Saying Come on over here, Brother.

A. rhyme
B. personification
C. consonance
D. all the above

____ 17. In "Almost a Summer Sky," why does the speaker mention Miss Edna's Sunday cooking and Lily's pretty dresses and great big smile?
A. to show that he is a keen observer
B. to stress how happy he is at home with his foster family
C. to suggest that Rodney was wrong to live upstate
D. to prove to Ms. Marcus that he has the heart of a poet

____ 18. Which statement about "Describe Someone" and "Almost a Summer Sky" is true?
A. They have the same speaker.
B. They are both written in free verse.
C. Ms. Marcus is a character in both poems.
D. all of the above

Essay

19. In "Describe Somebody" and "Almost a Summer Sky," Jacqueline Woodson uses many details to create a vivid picture of Lonnie and his surroundings. In an essay, select one of the poems, and identify three details that you think are especially important in that poem. Then, tell what kind of atmosphere, or mood, those details contribute to. Finally, discuss how the details and the atmosphere suggest the theme of the poem, or its central insight or message.

20. Select one of the poems—"Describe Somebody" or "Almost a Summer Sky"—and tell why it can be described as a lyric poem. Then, for the poem you have selected, go on to give an example of its figurative language, images, or repetition.

21. **Thinking About the Big Question: What is the secret to reaching someone with words?** In the poems "Describe Somebody" and "Almost a Summer Sky," Lonnie realizes that words can reach people powerfully. Choose one of the poems, and then explain what Lonnie learns about reaching someone with words. Use details from the poem to support your response.

Vocabulary Warm-up Word Lists

Study these words from the poetry of Eleanor Farjeon, Walter de la Mare, and Georgia Douglas Johnson. Then, complete the activities that follow.

Word List A

gleam [GLEEM] *v.* shine
I like how our wood floors gleam after we clean them.

horizon [huh RY zuhn] *n.* where the land or water seems to meet the sky
Watching the sun sink beneath the horizon is a wondrous sight.

peers [PEERZ] *v.* looks hard at something as if to see it more clearly
Jerry peers down the country road, waiting for a car to come.

scampering [SKAM per ing] *n.* running with short, quick steps
I saw the puppy scampering away with my shoe in its mouth.

scatter [SKAT er] *v.* to toss around here and there
The strong wind will surely scatter the leaves that I raked into a pile.

throbbed [THRAHBD] *v.* beat quickly; pulsed
My heart throbbed with excitement before my first plane ride.

Word List B

battered [BAT erd] *v.* hit something over and over
Ancient warriors battered castle gates with huge logs to get through them.

casements [KAYS muhnts] *n.* window frames built so the windows swing outward
We opened the casements wide, so a breeze could come in the windows.

immensity [i MEN si tee] *n.* hugeness or vastness
I was shocked at the immensity of the trees in the redwood forest.

slithery [SLITH er ee] *adj.* slippery
Misty loved watching the slithery eels in the huge tank.

thatch [THACH] *n.* dried straw used to make roofs
I would guess that insects live in the thatch on those old houses.

uttermost [UH ter mohst] *adj.* farthest away; outermost
I wonder how old the stars are at the uttermost parts of our galaxy.

Name ______________________________ Date ______________

Poetry Collection: Eleanor Farjeon, Walter de la Mare, Georgia Douglas Johnson

Vocabulary Warm-up Exercises

Exercise A *Fill in each blank in the paragraph below with an appropriate word from Word List A. Use each word only once.*

I stand at the front of the boat, watching the sun [1] ____________ and sparkle on the waves. As far as I can see, all the way to the [2] ____________, there is nothing but the sea. Standing beside me, my little brother [3] ____________ into the water. He wants to see a dolphin. I remember when I was his age and saw a whale emerge from the ocean. My whole body had [4] ____________ with excitement. My yells of joy had sent everyone [5] ____________ as fast as they could up the deck toward me. Now, years later, I hope my brother can see a whale, too. Suddenly, just ahead, a giant form seems to [6] ____________ the waves everywhere as it shoots up toward the sky. "A whale!" my brother and I scream.

Exercise B *Answer the questions with complete explanations.*

1. How do casements make windows different from those that move up and down?
____
____

2. Would you rather sleep on a mattress of thatch or one of cotton?
____
____

3. In which state, besides Hawaii, might you find a U.S. city at the uttermost point from a city in Alaska?
____
____

4. What would be happening if the ocean battered the rocky areas along the coast?
____
____

5. What do you think a small child might see as having immensity?
____
____

6. What, besides an animal, would you describe as slithery?
____
____

Name ______________________________ Date ______________

Poetry Collection: Eleanor Farjeon, Walter de la Mare, Georgia Douglas Johnson

Reading Warm-up A

Read the following passage. Pay special attention to the underlined words. Then, read it again, and complete the activities. Use a separate sheet of paper for your written answers.

As the sun sinks slowly over the horizon each evening, darkness creeps across the land. For many animals, this hour is the time to wake up and become active. As you prepare for bed, these nighttime creatures are just awakening.

In a forest setting, as a person peers into the growing gloom and hustles home before nightfall, small animals like the raccoon begin scampering around. These animals are starting their nightly search for food. Red foxes, mule deer, and badgers join the raccoons on the prowl. However, all are as silent as possible. Some do not want to be heard by those they hunt. Others are quiet to protect themselves from animals that hunt them.

The peacefulness of the night is rarely disturbed by loud animal sounds. If forest animals do make noise, they usually are raising an alarm. Perhaps an enemy or a fire has been sighted.

Up in the sky, the moon begins to gleam. Then, you can spot other creatures of the night. Bats whir along, black as death. A barn owl swoops gracefully through the night air, its white face shining. Its dive toward the ground will scatter all small animals aware of the owl's presence. They are afraid of becoming the mighty bird's evening meal.

If you are lucky, you might also catch sight of a flying squirrel one night. Its cousin, the tree squirrel, whose body throbbed with activity and excitement all day, peacefully sleeps the night away in a snug nest. The flying squirrel, on the other hand, soars through the trees until morning. Always on the go, it watches the action above and below its path.

So, as you drift off into the land of dreams tonight, imagine creatures large and small roaming the night. If you listen very carefully, maybe you'll hear the quiet whoosh of a flying squirrel or the soft patter of a fox.

1. Underline the words that tell what happens at the horizon each evening. Then, explain what the ***horizon*** is.
2. Circle the words naming where a person in the forest peers. Then, explain why the word ***peers*** is a good word to use in describing this action.
3. Underline the words that tell what a person does while the small animals begin scampering. Then, explain what ***scampering*** means.
4. Circle the word naming what begins to gleam. Then, describe something else that might ***gleam*** at night.
5. Underline the sentence telling why the owl will scatter small animals. Then, explain what ***scatter*** means.
6. Circle the words telling with what the tree squirrel's body throbbed all day. Then, explain what ***throbbed*** means.

Name ______________________________ Date ______________

Poetry Collection: Eleanor Farjeon, Walter de la Mare, Georgia Douglas Johnson

Reading Warm-up B

Read the following passage. Pay special attention to the underlined words. Then, read it again, and complete the activities. Use a separate sheet of paper for your written answers.

Since earliest times, long before thatch covered the tops of makeshift shelters, people have looked at the sky and dreamed of soaring above the world. Every night across our planet, casements are thrown open so people can lean out and look up at the heavens. As we wish upon stars, we wonder if we might ever reach them.

Each year, a few highly trained people get to move beyond these dreams to soar through the skies. Unafraid of the immensity of the universe, these people explore space. The first person to travel in space was the Soviet cosmonaut Yuri Gagarin. On April 12, 1961, his rocket shot into space. It traveled once around Earth and then returned home. On July 20, 1969, American astronaut Neil Armstrong became the first person to stand on ground in a place other than Earth. On that day, he walked on the moon. Since then, many astronauts have traveled to space and back aboard space shuttles. Others have lived in space for months in a space station.

Space flight is not always a comfortable experience. Astronauts have to learn to move around in a weightless state. They hold onto lines, using twisting movements to avoid one another and all of the equipment. The bottoms of their shoes and the floor of the space vehicle are made of fabric that sticks together, which also helps the astronauts move around. Slithery surfaces would be a disaster for these space travelers.

Many astronauts suffer from space sickness during the first few days of flight. Whether the trip is smooth or the vehicle is battered by forces in space, astronauts might experience headaches, nausea, and heavy sweating.

Despite these and other uncomfortable parts of space flight, each trip is unforgettable. Astronauts describe the beauty of space and the amazing views of Earth from far away. As humans continue to explore the uttermost limits of our universe, people will always want to be part of the great adventure.

1. Underline the words describing where thatch was found. Then, explain what ***thatch*** is.
2. Circle the words naming the action that is taken with casements. Then, without using the word ***casements***, rewrite the sentence in your own words.
3. Underline the name of something that has immensity. Then, explain why some people might be afraid of this ***immensity***.
4. Circle the words in the previous sentence that are the opposite of slithery. Then, explain why ***slithery*** surfaces would be a disaster.
5. Circle the word that describes the opposite of a battered flight. Then, name some forces in space that might have ***battered*** space vehicles or stations.
6. Circle the word that tells what has uttermost limits. Explain why humans want to explore the ***uttermost*** limits.

Name ______________________________ Date ______________

Poetry Collection: Eleanor Farjeon, Walter de la Mare, Georgia Douglas Johnson

Writing About the Big Question

THE BIG ?

What is the secret to reaching someone with words?

Big Question Vocabulary

benefit	connection	cultural	experience	express
feedback	individuality	inform	meaningful	media
misunderstand	relevant	sensory	significance	valid

A. *Use one or more words from the list above to complete each sentence.*

1. When Kirsten wrote her summary, she included only ______________ information.
2. Justin hoped that Sarah didn't ______________ his question.
3. To paint a picture with words, poetry uses ______________ details.
4. Jasmine chose to express her ______________ through her writing.
5. Zoe appreciated the ______________ she received from her teacher.

B. *Follow the directions in responding to each of the items below.*

1. Write two sentences describing a personal connection you have formed in the last year.

   ____.

   ____.

2. Write two sentences explaining how to resolve conflicts over cultural differences. Use at least two of the Big Question vocabulary words.

   ____

   ____

C. *Complete the sentence below. Then, write a short paragraph in which you connect this idea to the Big Question.*

Poets use sounds and rhythms to ______________________________

____

____

____

Name ______________________________ Date ______________

Poetry Collection: Eleanor Farjeon, Walter de la Mare, Georgia Douglas Johnson

Reading: Preview to Determine Meanings From Context

Poetry often contains unusual words with which you may not be familiar. When you read a poem, it is a good idea to **preview** it, or examine it in advance, to identify any unfamiliar words. Then, as you read the poem more closely, look for clues in the **context** that can help you determine the meanings of these words. The **context** consists of the other words and phrases that surround a particular word. The following chart shows common types of context clues and an example of each. In the examples, the possibly unfamiliar words are underlined, and the context clues are in italics.

Clue	**Synonym/Definition:** words that mean the same as the unfamiliar word
Example	Knowing the importance of *exercise*, she does calisthenics every day.
Clue	**Antonym/Contrast:** words that mean the opposite of the unfamiliar word
Example	She does calisthenics every day, *but her brother is a couch potato.*
Clue	**Explanation:** words that give more information about the unfamiliar word
Example	Calisthenics *can improve your muscle tone and breathing.*
Clue	**Example:** a word or words that illustrate the unfamiliar word
Example	Calisthenics include *pushups and situps.*
Clue	**Sentence Role:** structural clue that indicates the unfamiliar word's part of speech
Example	Joanna *does* calisthenics every morning. [clearly a noun; seems to be an activity]

DIRECTIONS: *Answer these questions about words in the three poems in this collection.*

1. What synonym later in the poem shows the meaning of *git* in line 11 of "Cat!"? ______

____

2. A. In lines 26–27 of "Cat!" what does the context suggest that a *sycamore* is?

____

B. What other word is a clue to the meaning of *sycamore*? ______________

____

3. In line 3 of "Silver," what synonym shows the meaning of *peers*? ______________

____

4. In lines 5–6 of "Your World," what words give an explanation of *horizon*? ______

____

5. A. Looking at the role of *reaches* in line 11, what part of speech is it? __________

____

B. From the context, what do you think *reaches* means here? ______________

____

Name ______________________________ Date ______________

Poetry Collection: Eleanor Farjeon, Walter de la Mare, Georgia Douglas Johnson

Literary Analysis: Sound Devices

Poets often use **sound devices** to make their poems more musical and memorable. Four of the most popular sound devices are rhythm, rhyme, alliteration, and onomatopoeia.

- **Rhythm** is the pattern of strong and weak beats, as in TWINkle TWINkle LITtle STAR.
- **Rhyme** is the repetition of sounds at the ends of words, as in *star* and *far.*
- **Alliteration** is the repetition of consonant sounds at the beginnings of nearby words, as in *twinkle* and *twist.*
- **Onomatopoeia** is the use of words that imitate sounds, such as *bang* and *sizzle.*

DIRECTIONS: *As you read the three poems in this collection, record on this chart examples of rhythm, rhyme, alliteration, and onomatopoeia.*

Poem	Rhythm	Rhyme	Alliteration	Onomatopoeia
"Cat!"				
"Silver"				
"Your World"				

Name ______________________________ Date ______________

Poetry Collection: Eleanor Farjeon, Walter de la Mare, Georgia Douglas Johnson

Vocabulary Builder

Word List

flatterer horizon immensity kennel rapture reeds scampering

A. Directions: *Using your knowledge of the underlined Word List words, circle* T *if the statement is true or* F *if the statement is false.*

T / F 1. Someone experiencing rapture is probably frowning.

T / F 2. A flatterer always tells the truth.

T / F 3. Dogs may be housed in a kennel.

T / F 4. You might find reeds along the banks of a pond.

T / F 5. An elephant is likely to be seen scampering through the savannah.

T / F 6. The immensity of a task can be overwhelming.

T / F 7. The sun appears to set on the horizon.

B. Directions: *Answer each question with a sentence that uses one of the Word List words. Use each Word List word only once.*

1. What sort of person lavishly praises someone else?

____

____

2. Where might you keep your pet?

____

____

3. How might a person who is feeling absolutely wonderful describe his or her state?

____

____

C. Word Study: *The prefix* im- *means "not." Use the context of the sentences and what you know about the Latin prefix* im- *to explain your answer to each question.*

1. Would talking with your mouth full be consider *improper*? Explain.

____

____

2. How would an *impatient* person likely act?

____

____

Name ______________________________ Date ______________

Poetry Collection: Eleanor Farjeon, Walter de la Mare, Georgia Douglas Johnson

Enrichment: Phases of the Moon

The light of the moon seen from Earth is the reflected light of the sun. The amount of light depends on the moon's position in relation to the sun and Earth. The different stages in the moon's appearance are called the **phases** of the moon. The moon goes through its phases every 29.5 days, or in just about one month.

The phases start with a **new moon,** when the moon is between the sun and Earth. The side facing Earth is completely dark. As the moon moves in its orbit, a thin curve becomes visible, called a **crescent moon.** When the moon reaches the point where it is at right angles to Earth and the sun, people call it a **half moon** because half the surface we think of as the moon is visible. As the moon grows bigger, it is called a **gibbous moon.** Finally, halfway through its cycle, it reaches the phase called the **full moon,** when Earth is between the moon and the sun, and the entire side of the moon facing Earth is lighted. The phases then move in reverse. During the period when the moon seems to become larger, it is said to be **waxing.** During the period when it seems to become smaller, it is said to be **waning.**

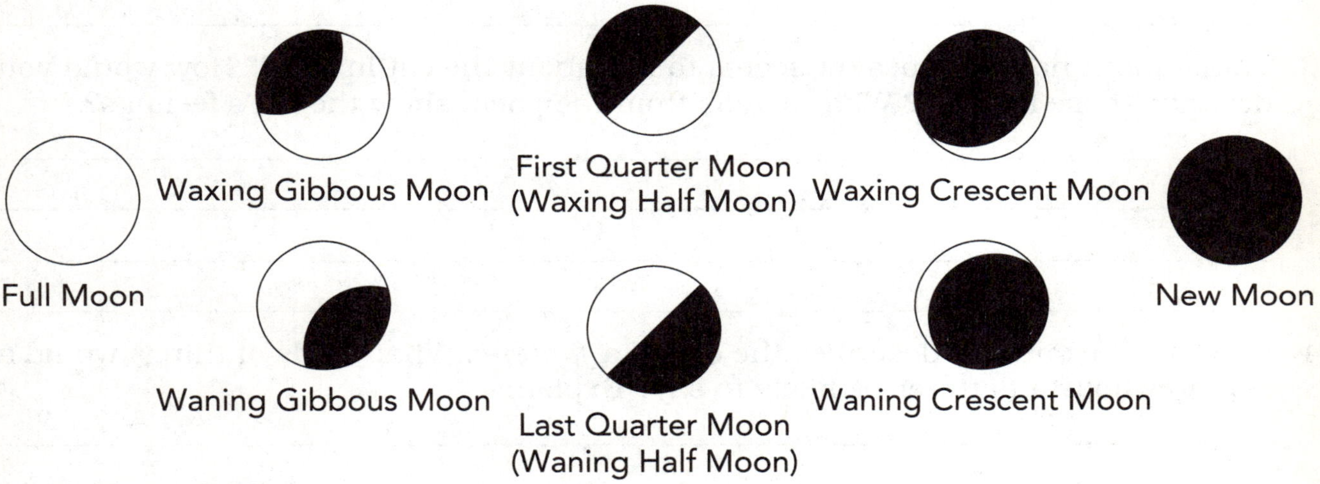

DIRECTIONS: *Answer these questions based on what you have read.*

1. The word *month* has the same origins as the word *moon*. Explain the relationship.

   ____

2. Before the use of electricity, why do you think people who had to travel at night preferred to do so during a full moon? ______________________________

   ____

3. Before the use of electricity, during what phase of the moon did criminals most often commit their nighttime crimes? Why? ______________________________

   ____

4. The verbs *wax* and *wane* can describe situations not related to the moon. Explain what they mean. Then, use *wane* in a sentence that is not about the moon. ______

   ____

Name ______________________________ Date ______________

Poetry Collection: Eleanor Farjeon, Walter de la Mare, Georgia Douglas Johnson

Open-Book Test

Short Answer *Write your responses to the questions in this section on the lines provided.*

1. *Onomatopoeia* is words that imitate sounds. In "Cat!" the word *scritching* is a made-up onomatopoeic word. What sound does *scritching* imitate? Explain.

____

____

____

2. Rhythm is the pattern of strong and weak beats in a poem. How do the very short lines in "Cat!" affect the poem's rhythm?

____

____

____

____

3. Think about how the speaker seems to feel about the cat in "Cat!" How would you describe those feelings? What details from the poem show the cat's feelings?

____

____

____

____

4. In "Cat!" the speaker describes the cat as a *flatterer.* What kinds of things would a person who is a flatterer be likely to say? Explain.

____

____

____

____

5. In "Silver," the poet writes that the moon "peers, and sees/Silver fruit upon silver trees." What does *peers* mean in this line? What other word helps you guess the meaning of *peers*?

____

____

____

____

Name ______________________ Date ______________

6. In "Silver," the moon "walks the night in her silver shoon." What word from this line helps you figure out the meaning of the word *shoon*? How does this word help?

7. Walter de la Mare uses the word *silver* many times in his poem "Silver." Why does he repeat this word so often?

8. Think about the first line in "Your World." How do words such as "distant horizon" and "immensity" expand on the meaning of that first line?

9. Rhyme is the repetition of sounds at the ends of words. In "Your World," which lines end in rhyming words? Include the rhyming words in your answer.

10. Under each sound device listed at the top, supply an example and tell which poem it is from—"Cat!" "Silver," or "Your World." After you have completed the chart, choose one example and tell what effect it has on the reader.

	Onomatopoeia	**Alliteration**	**Rhyme**
Example			
Poem			

Name ______________________ Date ______________

Essay

Write an extended response to the question of your choice or to the question or questions your teacher assigns you.

11. Which of the three poems—"Cat!" "Silver," or "Your World"—do you think is the most musical? State your opinion in a short essay. Then, support your opinion with at least two examples of the poem's sound devices, such as rhythm, rhyme, onomatopoeia, and alliteration.

12. In a brief essay, describe the feeling created in the poem "Silver." Explain how the poem's details, including its sound devices, help create this feeling.

13. Think about the worldview expressed in the poem "Your World." In an essay, restate that view in your own words. Be sure to cite examples from the poem to support your general statement about it. Then, explain whether or not you agree with the poem's observations, and why.

14. **Thinking About the Big Question: What is the secret to reaching someone with words?** In "Cat!" "Silver," and "Your World," the poets use words to create images for the reader. Which poem touched you most with its use of words? Give examples of the words the poet used to reach out to readers.

Oral Response

15. Go back to question 3, 4, 7, or 8 or to the question your teacher assigns you. Take a few minutes to expand your answer and prepare an oral response. Find additional details in "Cat!" "Silver," or "Your World" that will support your points. If necessary, make notes to guide your response.

Name ______________________ Date ______________

Poetry Collection: Eleanor Farjeon, Walter de la Mare, Georgia Douglas Johnson

Selection Test A

Critical Reading *Identify the letter of the choice that best answers the question.*

____ **1.** What seems to be happening in the poem "Cat!"?

A. The speaker is chasing a cat.
B. The speaker is feeding a cat.
C. The speaker is petting a cat.
D. The speaker is looking for a lost cat.

____ **2.** Which of these words from "Cat!" is an example of onomatopoeia?

A. ark
B. wuff
C. cat
D. green

____ **3.** Which statement best expresses the speaker's feelings about the cat in "Cat!"?

A. The speaker loves it.
B. The speaker admires its beauty.
C. The speaker dislikes it and wants to drive it off.
D. The speaker is afraid of it and does not like to go near it.

____ **4.** What does the word *git* mean in the context of these lines from "Cat!"?

Git her, git her,
Whiskery spitter!
Catch her, catch her,
Green-eyed scratcher!

A. catch
B. scram
C. scratch
D. a small insect

____ **5.** What does the poem "Silver" describe?

A. the many stars in the nighttime sky
B. a dark evening in a city
C. an eerie, dead landscape
D. a scene slowly lit up by moonlight

Name ______________________ Date ______________

___ 6. Which words in this line from "Silver" are an example of alliteration?

This way, and that, she peers, and sees

A. *this* and *way*

B. *this* and *that*

C. *peers* and *sees*

D. none of the above

___ 7. In these lines from "Silver," what synonym for *peers* points to the word's meaning?

This way, and that, she peers, and sees
Silver fruit upon silver trees.

A. way

B. sees

C. silver

D. trees

___ 8. Which word does the poet repeat most often in "Silver"?

A. slowly

B. silently

C. silver

D. moon

___ 9. What does the speaker in "Your World" compare herself to?

A. a world

B. a bird

C. a rope

D. a song

___ 10. According to the speaker in "Your World," how big is a person's world?

A. as big as he or she makes it

B. not as big as he or she thinks

C. as big as time will allow

D. as big as a star

___ 11. What does the word *horizon* mean in the context of these lines from "Your World"?

But I sighted the distant horizon
Where the sky-line encircled the sea

A. a ship

B. the imaginary circle around the center of Earth

C. the line where the sky seems to meet the land or sea

D. the sound of ringing bells

Name ______________________ Date ______________

___ 12. Of "Cat!" "Silver," and "Your World," which poems use a regular pattern of rhyme at the ends of lines?

A. "Cat!" and "Silver"

B. "Silver" and "Your World"

C. "Your World" and "Cat!"

D. all three poems

___ 13. Which phrase from "Your World" best illustrates alliteration?

A. narrowest nest

B. close to my side

C. distant horizon

D. this immensity

Vocabulary and Grammar

___ 14. What kind of subject complement is used in this sentence?

That cat is a green-eyed little monster.

A. predicate noun

B. predicate pronoun

C. predicate adjective

D. There is no subject complement.

___ 15. Which word is most nearly *opposite* in meaning to the word *rapture*?

A. joy

B. opening

C. silence

D. depression

Essay

16. Write a short essay in which you explain what is happening in "Cat!" Tell what the speaker and the cat are doing and how the speaker feels about the cat.

17. Which of the three poems—"Cat!" "Silver," or "Your World"—do you think is the most musical? State your opinion in a short essay. Then, support your opinion with at least two examples of the poem's sound devices, such as rhythm, rhyme, onomatopoeia, and alliteration.

18. **Thinking About the Big Question: What is the secret to reaching someone with words?** In "Cat!", "Silver," and "Your World," the poets use words to create images for the reader. In an essay, explain which poem touched you most with its use of words. Give examples of the words the poet used to reach out to readers.

Name ______________________________ Date ______________

Poetry Collection: Eleanor Farjeon, Walter de la Mare, Georgia Douglas Johnson

Selection Test B

Critical Reading *Identify the letter of the choice that best completes the statement or answers the question.*

____ 1. In "Cat!" how does the speaker seem to feel about the cat?
- A. pleased
- B. annoyed
- C. affectionate
- D. sad

____ 2. Which word best describes the cat in "Cat!"?
- A. lazy
- B. cuddly
- C. spooky
- D. fast

____ 3. In these lines from "Cat!" what sound does the made-up onomatopoeic word *scritching* try to imitate?

Scritching the bark
Of the sycamore tree,

- A. the sound of scratching
- B. the sound of barking
- C. the sound of chewing
- D. the sound of weeping

____ 4. Which statement best describes the rhythm in "Cat!"?
- A. The short rhythmic lines capture the sound of the running animals.
- B. The even-numbered lines all have fewer beats than the odd-numbered lines.
- C. Every line opens with a stressed syllable followed by an unstressed syllable.
- D. all of the above

____ 5. Which phrase best describes the mood of the scene in "Silver"?
- A. magical and peaceful
- B. tense and scary
- C. dark and depressing
- D. beautiful but sad

____ 6. Based on the context, what does *shoon* mean in these lines from "Silver"?

Slowly, silently, now the moon
Walks the night in her silver shoon.

- A. hat
- B. shoes
- C. moonlight
- D. night

Name ________________________________ Date ________________

____ 7. Which sound is repeated most often at the start of words in "Silver"?
A. the *s* sound
B. the *k* sound
C. the *l* sound
D. the *th* sound

____ 8. How many strong beats occur in the following line from "Silver"?

Slowly, silently, now the moon

A. one
B. two
C. three
D. four

____ 9. What change in herself does the speaker in "Your World" describe?
A. She was once bold and daring, but now she is less confident.
B. She was once like a child, but now she is more mature.
C. She once lived a narrow life, but in time she grew more adventurous.
D. She once was more worldly, but now she has become more spiritual.

____ 10. What does the context suggest that *abide* means in these lines from "Your World"?

I know, for I used to abide
In the narrowest nest in a corner

A. obey
B. welcome
C. conceal
D. remain

____ 11. Based on the following line, how many strong beats are there in each line of "Your World"?

Your world is as big as you make it

A. one
B. two
C. three
D. four

____ 12. Based on the following lines, which statement most accurately describes the rhyme pattern in "Your World"?

1 Your world is as big as you make it
2 I know, for I used to abide
3 In the narrowest nest in a corner
4 My wings pressing close to my side

A. The last words in each pair of lines rhyme.
B. The last words in lines 1 and 3 rhyme, as do the last words in lines 2 and 4.
C. The last words in lines 2 and 4 rhyme, but the last words in lines 1 and 3 do not.
D. There is no rhyme pattern in "Your World."

Name ______________________________ Date ______________

____ 13. Which poem in this collection makes the most frequent use of onomatopoeia?
A. "Cat!"
B. "Silver"
C. "Your World"
D. none of the above

Vocabulary and Grammar

____ 14. Where would you most likely find a *kennel?*
A. in a movie theater
B. in a hospital
C. in the attic of a house
D. in someone's backyard

____ 15. Which sentence uses the underlined vocabulary word correctly?
A. The <u>rapture</u> sang several songs on his latest album.
B. The gift boxes were covered in bright <u>rapture</u> and ribbons.
C. Staying up all night studying for a test is <u>rapture.</u>
D. The team was in <u>rapture</u> after winning the county finals.

____ 16. Which sentence contains a predicate adjective as subject complement?
A. The moon shone brightly.
B. The moon becomes more lovely on a clear night.
C. The moonlight is a beautiful beacon.
D. all of the above

____ 17. Which sentence correctly uses a subject pronoun as a subject complement?
A. The winners were Nancy and I.
B. The last visitors were Jack and me.
C. She looks like my sister and I.
D. Her older brother became her mentor.

Essay

18. Write an essay about the mood, or atmosphere, in the poem "Silver." Explain how the poem's details, including its sound devices, help create that mood.

19. Write an essay about the worldview expressed in "Your World." First, restate that view in your own words. Be sure to cite examples from the poem to support your general statement about it. Then, react to the worldview, telling whether or not you agree with the poem's observations, and why.

20. **Thinking About the Big Question: What is the secret to reaching someone with words?** In "Cat!", "Silver," and "Your World," the poets use words to create images for the reader. Which poem touched you most with its use of words? Give examples of the words the poet used to reach out to readers.

Vocabulary Warm-up Word Lists

Study these words from the poetry of Eve Merriam; Nikki Giovanni; and Alfred, Lord Tennyson. Then, complete the activities that follow.

Word List A

ancient [AYN shuhnt] *adj.* from times long ago
The Olympic Games began in ancient Greece.

captured [KAP cherd] *v.* taken by force
When enemy troops are captured, they must be treated decently.

foul [FOWL] *adj.* horrible
Why do shoes always have such a foul smell when they get wet?

funeral [FYOO ner uhl] *adj.* having to do with a ceremony held after a person has died
The funeral flowers brought beauty to a sad day.

interior [in TEER ee uhr] *adj.* inside; of a person's private self
My diary told about the thoughts and feelings of my interior world.

triumph [TRY uhmf] *n.* a feeling of joy because of success
Our triumph at finally winning the state spelling bee was huge.

Word List B

atom [AT uhm] *n.* the smallest part of a simple substance
An atom is the building block of every element in nature.

imprint [im PRINT] *v.* to fix in the mind or memory for a long time
I wish I could imprint that song in my brain forever.

mournful [MAWRN fuhl] *adj.* filled with deep sadness
I will never forget the mournful cry of our cat when she lost her kitten.

signature [SIG nuh cher] *n.* one's name written in one's own handwriting
The bank will double-check the signature on a large check.

slander [SLAN der] *n.* bad and untrue things said about someone
People have taken others to court for slander.

whorls [HWURLZ] *n.* the circular ridges on the pads of your fingers
When I saw my fingerprint next to yours, I could see the difference in the whorls.

Name ______________________________ Date ______________

Poetry Collection: Eve Merriam; Nikki Giovanni; Alfred, Lord Tennyson

Vocabulary Warm-up Exercises

Exercise A *Fill in each blank in the paragraph below with an appropriate word from Word List A. Use each word only once.*

Since [1] ______________ times, people have had special ways to celebrate the lives of those who die. In addition to holding fancy [2] ______________ services, people have built great structures to honor the dead. The best examples are the pyramids of Egypt. If a pharaoh [3] ______________ enemies or gained great wealth, for example, paintings and statues tell the story. They show the [4] ______________ the rulers felt after such victories. The Egyptians even figured out how to avoid the [5] ______________ odor of a dead body. If only we could know the [6] ______________ minds of these brilliant people! The way they preserved the bodies is amazing! Looking at the mummies, you almost believe that the world of the pharaohs is still alive.

Exercise B *Answer the questions with complete explanations.*

1. What do your <u>signature</u> and the <u>whorls</u> on your fingertips have in common?

   ____

   ____

2. What would be required to see an <u>atom</u>?

   ____

   ____

3. What important fact or understanding would you like to <u>imprint</u> on the mind of every human?

   ____

   ____

4. Why do people take others to court for <u>slander</u>?

   ____

   ____

5. What has happened in your life, or in the lives of others, that has made you feel <u>mournful</u>?

   ____

   ____

Name ______________________________ Date ______________

Poetry Collection: Eve Merriam; Nikki Giovanni; Alfred, Lord Tennyson

Reading Warm-up A

Read the following passage. Pay special attention to the underlined words. Then, read it again, and complete the activities. Use a separate sheet of paper for your written answers.

Dr. Martin Luther King, Jr., brought about many important changes in American life. His words and deeds have served as a model for creating change without violence or <u>foul</u> actions. At age thirty-five, King became the youngest person to receive the Nobel Peace Prize. By this time, he had helped many African Americans begin to feel the <u>triumph</u> of gaining equal rights.

How did he do it? King never chose the easy path. Instead, he encouraged peaceful protest. With thousands of followers, he staged boycotts and marches to speak out against injustices in America. King was <u>captured</u> and taken to jail again and again. Yet, despite being taken by force, he continued to encourage peaceful protests.

King traveled more than 6 million miles and spoke some 2,500 times. His words inspired people from all corners of the country to work for social change. This included changes in education and employment opportunities for the poor and the blacks in America. Few have spoken as well and as honestly about the need for equal treatment for all.

King was a brilliant man whose <u>interior</u> life must have been extraordinary. He graduated from high school at fifteen, and received many degrees and awards during his lifetime. King's speeches are among the most famous of modern times. Some have compared his ability to inspire others to that of the greatest speakers of <u>ancient</u> times.

Sadly, King was shot to death at age thirty-nine. This tragic event touched all Americans. Two <u>funeral</u> services were held: one at his home church in Atlanta, and the other at his college. The president of the United States honored King's memory by ordering that all American flags fly at half-mast that day. The entire nation felt the terrible loss of Dr. Martin Luther King, Jr. Each January, a national holiday reminds us of the importance of Dr. King's life.

1. Underline the word that is described by <u>foul</u>. Give an example of ***foul*** behavior prompted by violence.

2. Underline the words that tell what led people to feel <u>triumph</u>. Then, tell about a time when you have had a feeling of ***triumph***.

3. Underline the sentence that tells what resulted in King's being <u>captured</u> and taken to jail. Explain what ***captured*** means.

4. Circle the word describing King's <u>interior</u> life. Then, explain why a very smart person might have an interesting ***interior*** life.

5. Underline the word in the previous sentence that means the opposite of <u>ancient</u>. Give an example of an ***ancient*** time or civilization.

6. Circle the words that tell where the <u>funeral</u> services for King were held. Write a sentence describing one ***funeral*** service for King as you imagine it might have been.

Name ______________________________ Date ______________

Poetry Collection: Eve Merriam; Nikki Giovanni; Alfred, Lord Tennyson

Reading Warm-up B

Read the following passage. Pay special attention to the underlined words. Then, read it again, and complete the activities. Use a separate sheet of paper for your written answers.

Many scientists are working in a new field called biometrics. They are looking for reliable ways to identify individuals. In other words, they want you, and nobody but you, to be able to identify yourself.

The days of a person's signature being proof of identity are gone. Too many people are able to copy the handwriting of others.

More modern approaches to identification look at the human body and things that are unique to each person. These include the whorls on the pads of your fingers, the pattern in the colored part of your eyes, and the structure of your face and palms. Taking fingerprints and then scanning a person's fingers to check for a match is one new way to identify people. Researchers at Michigan State University have created "the ID mouse." It looks like a computer mouse but has a scanner built in to check a person's fingerprints.

Other researchers focus on photography that computers will recognize. Although people often imprint others' faces in their minds, mistaken identity can happen. One person might look a lot like another person. With this new method, a scan of a person's face, eye, or palm must match what is in a computer to prove identity.

Many people are mournful about these new developments. They fear the consequences of too much personal information residing in one place. A new card being tested with airport workers, for example, includes fingerprints, eye scans, palm geometry, and a digital photo. If someone steals and uses this information, the theft of a person's identity would be complete. Imagine accusing the true cardholder of a crime committed by the identity thief! That person could then sue you for slander. All this because of a stolen identity!

Scientists have figured out how to split an atom, but biometrics might be some of the trickiest research ever.

1. Underline the word in the next sentence that gives a clue about the meaning of signature. Then, explain what a ***signature*** is.
2. Underline the words telling where whorls are located. Then, write a sentence using ***whorls***.
3. Circle the words naming what people can imprint in their minds. Then, tell about something you want to ***imprint*** on someone's mind.
4. Underline the words explaining what people are mournful about. Then, rewrite the sentence using a synonym for ***mournful***.
5. Underline the sentence that tells why you might be sued for slander. In your own words, explain why this is ***slander***.
6. Circle the word telling what scientists learned to do to an atom. Based on what you know about an ***atom***, why would this be so difficult?

Name ______________________________ Date ______________

Poetry Collection: Eve Merriam; Nikki Giovanni; Alfred, Lord Tennyson

Writing About the Big Question

What is the secret to reaching someone with words?

Big Question Vocabulary

benefit	connection	cultural	experience	express
feedback	individuality	inform	meaningful	media
misunderstand	relevant	sensory	significance	valid

A. *Use one or more words from the list above to complete each sentence.*

1. The politician wrote a speech to ______________________ his audience about his positions.
2. Amanda wanted a career in print ______________________,—at a newspaper, for example.
3. One ______________________ of written works is that they can be reviewed.
4. Barb had a hard time expressing the personal ______________________ she found in the poem.
5. To form a ______________________ argument, one must base it on facts.

B. *Follow the directions in responding to each of the items below.*

1. Write two sentences using sensory details to describe an object.

   ____.

   ____.

2. Describe the possible results of a misunderstanding. Use at least two of the Big Question vocabulary words.

   ____

   ____

C. *Complete the sentence below. Then, write a short paragraph in which you connect this experience to the big question.*

Poetry and songs touch people in ways that are ______________________

____

____

____

Name ______________________________ Date ______________

Poetry Collection: Eve Merriam; Nikki Giovanni; Alfred, Lord Tennyson

Reading: Preview to Determine Meanings From Context

Context consists of the words and phrases that surround a particular word. When you read a poem, first **preview** it, or examine it in advance, to identify any unfamiliar words. Then, as you read the poem more closely, look for clues in the **context** that can help you determine the meanings of those words. The following list shows common types of context clues and an example of each. In the examples, the possibly unfamiliar words are underlined, and the context clues are in italics.

- **Synonym or Definition:** words that mean the same as the unfamiliar word

  It will soon be time to commence the race, so please get ready to *start.*

  She shopped in a boutique, *a small specialty store.*

- **Antonym or Contrast:** words that mean the opposite of the unfamiliar word or tell what the unfamiliar word is *not*

  The race will commence at 6 o'clock and *end* three hours later.

  Did you buy that in a boutique or in *a large chain store?*

- **Explanation:** words that give more information about an unfamiliar word

  A feline is *any animal of the cat family.*

- **Example:** words that illustrate the unfamiliar word

  Felines include *lions, tigers, and leopards.*

- **Sentence Role:** structural clue that indicates the unfamiliar word's part of speech. For example, in the following sentence, a reader can figure out that a *boutique* is a noun and that it is not abstract, since it can be entered.

  The two friends *entered* the boutique.

DIRECTIONS: *The chart below lists three words from this collection's poems. You may not be certain of their meanings. Use context clues to help you understand the words, and on the chart, write the clues you use and your best guess about each word's meaning. Then, check a dictionary to see if you were right about the meaning.*

Word	***unique***	***kettles***	***slander***
Location	"Thumbprint," line 3	"The Drum," line 4	"Ring Out, Wild Bells," line 22
Context Clues			
Likely Meaning			
Dictionary Meaning			

Name ______________________________ Date ______________

Poetry Collection: Eve Merriam; Nikki Giovanni; Alfred, Lord Tennyson

Literary Analysis: Sound Devices

Poets often use **sound devices** to make their poems more musical and memorable. The chart below shows four of the most popular sound devices.

Sound Device	**Definition**	**Example**
rhythm	the pattern of strong and weak beats	*HICKory DICKory DOCK*
rhyme	the repetition of sounds at the ends of words	*dock* and *clock*
alliteration	the repetition of consonant sounds at the start of nearby words	*clock* and *close*
onomatopoeia	the use of words that imitate sounds	*fizz, bubble*

Directions: *Answer these questions about the sound devices used in the poems in this collection. Include the line numbers of any examples you list.*

1. What are two examples of alliteration in "Thumbprint"? ______________________________

____

2. List two examples of onomatopoeia in "The Drum." Also, explain what sound each example imitates. ______________________________

____

3. List one example of alliteration and one example of onomatopoeia in "Ring Out, Wild Bells." Also, explain what the onomatopoeia imitates. ______________

____

4. Of the three poems in this collection, which one follows a pattern of rhymes at the ends of lines? Describe that pattern. ______________________________

____

5. Focus on the rhythm of "The Drum" as you say the lines to yourself. What rhythm is the poet trying to imitate? ______________________________

____

6. Given the subject, why is it appropriate that "Ring Out, Wild Bells" is such a musical poem? ______________________________

____

Name ______________________ Date ______________

Poetry Collection: Eve Merriam; Nikki Giovanni; Alfred, Lord Tennyson

Vocabulary Builder

Word List

imprint modes resounding singularity spite strife

A. Directions: *Answer each question with a sentence that uses one of the Word List words. Use each Word List word only once.*

1. Was there a lot of misery in the world during the twentieth century?

2. What quality might an independent person display?

3. What sort of music might you hear at a loud concert?

4. How might a person feel toward his enemy?

5. What do publishers use to identify themselves in books?

6. What can you call different ways of doing something, such as learning?

B. Word Study: *The Latin prefix* im- *means "in" or "into." Use the context of the sentences and what you know about the Latin prefix* im- *to explain your answer to each question.*

1. What is something that can be *implanted*?

2. Is someone who is *imperiled* safe? Explain.

Name ______________________________ Date ______________

Poetry Collection: Eve Merriam; Nikki Giovanni; Alfred, Lord Tennyson

Enrichment: Fingerprints

The skin on the tips of our fingers has small ridges that help us grasp and hold on to things. These ridges form a pattern. When we touch something, oils from our skin leave an impression of this pattern on the surface we touch. This impression is called a fingerprint.

"Thumbprint" recognizes something that was not widely known until the late nineteenth century: except for identical twins, no two people's fingerprints are exactly alike. William Herschel, a British official in India in the 1870s, was one of the first to understand this important quality of fingerprints. He collected fingerprints as a hobby and noticed that each person's was a unique pattern. Herschel ended up using fingerprints as a way to identify people.

Eventually, police organizations came to understand the importance of fingerprints in identifying criminals. In 1892, Argentina became the first nation in the world to use fingerprinting as standard police procedure. Soon police forces in Europe and North America began collecting prints left at crime scenes and using them to help identify criminals. Today, the FBI fingerprint file contains millions of prints. All the information is computerized and shared with state and local police agencies across the country. Police use not only fingerprints but also footprints, hairs, fibers, blood, and genetic evidence based on traces of DNA left behind at crime scenes.

A. DIRECTIONS: *Answer these questions based on the information you just read and your own knowledge.*

1. How can the FBI fingerprint file help tie crimes together?

____

2. What kinds of surfaces do you think would probably provide the clearest fingerprints?

____

3. What environmental factors might spoil fingerprints left at crime scenes?

____

4. How might a criminal avoid leaving his or her fingerprints at a crime scene?

____

5. For what purposes other than crime investigation might fingerprints be used?

____

B. DIRECTIONS *In the space below or on a separate sheet of paper, write a description of your own thumbprint or someone else's. Your description can be factual or more imaginative—telling what the pattern reminds you of, for example.*

____

____

____

Name ______________________________ Date ______________

Poetry Collections: Eleanor Farjeon, Walter de la Mare, Georgia Douglas Johnson; Eve Merriam; Nikki Giovanni; Alfred, Lord Tennyson

Integrated Language Skills: Grammar

Subject Complements

A **subject complement** is a word that follows a linking verb and tells something about the subject. One kind of subject complement is called a *predicate adjective*. It describes the subject. Other kinds of subject complements are called a *predicate noun* and a *predicate pronoun*. They further identify the subject. A predicate pronoun uses the subject, not object, form.

Predicate Adjective:	The visitor seems lost. [*Lost* describes the subject, *visitor.*]
Predicate Noun:	He was the best *player* on the team. [*Player* further identifies the subject, *He.*]
Predicate Pronoun:	The winner is *she.* [*She* further identifies the subject, *winner.*]

A. Practice: *Circle the subject complement in each sentence that contains a subject complement. On the line before the sentence, write* PN *if the subject complement is a predicate noun,* PP *if it is a predicate pronoun, and* PA *if it is a predicate adjective. If the sentence does not contain a subject complement, write* none *on the line.*

___ 1. Poems are often very musical.

___ 2. That word is an example of onomatopoeia.

___ 3. The last speaker in the choral reading was I.

___ 4. The rhythm of the poem sounded familiar to me.

___ 5. The bell sounded at the end of English class.

B. Writing Application: *Add to each subject in the items below to build a sentence that includes a linking verb and a subject complement. Include at least one predicate noun, one predicate pronoun, and one predicate adjective in your sentences.*

1. The cat ______________________________
____

2. Martin Luther King, Jr., ______________________________
____

3. The fingerprint ______________________________
____

4. The bravest person ______________________________
____

5. The bells ______________________________
____

Name ______________________ Date ______________

Poetry Collection: Eleanor Farjeon, Walter de la Mare, Georgia Douglas Johnson; Eve Merriam; Nikki Giovanni; Alfred, Lord Tennyson

Integrated Language Skills: Support for Writing a Poem That Uses Rhythm and Sound Devices

Use this chart to jot down your ideas about what to include in your poem.

Title	
Author	
Subject	
Main Idea	
Sound Devices	Rhyme:
	Meter:
	Alliteration:
	Other:

Name ______________________________ Date ______________

Poetry Collection: Eleanor Farjeon, Walter de la Mare, Georgia Douglas Johnson; Eve Merriam; Nikki Giovanni; Alfred, Lord Tennyson

Integrated Language Skills: Support for Extend Your Learning

Listening and Speaking

Use this chart to record details about the sound devices and the mood they create.

Poem Title and Author	
Mood of Poem	
Rhyme	
Rhythm	
Alliteration	
Onomatopoeia	

Name ______________________ Date ______________

Poetry Collection: Eve Merriam; Nikki Giovanni; Alfred, Lord Tennyson

Open-Book Test

Short Answer *Write your responses to the questions in this section on the lines provided.*

1. In "Thumbprint," the speaker says, "Imprint my mark upon the world." What does the word *imprint* mean in this context? How do you know?

2. In "Thumbprint," the speaker compares her thumbprint to her signature. What is similar about the thumbprint and the signature? Support your answer with details from the poem.

3. In this line from "Thumbprint," what does *base* mean? What antonym helps you define it?

   No other, however grand or base,
   Can ever contain the same.

4. In "The Drum," the poet mentions the Pied Piper, Kunta Kinte, Thoreau, and Martin Luther King, Jr. Why does she mention all these people? What do they have in common?

5. Words that imitate sounds are called *onomatopoeia.* Give two examples of onomatopoeia found in "The Drum." What sound do these words imitate?

6. Alliteration is the repetition of consonant sounds at the start of words. Which poems—"Thumbprint," "The Drum," or "Ring Out, Wild Bells"—use alliteration? Include examples in your answer.

Name ______________________________ Date ______________

7. "Ring Out, Wild Bells" compares present problems with remedies that might come in the future. For each problem shown in the chart below, write the solution suggested in the poem. Pick one solution. Tell whether you think it is realistic, and why.

Problem	**Solution**
Inequality between rich and poor	
Worry and sadness	

____

____

____

8. What does the speaker of "Ring Out, Wild Bells" mean when he says, "Ring out false pride in place and blood"?

____

____

____

9. Each stanza in "Ring Out, Wild Bells" has the same rhyme pattern. Which lines in each stanza end in words that rhyme? Give examples of rhymes from two stanzas.

____

____

____

____

10. In the fourth stanza of "Ring Out, Wild Bells," the speaker says he wants to ring out *strife*. What does he think should replace strife? Explain, focusing on the meaning of *strife*.

____

____

____

Name ________________________________ Date ________________

Essay

Write an extended response to the question of your choice or to the question or questions your teacher assigns you.

11. The speaker of "Thumbprint" has very strong feelings about her thumbprint. Write an essay in which you explain how she feels. Using details from the poem, tell what the thumbprint means to her, and why.

12. "The Drum" uses several different sound devices. In an essay, describe at least two of the sound devices and explain how they help to make the poem more effective. Cite specific examples in your essay.

13. Think about the world the speaker of "Ring Out, Wild Bells" wants to ring in. In an essay, describe that world. Use examples from the poem to illustrate your response. Then, tell whether you think such a world could ever be achieved, and why.

14. **Thinking About the Big Question: What is the secret to reaching someone with words?** In "Thumbprint," "The Drum," and "Ring Out, Wild Bells," the poets use rhythmic or repetitive words to make a strong statement. Choose one of the poems and explain how the poet's use of these words helps convey the poem's message. Include specific words from the poem in your response.

Oral Response

15. Go back to question 1, 5, or 8 or to the question your teacher assigns you. Take a few minutes to expand your answer and prepare an oral response. Find additional details in "Thumbprint," "The Drum," and "Ring Out, Wild Bells" that will support your points. If necessary, make notes to guide your response.

Name ______________________________ Date ______________

Poetry Collection: Eve Merriam; Nikki Giovanni; Alfred, Lord Tennyson

Selection Test A

Critical Reading *Identify the letter of the choice that best answers the question.*

____ 1. In "Thumbprint," what does the speaker stress most about her thumbprint?

A. It is slim and beautiful.
B. It is strong and thick.
C. It is smooth and unlined.
D. It is one of a kind.

____ 2. To what does the speaker in "Thumbprint" compare her thumbprint?

A. a signature
B. a gold mine
C. an atom bomb
D. a math problem

____ 3. Which word from "Thumbprint" is an example of onomatopoeia?

A. whirls
B. treasure
C. universe
D. atom

____ 4. What does the word *imprint* mean in the context of these lines from "Thumbprint"?

Imprint my mark upon the world,
Whatever I shall become.

A. publish
B. leave
C. use block letters
D. travel

____ 5. Which of these statements best sums up "The Drum"?

A. It is about the achievements of Martin Luther King, Jr.
B. It is about a drum that was made in Africa and brought to America.
C. It is about the drums of war.
D. It tells of some associations that the poet has with drums.

____ 6. What does "The Drum" tell us about Kunta Kinte?

A. He beat a drum as he led the rats from town.
B. He played a drum when he recited poetry.
C. He said, "I was a Drum Major for peace."
D. He was making a drum when he was captured.

Name ______________________________ Date ______________

____ 7. In "The Drum," what examples of onomatopoeia help capture the sound of a drum?

A. *pa-Rum* and *rat-tat-tat*

B. *oompah* and *rat-a-tat*

C. *pa-dum* and *boom boom boom*

D. *ba-da-da* and *boom*

____ 8. Why does the poet mention the Pied Piper, Kunta Kinte, Thoreau, and King in "The Drum"?

A. They all played drums.

B. They used or spoke about drums.

C. They were each drummed out of town.

D. They were drum majors.

____ 9. For what occasion are the bells ringing in "Ring Out, Wild Bells"?

A. a wedding

B. a funeral

C. the new year

D. Easter

____ 10. What does the speaker of Tennyson's poem mean by the expression "ring out" in the following line?

Ring out the old, ring in the new,

A. squeeze dry

B. grow silent

C. welcome

D. send away

____ 11. What does the word *want* mean in the context of this line from "Ring Out, Wild Bells"?

Ring out the want, the care, the sin,

A. desire

B. need

C. value

D. immorality

____ 12. Which word in "Ring Out, Wild Bells" is an example of onomatopoeia?

A. ring

B. wild

C. grief

D. rhymes

Name ______________________________ Date ______________________

____ 13. Which poem in this collection uses a regular pattern of rhyme at the ends of lines?

A. "Thumbprint"

B. "The Drum"

C. "Ring Out, Wild Bells"

D. none of the above

Vocabulary and Grammar

____ 14. Which word is most nearly *opposite* in meaning to the word *strife*?

A. joy

B. opening

C. silence

D. misery

____ 15. What kind of subject complement is used in the following sentence?

That drum seems louder.

A. predicate noun

B. predicate pronoun

C. predicate adjective

D. none

Essay

16. Write a short essay in which you explain how the speaker in "Thumbprint" feels about her thumbprint. Tell what the thumbprint means to her.

17. Which of the three poems—"Thumbprint," "The Drum," or "Ring Out, Wild Bells"—do you think is the most musical? State your opinion in a short essay. Then, support your opinion with examples of the poem's sound devices, such as alliteration, onomatopoeia, rhythm, and rhyme.

18. **Thinking About the Big Question: What is the secret to reaching someone with words?** In "Thumbprint," "The Drum," and "Ring Out, Wild Bells," the poets use rhythm or repeated words to make a strong statement. Choose one of the poems, and write a brief essay about how the poet's use of rhythm or repeated words helps get the message across to the reader.

Name ______________________________ Date ______________

Poetry Collection: Eve Merriam; Nikki Giovanni; Alfred, Lord Tennyson

Selection Test B

Critical Reading *Identify the letter of the choice that best completes the statement or answers the question.*

____ 1. In discussing her thumbprint, what does the speaker in "Thumbprint" recognize about herself?
A. She is a part of nature.
B. She is a criminal.
C. She is her mother's daughter.
D. She is unique.

____ 2. Which of these lines from "Thumbprint" does *not* contain alliteration?
A. In the heel of my thumb
B. Are whorls, whirls, wheels
C. Can ever contain the same
D. all of the above

____ 3. Why does the speaker compare her thumbprint to her signature?
A. Both are unique indications of her individuality.
B. Both are made in blue ink and appear on the same sheet of paper.
C. Both control her "interior weather."
D. Both are made with her right hand.

____ 4. Which is the correct meaning of *impress* in these lines from "Thumbprint"?

My universe key,
My singularity.
Impress, implant,

A. to inspire admiration
B. to leave a mark
C. to force to join the navy
D. to seize for public use

____ 5. Which word is an antonym clarifying the meaning of *base* in these lines from "Thumbprint"?

No other, however grand or base,
Can ever contain the same.

A. other
B. grand
C. contain
D. same

____ 6. Which two sound devices contribute most to the drumlike sound in "The Drum"?
A. alliteration and rhyme
B. rhyme and onomatopoeia
C. onomatopoeia and rhythm
D. rhythm and rhyme

Name ______________________________ Date ______________

___ 7. What does *kettles* mean in the context of this line from "The Drum"?

The big bass drums . . . the kettles roar . . . the sound of animal flesh

A. pots
B. guitars
C. lions
D. types of drums

___ 8. In "The Drum," what is the meaning of the remark "I was a Drum Major for peace" by Martin Luther King, Jr.?
A. I constantly tried to encourage peace.
B. I eventually found an inner peace.
C. I saw the need for war as well as peace.
D. I tried to silence the cries for peace.

___ 9. What does "The Drum" seem to be saying about life in general?
A. Life is made up of all sorts of experiences, both good and bad.
B. The person who makes the most noise gets the most.
C. War is sometimes an easier choice than peace.
D. It is dangerous to disturb the rhythms of nature.

___ 10. What is the speaker's main purpose in "Ring Out, Wild Bells"?
A. to describe the sound of the bells
B. to encourage people to behave morally
C. to celebrate an important occasion in someone's life
D. to express a message of hope at the new year

___ 11. What does the speaker mean by the following line from "Ring Out, Wild Bells"?

Ring out false pride in place and blood,

A. Send away false pride in one's social position or birth.
B. Send away pride, which is a false value that keeps us from forgiving loved ones.
C. Send away false pride instead of true pride in one's family background.
D. Send away false pride in wealth or skill at warfare.

___ 12. In "Ring Out, Wild Bells," what is the effect of the repetition of *ring out* and *ring in*?
A. It captures the sound of the bells ringing over and over.
B. It stresses how cold and wild the winter weather is.
C. It emphasizes how exasperated and angry the speaker is.
D. It communicates a playful and somewhat puzzling tone.

Name ______________________________ Date ________________

____ 13. Which statement most accurately describes the rhyme pattern in these lines from "Ring Out, Wild Bells"?

1 Ring out the grief that saps the mind,
2 For those that here we see no more;
3 Ring out the feud of rich and poor,
4 Ring in redress to all mankind.

A. The last words in each pair of lines rhyme.
B. The last words in lines 1 and 3 rhyme, and the last words in lines 2 and 4 rhyme.
C. The last words in lines 2 and 4 rhyme, but the last words in lines 1 and 3 do not rhyme.
D. The last words in lines 1 and 4 rhyme, and the last words in the middle two lines rhyme.

Vocabulary and Grammar

____ 14. Which choice is a good example of *strife*?
A. war
B. peace
C. spring
D. loud music

____ 15. Which choice means the opposite of *singularity*?
A. charity
B. duplicity
C. conformity
D. marriage

____ 16. Which sentence contains a predicate adjective as subject complement?
A. The bells rang loudly.
B. The bells grow louder every year.
C. The bells are a beautiful sound.
D. all of the above

____ 17. Which sentence correctly uses a predicate pronoun as a subject complement?
A. The last arrivals were Joe and I.
B. This year's soccer champions were Lana and me.
C. The tribute deeply touched my brother and I.
D. My boyfriend became my best friend.

Essay

18. Write a brief essay in which you explain how the sound devices in "The Drum" help make the poem more effective. Discuss at least two different kinds of sound devices, citing specific examples.

19. Write a brief essay about the central message of "Ring Out, Wild Bells." Explain how the poem's details, including its sound devices, help convey that message.

20. **Thinking About the Big Question: What is the secret to reaching someone with words?** In "Thumbprint," "The Drum," and "Ring Out, Wild Bells," the poets use rhythmic or repetitive words to make a strong statement. Choose one of the poems, and explain how the poet's use of these words helps convey the poem's message. Include specific words from the poem in your response.

Vocabulary Warm-up Word Lists

Study these words from the poetry of Patricia Hubbell, Richard García, and Langston Hughes. Then, complete the activities that follow.

Word List A

bulging [BUHLJ ing] *adj.* swelling out in a round shape or lump
The huge frog, with bulging eyes, jumped into the water.

dew [DOO] *n.* small drops of water that form overnight outdoors
I got up early, before the sun had dried up the dew on the grass.

direct [di REKT] *v.* to aim something in a particular direction
Would you please direct the heat vents more to my side of the car?

hose [HOHZ] *v.* to wash or pour water on something with a hose
Hose off your muddy shoes before you come inside!

muck [MUHK] *n.* a substance that is sticky, wet, and dirty; mud
After the floodwaters dried, the town was covered in muck.

perch [PERCH] *v.* to sit on the edge or on top of something
We like to perch on the very top of the mountain and watch the sunset.

Word List B

concrete [KAHN kreet] *n.* building material made of cement, small stones, sand, and water
The new art museum has strong walls of concrete with tiny windows.

elevator [EL uh vay ter] *n., used here as adj.* an enclosure raised or lowered in a vertical shaft to transport people or freight
We pushed all the elevator buttons but still the doors would not close.

raising [RAYZ ing] *v.* building; causing to rise to a standing position
The workers were raising the house quickly to finish before winter.

tenders [TEN derz] *n.* caretakers
The mayor hired three tenders to keep an eye on the town bonfire.

trough [TRAWF] *n.* long, open container for holding or mixing something
The workers mixed cement in a large trough near the building site.

urban [UHR buhn] *adj.* having to do with a city
In an urban area, life is often more hectic than in the country.

Name ______________________ Date ______________

Poetry Collection: Patricia Hubbell, Richard García, Langston Hughes

Vocabulary Warm-up Exercises

Exercise A *Fill in each blank in the paragraph below with an appropriate word from Word List A. Use each word only once.*

My shoes got wet with morning [1] ______________ as I crossed the lawn to get the newspaper. The [2] ______________ plastic bag indicated a free sample inside. Sure enough, when I opened the bag, I found a pouch of moist dog food, and it was leaking onto the paper. I headed back to the house, knowing that I could never [3] ______________ off the paper and still read it. Just then, a red-throated bird flew in front of me to [4] ______________ on a high branch of the cherry tree. While I followed it with my gaze, I stepped in a hole of gooey [5] ______________ in the middle of the dirt-and-gravel path. Now, the paper wasn't the only thing that needed cleaning off. It was only seven o'clock, but I had to [6] ______________ my attention to two sloppy jobs before breakfast.

Exercise B *Revise each sentence so that the underlined vocabulary word is used in a logical way. Be sure to keep the vocabulary word in your revision.*

1. The <u>elevator</u> doors opened and we began to move sideways, from the shoe department to sporting goods.

   ____

   ____

2. We mixed cement in the sink while the vegetables drained in the <u>trough</u>.

   ____

   ____

3. The coal <u>tenders</u> let the supply of fuel run out.

   ____

   ____

4. Some <u>urban</u> shopping centers are far away from big cities.

   ____

   ____

5. The farmer is <u>raising</u> a new barn all by himself in just one day.

   ____

   ____

6. A floor made of <u>concrete</u> is much more likely to catch fire than one made of wood.

   ____

   ____

Name ______________________ Date ______________

Poetry Collection: Patricia Hubbell, Richard García, Langston Hughes

Reading Warm-up A

Read the following passage. Pay special attention to the underlined words. Then, read it again, and complete the activities. Use a separate sheet of paper for your written answers.

The dew is still heavy on the grass. I take my dog, Rex, for his morning walk. The sun has risen just enough for us to walk safely without a flashlight. A nervous squirrel runs across our path. Then, it scurries up a tree to perch on a high branch and scold us from afar.

As I turn the corner, I see I am not the only one awake this early on a summer weekend. Justin is standing in front of his house. Alongside him is his white terrier, Terry. The dog has managed to get brown muck all over his coat. The bucket, brush, and shampoo bottle on the grass tip me off to what is about to happen.

Rex and I watch from a polite distance. Justin pulls out a ten-foot length of garden hose and turns on the faucet at the side of the house. He attempts to direct the stream of water at Terry. Of course, by now the dog has gotten wise to what is going on and high-tails it around to the other side of the house. I begin to doubt that Justin will manage to hose down anything but the front lawn.

From experience, I could tell Justin that he must get Terry on the leash in order to wash him, but I am curious to see if he will figure that out himself. When Justin disappears from sight, I think that is exactly what he has gone to do. Instead, he comes running back—not with Terry on a leash but with one pocket bulging at the side.

The next thing I know, Terry comes charging after him. He snaps his muzzle right on Justin's swollen pocket. Whatever is in the pocket must smell so good that Terry has risked a bath to follow its odor. Justin picks up the garden hose. With Terry still hanging onto his pocket, Justin begins washing off the slimy dirt. Now, why had not I thought of that?

1. Circle the sentence in the paragraph that explains why the dew is still on the grass. In your own words, explain what ***dew*** is.
2. Underline the place where the squirrel goes to perch. Give an example of some place you like to ***perch.***
3. Circle the three objects named in the next sentence that give a clue to what muck is. Write about a time when you or someone else got covered in ***muck.***
4. Circle what Justin attempts to direct at Terry. Rewrite the sentence, using a different word or words for ***direct.***
5. Circle the words in the paragraph that help the reader understand hose. Explain whether you should ***hose*** down things inside a house.
6. Underline the word that tells what was bulging. Describe what you think was causing it to be ***bulging.***

Name ______________________________ Date ______________

Poetry Collection: Patricia Hubbell, Richard García, Langston Hughes

Reading Warm-up B

Read the following passage. Pay special attention to the underlined words. Then, read it again, and complete the activities. Use a separate sheet of paper for your written answers.

If you live in a big urban area, you may take for granted the tall buildings that reach many stories above the city streets. Workers have been raising such tall buildings for only a little more than a hundred years. There are a number of reasons for this.

Materials had to be strong enough to hold up tall structures. In older buildings, the walls carried the load, or weight, of the upper stories. There was a limit to how many floors could be built.

Then, some new building materials appeared. With these, builders could shift the load from walls to columns and beams.

One of these materials was ready-made steel that came from factories. Another was concrete that could arrive at a building site already formed into blocks. Sometimes, however, workers would make this substance at the building site by mixing cement, water, and other things inside a big trough. Then, they would pour the substance into molds.

Machines, such as cranes, had to be invented that could lift these huge blocks and pieces of steel high into the sky. Tenders of such heavy equipment have an important job. Safety rests on the shoulders of these workers who watch over bulldozers, cement mixers, cranes, and other heavy machinery. These people must be sure that everyone working on the buildings as well as those who will work or live inside them will be safe.

The elevator was a nineteenth-century invention. Still, it waited patiently to rise to new heights until architects and builders created taller buildings. Advances in electricity, plumbing, heating, and air conditioning also helped make taller buildings possible. In addition, using aluminum and glass on the sides of new buildings allowed outer walls to be lighter and to let in more light.

Even with all the advances in high-rise buildings, some critics believe that construction is an industry of low technology. We will see what changes as the twenty-first century progresses.

1. Underline two words that give clues to the meaning of urban. Explain whether or not you live in an ***urban*** area.
2. Circle what workers have been raising. Name some types of buildings that workers are ***raising*** in your town or state.
3. Underline what concrete is made of. Then, name something other than a high-rise building that is made of ***concrete.***
4. Circle the words that tell what the trough was used for. Describe what else a ***trough*** might be used for.
5. Underline the words in the next sentence that tell what tenders of heavy equipment do. Write about a time that you were a ***tender.***
6. Underline the pun (play on words) that the writer makes about the elevator in the next sentence. Describe a trip you have made in an ***elevator.***

Name ______________________________ Date ______________

Poetry Collection: Patricia Hubbell, Richard García, Langston Hughes

Writing About the Big Question

What is the secret to reaching someone with words?

Big Question Vocabulary

benefit	connection	cultural	experience	express
feedback	individuality	inform	meaningful	media
misunderstand	relevant	sensory	significance	valid

A. *Use one or more words from the list above to complete each sentence.*

1. Jamie recorded her camping ______________ for her friends to enjoy.
2. Alex wanted to ______________ his gratitude for his parents' help.
3. Meg and her grandson had a ______________ conversation about her history.
4. After their conversation, Lynn and Ronnie felt the ______________ of true friendship.
5. The poet reading his work aloud provided a true ______________ experience: we felt as though we were there.

B. *Follow the directions in responding to each of the items below.*

1. Write two sentences about the media. Consider media's role in society.

   ____.

   ____.

2. Write about a way you express your individuality. Use at least two of the Big Question vocabulary words.

   ____

   ____

C. *Complete the sentence below. Then, write a short paragraph in which you connect this idea to the Big Question.*

The sounds of language influence meaning in literature by ______________

____

____

____

Name ______________________________ Date ______________

Poetry Collection: Patricia Hubbell, Richard García, Langston Hughes

Reading: Reread and Read Ahead to Determine Meanings From Context

Poetry often contains unusual words with which you may not be familiar. Nevertheless, you can often understand these words if you examine the **context**—the words and phrases surrounding an unfamiliar word. When you find an unfamiliar word, **reread and read ahead** for context clues that will help you figure out the meaning. When you think you have come up with a possible meaning, insert the meaning in place of the unfamiliar word, and reread the sentence. If it does not make sense, look for more context clues, or consult a dictionary.

In "Concrete Mixers" by Patricia Hubbell, for example, the word *ponderous* may be unfamiliar, but the context provides clues to its meaning.

> Tough gray-skinned monsters standing *ponderous*,
> Elephant-bellied. . . .

If you reread the line with *ponderous* and focus on "monsters standing" and then read ahead to "elephant-bellied," you can figure out from these clues that *ponderous* probably means "big and heavy."

Directions: *Reread the poem "Concrete Mixers," looking for clues to the meaning of the underlined word in each item below. On the lines provided, write your best guess about the meaning of the word, and write the clue, if any, that pointed you to that meaning. When you have finished, you can check the meanings in a dictionary.*

1. Likely meaning of hose in line 2: ______________________________

   Clue(s): ______________________________

2. Likely meaning of muck in line 5: ______________________________

   Clue(s): ______________________________

3. Likely meaning of perch in line 7: ______________________________

   Clue(s): ______________________________

4. Likely meaning of bellow in line 14: ______________________________

   Clue(s): ______________________________

5. Likely meaning of urban in line 16: ______________________________

   Clue(s): ______________________________

Name ______________________________ Date ______________

Poetry Collection: Patricia Hubbell, Richard García, Langston Hughes

Literary Analysis: Figurative Language

Poets often use imaginative **figures of speech,** or **figurative language,** to make their poems more musical and memorable. Figures of speech often compare unlike things. A **simile** directly states the comparison of two unlike things by using a word such as *like* or *as.* A **metaphor** suggests a comparison between two unlike things by saying that one *is* the other. **Personification** compares something nonhuman to a human being by giving it human characteristics.

Similes: Life is like a dance. The ocean is as moody as a child.

Metaphor: Life is a dance.

Personification: The ocean laughs and cries.

DIRECTIONS: *On the chart below, record the desired examples.*

	Line Number(s)	What Two Things Are Compared
1. Simile in "Concrete Mixers"		
2. Metaphor in "Concrete Mixers"		
3. Personification in "Concrete Mixers"		
4. Personification in "The City Is So Big"		

Name ______________________ Date ______________

Poetry Collection: Patricia Hubbell, Richard García, Langston Hughes

Vocabulary Builder

Word List

bellow dew ponderous roam urban

A. Directions: *Answer each question with a sentence that uses one of the Word List words. Use each Word List word only once.*

1. What might a suitcase with lots of travel labels show about its owner?

2. What kind of suitcase would be hard to carry?

3. How might you describe a roar of a lion?

4. What might cover flowers' petals on a spring morning?

5. How might you describe a photograph of a city?

B. Word Study: *The suffix* -ous *means "characterized by" or "full of." Use the context of the sentences and what you know about the suffix* -ous *to explain your answer to each question.*

1. Does something *instantaneous* take a long time? Explain.

2. Is something *frivolous* necessary? Explain.

Name ______________________________ Date ______________

Poetry Collection: Patricia Hubbell, Richard García, Langston Hughes

Enrichment: Concrete

Concrete, like that discussed in Patricia Hubbell's poem, is made from a mixture of cement, water, and inert materials such as sand or gravel. The inert materials are called aggregate. In a chemical process known as hydration, the cement reacts with the water (and the air that gets into the mixture naturally) to form a kind of paste that gradually hardens and holds together the inert materials, which do not participate in the reaction.

The ancient Egyptians knew how to make concrete. So did the ancient Romans, who used it at the base of monuments. Over time, however, the process of making concrete was nearly lost. It was revived in 1824 when a new kind of cement, called portland cement, was developed. Today, concrete is the most widely used construction material in the world.

There are three important factors in mixing concrete. The type of aggregate is one factor. Depending on the job, concrete is generally made with either a fine aggregate, such as sand, or a coarse aggregate, such as gravel. Generally, jobs requiring extremely strong concrete, like dams, need the coarsest aggregate. The water/cement ratio—the amount of water compared with the amount of cement—is another factor in mixing concrete. The higher the water/cement ratio, the more easily the concrete will flow before it hardens; the lower the water/cement ratio, the stronger the concrete will be later. The final factor in the mixing process is heat: The temperature must be kept steady to avoid cracking problems later.

A. Directions: *Based on the passage above, write the definitions of each term below. Use context clues to help you with the meanings. Then, check the meanings in a dictionary.*

1. concrete: ______________________________
____
2. inert: ______________________________
3. aggregate: ______________________________
____
4. hydration: ______________________________
____
5. water/concrete ratio: ______________________________
____
6. portland cement: ______________________________
____

B. Directions: *Imagine that you are an engineer at a construction site. On the lines below, list three questions you need to ask before you mix the concrete.*

1. ______________________________
2. ______________________________
3. ______________________________

Name ______________________________ Date ______________

Poetry Collection: Patricia Hubbell, Richard García, Langston Hughes

Open-Book Test

Short Answer *Write your responses to the questions in this section on the lines provided.*

1. "Concrete Mixers" uses similes and metaphors to create comparisons. To what or whom does the poem compare the mixing machines? Explain your answer using examples from the poem.

2. The concrete mixers are described as *ponderous.* How would a ponderous machine move? Why?

3. In these two lines from "Concrete Mixers," what does *urban* mean? How does the context give its meaning?

   Concrete mixers are urban elephants,
   Their trunks are raising a city.

4. In "The City Is So Big," the speaker reveals certain feelings about the city. How does the speaker feel about the city? What details from the poem tell you how he feels?

5. In "The City Is So Big," the speaker says, "Its bridges quake with fear." What does the word *quake* probably mean in that context? How do you know?

6. Personification gives human characteristics to nonhuman things. What things are personified in "The City Is So Big"? Use details from the poem to explain your answer.

Name ______________________ Date ______________

7. In "Harlem Night Song," the speaker shares his feelings about Harlem. How does he feel? Choose two details from the poem and explain how they reveal the speaker's feelings.

8. In "Harlem Night Song," the speaker's mood comes through clearly. What is the speaker's mood? Explain your answer using details from the poem.

9. All three poems—"Concrete Mixers," "The City Is So Big," and "Harlem Night Song"—use comparisons. In the chart, give two examples of comparisons. Why do you think poets use comparisons? Write your answer on the line provided.

Poem	Thing Compared	Compared To

10. Langston Hughes uses the word *roam* to describe his walk in "Harlem Night Song." Why do you think he chose the word *roam*?

Essay

Write an extended response to the question of your choice or to the question or questions your teacher assigns you.

11. Richard García uses very simple words in "The City Is So Big." Why do you think he made that choice? In an essay, explain García's choice of words. Tell how the specific words help get across the message of the poem. Use examples from the poem to support your response.

12. Write a short essay in which you examine the figurative language in "Concrete Mixers." Explain what the concrete mixers are compared to, what the parts of the mixers are compared to, and what the drivers of the mixers are compared to. Then, show how the comparisons are related. Use details from the poem in your response.

13. Each poem—"Concrete Mixers," "Harlem Night Song," and "The City Is So Big"—includes impressions of city life. In an essay, compare and contrast the impressions in two of the poems. Then, react to the impressions by giving your own opinion of city life and citing examples or other details to support it.

14. **Thinking About the Big Question: What is the secret to reaching someone with words?** Which of the poems—"Concrete Mixers," "The City Is So Big," or "Harlem Night Song"—best uses words to create a vision or an idea of the city for you? In an essay, state your opinion and support it with words and phrases that the poet uses to reach you.

Oral Response

15. Go back to question 1, 4, or 6 or to the question your teacher assigns you. Take a few minutes to expand your answer and prepare an oral response. Find additional details in "Concrete Mixers," "The City Is So Big," and "Harlem Night Song" that will support your points. If necessary, make notes to guide your response.

Name ______________________________ Date ______________

Poetry Collection: Patricia Hubbell, Richard García, Langston Hughes

Selection Test A

Critical Reading *Identify the letter of the choice that best answers the question.*

____ 1. What does "Concrete Mixers" describe?
- A. a rural village in Africa
- B. a zoo in India
- C. a construction site in a modern city
- D. a large corporation

____ 2. To what or whom does "Concrete Mixers" compare the operators of the concrete mixers?
- A. elephants
- B. elephant drivers
- C. firefighters
- D. hoses

____ 3. To what or whom does "Concrete Mixers" compare the mixing machines?
- A. elephants
- B. elephant drivers
- C. fire trucks
- D. washing machines

____ 4. What does the word *perch* mean in the context of these lines from "Concrete Mixers"?

> Their drivers perch on their backs like mahouts,
> Sending the sprays of water up.

- A. water
- B. sneeze
- C. fish
- D. sit

____ 5. What is the speaker doing in "Harlem Night Song"?
- A. hoping to join a band
- B. asking someone to join him or her
- C. giving a tour
- D. worrying about the weather

Name ______________________________ Date ______________

____ 6. In "Harlem Night Song," whom does the speaker seem to be addressing?

A. a young child

B. an elderly parent

C. a homeless person

D. someone he or she loves

____ 7. What kind of figure of speech do these lines from "Harlem Night Song" contain?

Stars are great drops
Of golden dew.

A. simile

B. metaphor

C. personification

D. none

____ 8. In the context of these lines from "Harlem Night Song," which word tells you that *dew* is probably some kind of moisture?

Moon is shining,
Night sky is blue.
Stars are great drops
Of golden dew.

A. shining

B. blue

C. drops

D. golden

____ 9. What does "The City Is So Big" suggest about the city?

A. It is boring.

B. It is actually very small.

C. It is old and creaky.

D. It is frightening.

____ 10. According to "The City Is So Big," where do people in the city "disappear"?

A. in elevators

B. on bridges

C. on trains

D. on moving stairs

____ 11. What does the word *quake* probably mean in the context of this line from "The City Is So Big"?

Its bridges quake with fear

A. accident

B. shake

C. smile

D. stretch

____ 12. Which lines from "The City Is So Big" contain a simile?
- A. The city is so big / Its bridges quake with fear
- B. The lights sliding from house to house / And trains pass with windows shining
- C. And trains pass with windows shining / Like a smile full of teeth
- D. I have seen machines eating houses / And stairways walk all by themselves

____ 13. Which of these words often signal a simile?
- A. *like* and *as*
- B. *so* and *and*
- C. *for* and *like*
- D. none of the above

Vocabulary and Grammar

____ 14. Which word is most nearly *opposite* in meaning to the word *ponderous*?
- A. light
- B. strong
- C. awkward
- D. thoughtful

____ 15. What is the indirect object in the following sentence?

The supplier needs to give us more cement for the concrete.
- A. supplier
- B. us
- C. cement
- D. concrete

Essay

16. You have read three poems about cities—"Concrete Mixers" by Patricia Hubbell, "Harlem Night Song" by Langston Hughes, and "The City Is So Big" by Richard García. Now, write a letter from one of the poets to another one. What might the poet writing the letter say about the other poet's poem? For example, what might Langston Hughes say to Richard García about "The City Is So Big," or what might Richard García say to Patricia Hubbell about "Concrete Mixers"?

17. Which of the three poems—"Concrete Mixers," "Harlem Night Song," or "The City Is So Big"—do you like best? State your opinion in a short essay. Then, support your opinion with examples of what you like, including the figurative language.

18. **Thinking About the Big Question: What is the secret to reaching someone with words?** Which of the poems in this section—"Concrete Mixers," "The City Is So Big," or "Harlem Night Song"—best uses words to create a vision or idea of the city? In an essay, state your opinion, and then support it with words and phrases from the poem.

Name ______________________________ Date ______________

Poetry Collection: Patricia Hubbell, Richard García, Langston Hughes

Selection Test B

Critical Reading *Identify the letter of the choice that best completes the statement or answers the question.*

____ 1. What basic comparison controls the figures of speech in "Concrete Mixers"?
A. Concrete mixers are elephants, and their drivers are elephant tenders.
B. Concrete mixers are elephants, and their drivers are lions.
C. Concrete mixers are like elephants' trunks, and their drivers are like elephants.
D. Concrete mixers are like elephants, and their trunks are like hoses.

____ 2. In "Concrete Mixers," what seems to be the speaker's feelings about the concrete mixers?
A. She thinks they are an ugly eyesore in the city.
B. She thinks they are interesting and impressive.
C. She thinks they are mysterious and frightening.
D. She thinks they are boring and repetitious.

____ 3. Which of these lines in "Concrete Mixers" contains a metaphor?

The drivers are washing the concrete mixers;
Like elephant tenders they hose them down.
Tough gray-skinned monsters standing ponderous,

A. the first line
B. the second line
C. the third line
D. none of the above

____ 4. In these lines from "Concrete Mixers," which context word provides a synonym for *urban*?

Concrete mixers are urban elephants,
Their trunks are raising a city.

A. concrete
B. elephants
C. raising
D. city

____ 5. From the context of these lines in "Concrete Mixers," what can you assume about the word *bellow*?

Move like elephants
Bellow like elephants
Spray like elephants

A. *Bellow* is a verb.
B. *Bellow* is something elephants do.
C. *Bellow* probably does *not* mean "move."
D. all of the above

Name ______________________________ Date ______________

___ 6. What sort of night is described in “Harlem Night Song”?
A. cold and windy
B. bright and pleasant
C. quiet and eerie
D. dangerous but exciting

___ 7. Based on the content, what can you assume the speaker in “Harlem Night Song” enjoys?
A. literature
B. movies
C. music
D. sports

___ 8. From the details in “Harlem Night Song,” how do you think Langston Hughes felt about the New York City neighborhood known as Harlem?
A. He enjoyed it and found it a vibrant place.
B. He tolerated it.
C. He found it dull and stifling.
D. He found its people arty and snobbish.

___ 9. Which of these passages from “Harlem Night Song” uses figurative language?
A. Come / Let us roam the night together
B. Moon is shining.
C. Night sky is blue.
D. Stars are great drops / Of golden dew.

___ 10. Which word best describes the mood, or atmosphere, of “Harlem Night Song”?
A. tragic
B. angry
C. suspenseful
D. joyful

___ 11. In using the simile “like a smile full of teeth” to describe the passing train in “The City Is So Big,” what is the speaker suggesting about the train?
A. It is warm and welcoming.
B. It is somewhat menacing.
C. It is false and deceitful.
D. It spits out passengers at every stop.

___ 12. What is the logical explanation of “machines eating houses” near the end of “The City Is So Big”?
A. termites eating wood houses with machinelike speed
B. cars entering garages in houses
C. machinery knocking down old buildings to put up new ones
D. a computer game in which houses are gobbled

Name ______________________ Date ______________

____ 13. In what way do the people actually "disappear" in "The City Is So Big"?
A. They cannot be seen once they go inside the buildings.
B. They disappear behind closed elevator doors.
C. They are murdered.
D. They move to the suburbs.

____ 14. Which line from "The City Is So Big" is an example of personification?
A. Its bridges quake with fear
B. I have seen machines eating houses
C. And stairways walk all by themselves
D. all of the above

Vocabulary and Grammar

____ 15. Which of these things would you most likely describe as *ponderous*?
A. an unabridged dictionary
B. a bright green leaf
C. a leather wallet
D. a lace bedspread

____ 16. Which sentence contains an indirect object?
A. The city is my favorite place.
B. City life gave me wonderful experiences.
C. Riding the subway makes me nervous.
D. all of the above

____ 17. Which sentence correctly uses a pronoun as a direct object?
A. The best runners were Pedro and me.
B. My mom gave me a lift to school.
C. My sister resembles my mother and I.
D. Take me to the next bus stop, please.

Essay

18. Write a short essay in which you examine the figurative language in "Concrete Mixers." Explain what the concrete mixers are compared to, what the parts of the concrete mixers are compared to, and what the drivers of the concrete mixers are compared to. Then, show how all these comparisons are related.

19. Write an essay in which you compare and contrast the impressions of city life given in all three poems—"Concrete Mixers," "Harlem Night Song," and "The City Is So Big." Then, react to the impressions by giving your own opinion of city life and citing examples or other details to support it.

20. **Thinking About the Big Question: What is the secret to reaching someone with words?** Which of the poems—"Concrete Mixers," "The City Is So Big," or "Harlem Night Song"—best uses words to create a vision or an idea of the city for you? In an essay, state your opinion and support it with words and phrases that the poet uses to reach you.

Vocabulary Warm-up Word Lists

Study these words from the poetry of Pablo Neruda, Elizabeth Bishop, and Emily Dickinson. Then, complete the activities that follow.

Word List A

cicada [si KAY duh] *n.* a large, winged insect, the males of which make a loud, buzzing sound

I heard my first cicada of the summer humming in the tree.

drifting [DRIFT ing] *v.* moving slowly in the air or on water

The wind loosened the leaf that I saw drifting toward the ground.

limp [LIMP] *adj.* not firm

To keep the carrot strips from going limp, place them in ice water.

relieved [ri LEEVD] *adj.* glad because a worry or stress is gone

We were relieved when the tornado finally passed our town.

rut [RUHT] *n.* a deep track in the ground made by a wheel

We didn't see the rut in the road and drove over it bumpily.

sawing [SAW ing] *v., used here as adj.* cutting with a hand saw

The sawing noise coming from the garage woke us up early.

Word List B

boulevard [BOOL uh vahrd] *n.* a wide city street, often tree-lined

The boulevard, six lanes wide, had a grassy center strip.

diadem [DY uh dem] *n.* a crown worn as a sign of royalty

The queen wore a sparkling diadem on her head.

heron [HAIR uhn] *n.* a long-necked, long-legged, long-billed bird that lives along marshes and river banks

I saw a graceful white heron standing in the shallow water.

keys [KEEZ] *n.* small, low islands near the shore

During the hurricane, water washed over several keys in the bay.

latticework [LAT is wurk] *n.* a structure of crisscross strips

The tree's branches formed a natural latticework that let in little light.

mangrove [MAN grohv] *adj.* relating to tropical tree that grows near water and has thick roots

Mangrove trees grow in salty water along the shore.

Name ______________________________ Date ______________

Poetry Collection: Pablo Neruda, Elizabeth Bishop, Emily Dickinson

Vocabulary Warm-up Exercises

Exercise A *Fill in each blank in the paragraph below with an appropriate word from Word List A. Use each word only once.*

It was the kind of sunny, hot, muggy summer afternoon that made you feel tired and [1] ______________ right down to your bones. To add to my discomfort, one [2] ______________ after another was "serenading" me with its loud [3] ______________ noise. The sound, [4] ______________ through the air from trees far and near, had reached the level of annoyance that could drive a person crazy. Just as I thought there was no chance of being [5] ______________ of my discomfort, I noticed a low band of clouds headed in my direction. The sky briefly darkened, and a cool breath of fresh air ruffled the curtains. Rain suddenly burst from the clouds, quickly filling the [6] ______________ in the driveway with water. Just as suddenly, the rain stopped and the sun beat down anew.

Exercise B *Circle* T *if the statement is true or* F *if the statement is false. Then, explain your answer.*

1. A boulevard is usually narrower than a country lane.
   T / F ____
   ____

2. It is unlikely that a poor farmer would own a diadem.
   T / F ____
   ____

3. The mangrove tree is one of the few types of trees that grow high on a mountain.
   T / F ____
   ____

4. Keys are large, mountainous islands such as Iceland and Greenland.
   T / F ____
   ____

5. In wooden latticework, all the strips of wood run in the same direction.
   T / F ____
   ____

6. The heron is one of the few birds that live in high rocky places.
   T / F ____
   ____

Name ______________________________ Date ________________

Poetry Collection: Pablo Neruda, Elizabeth Bishop, Emily Dickinson

Reading Warm-up A

Read the following passage. Pay special attention to the underlined words. Then, read it again, and complete the activities. Use a separate sheet of paper for your written answers.

I was used to the fall lingering well into November, with roses still blooming as we sat eating Thanksgiving turkey. Here in the country, however, snow began dropping the first of November. Nearly a foot of the white stuff fell, drifting with the wind into mounds three feet high. That was only the beginning.

By the time the first crocus appeared during the last week of March, we had seen nearly a hundred inches of snow. The white blanket had been almost continuous for five months. The three-day thaw and rain in January had temporarily freed us from the snow, only to replace it with mudslides. Every rut in every road was filled with water or mud.

Spring took a while longer to arrive, and not without two more hefty snowstorms. Far from disappointing us, however, spring overwhelmed us. Hardly had the daffodils bloomed than tulips and irises followed. Before we knew it, wild roses and wisteria were spilling over the corral fence.

I had expected my first summer in the country to be a lot more bearable than in the city. It was true. The temperature and humidity were much lower. Also, we had gotten to the third week of July without so much as a sign—or sound—of a cicada. I didn't miss the loud sawing noise of that ugly insect all morning and afternoon.

Well, the cicadas did arrive, and the weather grew hot and muggy. I turned into the human counterpart of a wet, limp dishrag. It was not to last long, though. Fall arrived on a cool breeze in September, and my senses were relieved. Rain soon cleaned the air rather than making it stickier. I did not sneeze nonstop through September and October, as I usually did in the city.

When November rolled around again, I left the country, but it was not because of the weather. In fact, that year, with its dramatic seasons, would be one to remember forever.

1. Circle the cause of the drifting snow. Write a sentence that describes something else you might see *drifting*.

2. Underline the phrases that help you understand the meaning of rut. Tell about the damage a *rut* in a road can do.

3. Circle the words in the next sentence that tell what a cicada is and the sound it makes. Describe something else that makes a *sawing* noise.

4. Circle the words in the paragraph that tell why the writer felt like a wet, limp dishrag. Describe a *limp* handshake.

5. Underline what caused the writer's senses to be relieved. Tell about a time when you were *relieved* and explain what caused the change.

Name ______________________ Date ______________

Poetry Collection: Pablo Neruda, Elizabeth Bishop, Emily Dickinson

Reading Warm-up B

Read the following passage. Pay special attention to the underlined words. Then, read it again, and complete the activities. Use a separate sheet of paper for your written answers.

A mangrove tree is an unusual kind of tree. It grows along tropical shores, including the southern Gulf Coast of Florida. There are two reasons why mangrove trees can live in the muck and shallow water along the coast. First, unlike most other trees, they can survive in salty water. Second, their roots form a thick latticework that looks like twisted stilts. Some of these roots take in air so that the tree can "breathe" in the mud.

These amazing trees grow in mangrove keys, or low-lying islands. The so-called Ten Thousand Islands are hundreds of tiny keys that stretch along the Gulf Coast of Florida north of the Everglades National Park. They play an important role in the area's ecosystem. They protect the shore from winds and floods. When mangrove leaves and branches fall into the water, they become the first link in important food chains for both land and sea creatures.

Tiny marine creatures hatch and feed among the mangrove roots. They become food for shrimp, other shellfish, and fish. Those, in turn, become food for birds and turtles. White-tailed deer eat their fill of plants. All of these creatures may wind up as food for crocodiles.

During a storm, the gulf may flood a key. An area between thick growths of trees then becomes a watery boulevard where wading birds stroll, foraging for food. An egret stirs up mangrove roots to find a fish, a frog, or insects. A heron dips its long beak into the water and comes up with dinner.

A huge nest atop a mangrove tree has survived the storm. The bird's nest looks like a strange diadem, or crown, for a giant. Soon, it will be a safe place for young osprey to hatch and grow.

You can see that a mangrove key is the site of much activity. In recent years, people have realized that they must help protect the balance of life there.

1. Underline the words that tell you what a mangrove tree is. Tell whether a ***mangrove*** tree could grow where you live.
2. Circle the words that help give you a picture of what latticework is. In a sentence, describe what a pie's ***latticework*** top crust would look like.
3. Underline the definition of keys. Write a sentence using this meaning of ***keys***.
4. Underline the word that describes this boulevard. Describe a ***boulevard*** that you may have been on or heard of.
5. Circle the words in the paragraph that tell what kind of creature a heron is. Based on the description, what might be dinner for a ***heron***?
6. Circle the synonym for diadem. Tell about someone you have seen wearing a ***diadem***.

Name ____________________ Date ____________

Poetry Collection: Pablo Neruda, Elizabeth Bishop, Emily Dickinson

Writing About the Big Question

What is the secret to reaching someone with words?

Big Question Vocabulary

benefit	connection	cultural	experience	express
feedback	individuality	inform	meaningful	media
misunderstand	relevant	sensory	significance	valid

A. *Use one or more words from the list above to complete each sentence.*

1. The ____________________ of his message was expressed through his heartfelt emotion.
2. Everyone can ____________________ from communication.
3. Shawna made a ____________________ point when she said I didn't listen to her.
4. My ____________________ with communication suggests that my words must reflect my true feelings.
5. The ____________________ the poet received from the critics was positive.

B. *Follow the directions in responding to each of the items below.*

1. Write two sentences about a topic relevant to your communication with others.

____________________.

____________________.

2. Write two sentences that use sensory details to describe a conversation. Use at least two of the Big Question vocabulary words.

____

____

C. *Complete the sentence below. Then, write a short paragraph in which you connect this idea to the Big Question.*

Writers often respond to nature in poetry because ____________________

____

____

____

Name ______________________________ Date ______________

Poetry Collection: Pablo Neruda, Elizabeth Bishop, Emily Dickinson

Reading: Reread and Read Ahead to Determine Meanings From Context

Poetry often contains unusual words with which you may not be familiar. Nevertheless, you can often understand these words if you examine the **context**—the words and phrases surrounding an unfamiliar word. When you find an unfamiliar word, **reread and read ahead** for context clues that will help you figure out the meaning. When you think you have come up with a possible meaning, insert the meaning in place of the unfamiliar word, and reread the sentence. If it does not make sense, look for more context clues, or consult a dictionary.

DIRECTIONS: *The chart below lists three words from this collection's poems that you may not immediately be able to define. Use context clues to help you understand the words, and on the chart, write the clues you find and your best guess about each word's meaning. Then, check a dictionary to see if you were right about the meaning.*

Word	*latticework*	*heron*	*uninjured*
Location	"Ode to Enchanted Light," line 5	"Little Exercise," line 7	"Little Exercise," line 21
Context Clues			
Likely Meaning			
Dictionary Meaning			

Name ________________________ Date ____________

Poetry Collection: Pablo Neruda, Elizabeth Bishop, Emily Dickinson

Literary Analysis: Figurative Language

Poets often use **figures of speech,** or **figurative language,** to make their poems more musical and memorable. The chart below lists and explains three common figures of speech.

Figure of Speech	Definition	Example
simile	a comparison of two unlike things as if they were alike, using a comparing word such as *like* or *as* to state the comparison	The wind is like a cheerleader.
metaphor	a comparison of two unlike things as if they were alike, suggested by stating one thing *is* another	The wind is a cheerleader.
personification	a comparison of something nonhuman with something human, suggested by giving the nonhuman thing human characteristics	The wind sang in a loud, cheerful voice.

DIRECTIONS: *Answer these questions about the figurative language in "Ode to Enchanted Light." Include the line numbers of any examples you list.*

1. List two similes that help the reader picture the light in "Ode to Enchanted Light."
____

2. Which simile in the first nine lines do you think best captures the enchanted mood the poet wants to convey? Why? ____________________
____

3. Explain how the details about the cicada involve personification. ____________
____

4. With what metaphor does "Ode to Enchanted Light" conclude? ____________
____

5. What feelings, or mood, does the final metaphor help convey? ____________
____

Name ______________________ Date ______________

Poetry Collection: Pablo Neruda, Elizabeth Bishop, Emily Dickinson

Vocabulary Builder

Word List

boulevard cicada debates rut uneasily unresponsive

A. Directions: *Circle* T *if the statement is true or* F *if the statement is false.* Then, explain your answer.

T / F 1. A nightmare can make someone sleep uneasily.

____

____

T / F 2. Daydreamers are sometimes unresponsive when you ask them a question.

____

____

T / F 3. Every homeowner likes a big rut in the driveway.

____

____

T / F 4. Someone who debates all her decisions probably acts much too quickly.

____

____

T / F 5. It is hard to locate a cicada because it is so quiet.

____

____

T / F 6. Most boulevards are lined with trees.

____

____

B. Word Study: *The suffix* -ive *indicates a tendency toward a certain kind of action. Use the context of the sentences and what you know about the suffix* -ive *to explain your answer to each question.*

1. What is another way to describe a person who is *indecisive*?

____

____

2. How might an *impulsive* person act?

____

____

Name ______________________________ Date ______________

Poetry Collection: Pablo Neruda, Elizabeth Bishop, Emily Dickinson

Enrichment: Wind Force

Storms can cause a great deal of destruction on small islands like the mangrove keys in "Little Exercise." Scientists use the Beaufort scale to measure the force of the winds.

Beaufort Scale of Wind Force			
Beaufort Number	**Wind Speed (mph)**	**Description**	**Effect on Sea**
0	less than 1	Calm	Sea is like a mirror.
1	1–3	Light air	Ripples look like scales without foam crests.
2	4–7	Light breeze	Small wavelets appear; crests look glassy but do not break.
3	8–12	Gentle breeze	Large wavelets appear. Crests begin to break. Foam looks glassy, perhaps with scattered whitecaps.
4	13–18	Moderate breeze	Small waves appear, becoming longer; whitecaps are fairly frequent.
5	19–24	Fresh breeze	Moderate waves arise, taking a longer form; many white caps appear (with some chance of spray).
6	25–31	Strong breeze	Large waves; whitecaps everywhere, with some spray.
7	32–38	Moderate gale (high wind)	Sea heaps up, and white foam from breaking waves begins to blow in streaks.
8	39–46	Fresh gale	Moderately high, longer waves appear; edges of crests break. Foam is blown.
9	47–54	Strong gale	High waves appear. Sea begins to roll. Spray may affect visibility.
10	55–63	Whole gale	Very high waves with long crests. Sea looks white. Rolling of the sea becomes heavy. Visibility is affected.
11	64–72	Storm	Exceptionally high waves. (Small and medium-sized ships might be lost to view behind the waves.) The sea is covered with foam and froth. Visibility is affected.
12–17	73 and above	Hurricane	The air is filled with foam and spray. Sea is completely white with a driving spray. Visibility is seriously affected.

DIRECTIONS: *On a separate sheet of paper, write your own description of a bad storm as it approaches and hits a coastal area, an island, or a ship at sea. Trace the progress from a calm day to a nasty one by using the information in the Beaufort scale. If you like, you can write your description in the form of a poem.*

Name ______________________ Date ______________

Poetry Collections: Patricia Hubbell, Richard García, Langston Hughes; Pablo Neruda, Elizabeth Bishop, Emily Dickinson

Integrated Language Skills: Grammar

Direct and Indirect Objects

A **direct object** is a noun or pronoun that follows an action verb and receives the action of the verb. It answers the question *What?* or *Whom?* after the action verb. (A direct object does not appear after a linking verb.)

Sonya brewed some *tea.* [*What* did Sonya brew?]

The aroma tempted *them.* [*Whom* did the aroma tempt?]

An **indirect object** is a noun or pronoun that comes between an action verb and a direct object. It answers the question *To or for whom?* or *To or for what?* after an action verb. You cannot have an indirect object without a direct object.

Sonya brewed her *guests* some tea. [*For whom* did Sonya brew some tea?]

Sonya gave each *cup* a different flavor. [*To what* did Sonya give a different flavor?]

Pronouns used as direct or indirect objects require the object form of the pronoun.

Incorrect: We visited *Sue and he.* **Correct:** We visited *Sue and him.*

Incorrect: Sal gave *Dave and I* help. **Correct:** Sal gave *Dave and me* help.

A. Practice: *Underline the direct object and circle the indirect object in each sentence that contains one or both. If the pronoun form is incorrect, cross it out and write the correct form on the line after the sentence. If there is no direct or indirect object in the sentence, write* none *on the line.*

1. Nature plays a strong role in her poetry. ______________
2. The poem's speaker gives us advice about human relationships.
____
3. The last poem really impressed Nancy and I. ______________
4. The images show readers the speaker's feelings. ______________
5. The biggest fans of her poetry are Celia and Mary. ______________

B. Writing Application: *Add to each subject below to create a sentence that includes an action verb and a direct object. Also, include an indirect object in two of your sentences.*

1. The heavy machinery ______________
2. Great poets ______________
3. My thoughts ______________
4. The glowing light ______________
5. The islanders ______________

Name ______________________________ Date ____________________

Poetry Collections: Patricia Hubbell, Richard García, Langston Hughes; Pablo Neruda, Elizabeth Bishop, Emily Dickinson

Integrated Language Skills: Support for Writing a Study for a Poem

Use this chart to jot down ideas about the figurative language that you hope to include in your poem about a natural or city setting.

Comparison to Make	Wording to Use	Type of Figurative Language

Name ______________________________ Date ______________

Poetry Collections: Patricia Hubbell, Richard García, Langston Hughes; Pablo Neruda, Elizabeth Bishop, Emily Dickinson

Integrated Language Skills: Support for Extend Your Learning

Research and Technology

Use this form to record information about the poems you choose for your mini-anthology. Under "Ideas for My Introduction," jot down points to be made and details to be included.

POEM 1	
Title of Poem	Author
Subject of Poem	Source
Ideas for My Introduction	
POEM 2	
Title of Poem	Author
Subject of Poem	Source
Ideas for My Introduction	
POEM 3	
Title of Poem	Author
Subject of Poem	Source
Ideas for My Introduction	

Name ______________________________ Date ______________

Poetry Collection: Pablo Neruda, Elizabeth Bishop, Emily Dickinson

Open-Book Test

Short Answer *Write your responses to the questions in this section on the lines provided.*

1. In "Ode to Enchanted Light," the poet writes, "light/like a green/latticework of branches." What does *latticework* mean here? What other word is a hint to its meaning?

2. Pablo Neruda describes nature in "Ode to Enchanted Light." What impression of nature does he give in the poem? Support your answer with details from the poem.

3. A metaphor is a comparison of two unlike things. What example of metaphor does "Ode to Enchanted Light" contain?

4. The storm roams the sky *uneasily* in "Little Exercise." Why might a person react *uneasily* to news of the storm coming?

5. In "Little Exercise," the poet writes, "occasionally a heron may undo his head,/shake up his feathers." What is a *heron*? What in the lines helps you define the word?

6. In "Little Exercise," the palm trees are "suddenly revealed." What has happened to reveal them? What details in the poem help you infer what has happened?

Name ______________________________ Date ______________

7. In "Little Exercise," why does Elizabeth Bishop use the stage direction "Another part of the field"? What effect do these words create?

8. Look back at "Ode to Enchanted Light," "Little Exercise," and "The Sky Is Low . . ." to find one example each of personification, simile, and metaphor. Fill in the chart with the examples. Then, choose one example and describe its effect on the lines provided.

	Personification	**Simile**	**Metaphor**
Poem			
Example			

9. In "The Sky Is Low . . . ," a snowflake *debates* where it will go. If you and your friend *debate* where you will go this weekend, what kind of conversation are you having? Explain.

10. Emily Dickinson uses personification in "The Sky Is Low . . . ." What human quality does she give the wind? Use details from the poem to support your answer.

Essay

Write an extended response to the question of your choice or to the question or questions your teacher assigns you.

11. In an essay, explain what happens in "Little Exercise." Describe what the speaker observes from the beginning of the poem to the end. Tell what effect this observation has on you, the reader. Support your answer with details from the poem.

Name ________________________________ Date ________________

12. Pablo Neruda titled his poem "Ode to Enchanted Light." What does the poet seem to mean by "enchanted light"? In an essay, use details from the poem to support your explanation.
13. In an essay, explain how figurative language contributes to the theme of "The Sky Is Low . . . ." Be sure to provide examples of figurative language to support your ideas about the poem.
14. **Thinking About the Big Question: What is the secret to reaching someone with words?** "Ode to Enchanted Light," "Little Exercise," and "The Sky Is Low . . ." use words to create a moment in nature. Explain which poem affected you most strongly, and why. Use words and phrases from the poem to support your response.

Oral Response

15. Go back to question 2, 5, or 10 or to the question your teacher assigns you. Take a few minutes to expand your answer and prepare an oral response. Find additional details in "Ode to Enchanted Light," "Little Exercise," and "The Sky Is Low . . ." that will support your points. If necessary, make notes to guide your response.

Name ______________________________ Date ______________

Poetry Collection: Pablo Neruda, Elizabeth Bishop, Emily Dickinson

Selection Test A

Critical Reading *Identify the letter of the choice that best answers the question.*

____ 1. What kind of scene does "Ode to Enchanted Light" describe?
- **A.** a natural scene
- **B.** a city scene
- **C.** an underground scene
- **D.** an indoor scene

____ 2. What might be the light described "like a green latticework of branches" in "Ode to Enchanted Light"?
- **A.** moonbeams
- **B.** rays of sunlight
- **C.** rays from a searchlight
- **D.** none of the above

____ 3. What example of personification does "Ode to Enchanted Light" contain?
- **A.** It compares the light to a green latticework of branches.
- **B.** It compares the light to clean white sand.
- **C.** It describes cicadas sending their song into the air.
- **D.** It describes the world as a glass overflowing with water.

____ 4. How many similes do these lines from "Ode to Enchanted Light" contain?

light
like a green
latticework of branches,
shining
on every leaf,
drifting down like clean
white sand.

- **A.** none
- **B.** one
- **C.** two
- **D.** three

____ 5. In "Little Exercise," what sort of scene does the speaker ask us to picture?
- **A.** a hot day at a crowded beach
- **B.** a violent storm blowing up
- **C.** a battle scene
- **D.** a magical dark night

Name ______________________________ Date ______________

___ 6. What two things does this simile from "Little Exercise" compare?

Think of a storm roaming the sky uneasily
like a dog looking for a place to sleep in,

A. a storm and a dog
B. a storm and the sky
C. the sky and a dog
D. a dog and sleep

___ 7. In these lines from "Little Exercise," what does the context suggest that a *heron* is?

. . . occasionally a heron may undo his head,
shake up his feathers, . . .

A. an actor
B. the speaker
C. the poet
D. a bird

___ 8. What happens at the end of "Little Exercise"?

A. Someone drowns.
B. A bridge collapses.
C. The storm returns.
D. Someone sleeps through the storm.

___ 9. What sort of day does Emily Dickinson describe in "The Sky Is Low, the Clouds Are Mean"?

A. an unpleasantly hot summer day
B. a cold and nasty winter day
C. a beautiful but sad autumn day
D. a day of fresh spring rain

___ 10. What figure of speech does Dickinson use in this line from "The Sky Is Low, the Clouds Are Mean"?

A narrow wind complains all day

A. simile
B. metaphor
C. personification
D. none of the above

____ 11. What does *mean* mean in the line "The sky is low, the clouds are mean"?

A. high
B. average
C. cruel or nasty
D. signify

____ 12. Which of these words often signal a simile?

A. *like* and *as*
B. *so* and *and*
C. *for* and *like*
D. none of the above

Vocabulary and Grammar

____ 13. In which of these places would you most likely see a *rut*?

A. a dirt road
B. a museum hall
C. a movie theater
D. a skyscraper

____ 14. What is the indirect object in the following sentence?

Celia gave me two tickets to the new play.

A. Celia
B. me
C. tickets
D. play

____ 15. Which word is most nearly *opposite* in meaning to the word *unresponsive?*

A. reacting
B. quiet
C. puzzled
D. unanswered

Essay

16. Write a short essay in which you describe the scene in either "Ode to Enchanted Light" or "The Sky Is Low, the Clouds Are Mean." Show which details from the poem work to build the particular impression you identified.

17. Write a short composition in which you summarize the events in "Little Exercise." Trace what the speaker observes from the beginning of the poem to the end.

18. **Thinking About the Big Question: What is the secret to reaching someone with words?** "Ode to Enchanted Light," "Little Exercise," and "The Sky Is Low . . ." use words to re-create a moment in nature. In an essay, explain which poem affected you most strongly and why. Use words and phrases from the poem to support your response.

Name ______________________________ Date ______________

Poetry Collection: Pablo Neruda, Elizabeth Bishop, Emily Dickinson

Selection Test B

Critical Reading *Identify the letter of the choice that best completes the statement or answers the question.*

____ 1. What does the word *enchanted* suggest about the light in "Ode to Enchanted Light"?
A. It is pleasant and mysterious.
B. It is sad and mournful.
C. It is unpleasant and ugly.
D. It is the work of elves.

____ 2. Which attitude does the speaker display in "Ode to Enchanted Light"?
A. sensitivity to the needs of others
B. faith in human progress
C. a deep sense of wonder
D. a belief in scientific precision

____ 3. Which figure of speech from "Ode to Enchanted Light" is a metaphor?
A. light / like a green / latticework of branches
B. drifting down like clean / white sand
C. A cicada sends / its sawing song / high into the empty air.
D. The world / is a glass overflowing / with water.

____ 4. Which word in the context is a clue to the meaning of *latticework* in "Ode to Enchanted Light"?

light
like a green
latticework of branches

A. light
B. green
C. branches
D. none of the above

____ 5. What impression of nature does Pablo Neruda convey in "Ode to Enchanted Light"?
A. Nature is a source of comfort for human beings.
B. Nature is indifferent to human suffering.
C. Nature is not always pretty.
D. Nature is very far removed from city life.

____ 6. In these opening lines from "Little Exercise," to what does the word *growling* refer?

Think of the storm roaming the sky uneasily
like a dog looking for a place to sleep in,
listen to it growling.

A. the storm only
B. the dog only
C. both the storm and the dog
D. neither the storm nor the dog

Name ________________________________ Date ________________

____ 7. Where does "Little Exercise" take place?
A. in a tropical or semitropical coastal area
B. on a bleak island off the coast of New England
C. in the California desert
D. in the Arctic

____ 8. Which of these is an example of personification in "Little Exercise"?
A. mangrove keys / lying out there unresponsive to the lightning
B. a heron may undo his head, / shake up his feathers, make an uncertain comment
C. The boulevard / and its . . . sidewalks with weeds in every crack, / are relieved to be wet,
D. all of the above

____ 9. In these lines from "Little Exercise," which word is a clue to the meaning of *boulevard*?

It is raining there. The boulevard
and its broken sidewalks with weeds in every crack,
are relieved to be wet, the sea to be freshened.

A. raining
B. sidewalks
C. weeds
D. wet

____ 10. In "The Sky Is Low, the Clouds Are Mean," what human behavior does the snowflake display?
A. It cannot make up its mind.
B. It is mean and nasty.
C. It is full of complaints.
D. It has trouble getting along with others.

____ 11. In "The Sky Is Low, the Clouds Are Mean," what human behavior does the wind display?
A. It treats others badly.
B. It whines about being badly treated.
C. It keeps changing direction and is unable to make up its mind.
D. It is narrow in outlook and insensitive to the needs of others.

____ 12. Which of these things does Dickinson personify in her poem?
A. the sky
B. the sky, clouds, snowflake, and wind
C. the barn
D. the diadem

Name ______________________________ Date ______________

Vocabulary and Grammar

____ 13. Which word is an antonym of *uneasily*?
A. restfully
B. nervously
C. hardly
D. complicated

____ 14. In which sentence is *debates* used correctly?
A. She debates the pillow as she tries to fall asleep.
B. At the store, she debates whether or not to buy the scarf.
C. Joe debates Jack because they agree on everything.
D. all of the above

____ 15. Which sentence contains an indirect object?
A. The radio warned us of the storm.
B. The police gave everyone three hours to evacuate.
C. Carl remained at home on the island.
D. He escaped the storm in a boat.

____ 16. Which statement about indirect objects is accurate?
A. An indirect object can come after an action verb or a linking verb.
B. An indirect object is always a pronoun.
C. An indirect object comes before a direct object.
D. all of the above

____ 17. In which sentence is a pronoun correctly used as a direct object?
A. The stars of the play were Pablo and me.
B. My dad gave me his old watch.
C. Nan invited my sister and I to her party.
D. Ask me no more questions, please.

Essay

18. From the details in "Ode to Enchanted Light," what does Pablo Neruda seem to mean by "enchanted light"? Answer this question in a brief essay that uses details from the poem to support your explanation.

19. Explain how figurative language contributes to the theme and impact of "The Sky Is Low, the Clouds Are Mean." Be sure to provide examples of figurative language to support your ideas about the poem.

20. **Thinking About the Big Question: What is the secret to reaching someone with words?** "Ode to Enchanted Light," "Little Exercise," and "The Sky Is Low . . . " use words to create a moment in nature. Explain which poem affected you most strongly and why. Use words and phrases from the poem to support your response.

"Snake on the Etowah" by David Bottoms
"Vanishing Species" by Bailey White

Vocabulary Warm-up Word Lists

Study these words from the selections. Then, complete the activities.

Word List A

draped [DRAYPD] *v.* hung down loosely over something
Mom draped a piece of cloth over the couch to hide the ketchup stain.

eased [EEZD] *v.* moved or shifted slowly around or into
Max eased the car carefully into the narrow parking space.

majestic [muh JES tik] *adj.* grand and impressive
The wide, formal staircase and tall, carved columns outside the new library building give it a majestic look.

shudder [SHUD er] *n.* a brief trembling movement from fear or cold
Jackson felt a shudder when he heard the sound of the wolf's howl.

slumped [SLUMPT] *v.* fell or sunk down heavily and suddenly
Mira was so tired while doing her homework that her head slumped onto her math book.

smear [SMEER] *n.* a dirty mark left after one thing rubs against another
She ran her hand over the surface of the tire to look for a leak and came away with a smear of black grease on her palm.

Word List B

bellowing [BEL oh ing] *n.* a loud, powerful roar or howl
We heard the low, deep sound of bellowing from the bulls in the field.

flicker [FLIK r] *n.* a quick sparkling movement
Jamal watched the flicker of the candle flame.

flinch [FLINCH] *v.* to move backward suddenly in response to danger
He did not flinch at the high winds, but went on rounding up his sheep and brought them to safety.

hazy [HAY zee] *adj.* foggy or misty
The morning was so hazy that Arun could not see the bus stop that lay twenty-five yards from his front door.

snagged [SNAGD] *v.* caught on or ripped
The sharp edge of the table snagged Carla's dress.

spooked [SPOOKT] *v.* frightened, startled
My cat hid under the couch after being spooked by the sound of a dish crashing to the floor.

"Snake on the Etowah" by David Bottoms
"Vanishing Species" by Bailey White

Vocabulary Warm-up Exercises

Exercise A *Fill in each blank in the paragraph below with an appropriate word from Word List A. Use each word only once.*

The city spent three years and a lot of money to construct a [1] ____________ new baseball stadium. The place really did look impressive, Paul thought, as he walked through its stately green entry arch for the first time.

A lot of people wanted to see the new stadium, so the crowd was enormous. Paul kept a firm grip on his 4-year-old brother's hand. Winding this way and that, Paul [2] _______ them both through the crowd, and kept right behind their dad. Suddenly, another visitor collided with the two boys. Ramon let go of Paul, who felt an instant [3] _______ go through his body, thinking he might have lost the little guy. Fortunately, Ramon had not gone far. The boys were soon back together.

When they arrived at their seats, they found a number of empty ones in their row, despite the crowd. The boys [4] ________ their legs over a couple of the vacant seats. Their dad reminded them this was not polite. Besides, other people would be arriving. Sure enough, a few minutes later a man plopped down heavily next to Paul. As this man [5] _________ in his seat, the hot dog he had been carrying slid off its plate, into Paul's lap. The man apologized, but mustard had rubbed all over Paul's shirt and left a [6] ____________. Paul was quite happy when a lady came around handing out free tee-shirts to celebrate the opening of the stadium. He put his on right away.

Exercise B *Respond to each item with a complete explanation.*

1. If you saw a man sitting calmly reading a book and sipping tea, would you say he looked spooked?
   ____
2. If you hear a weather report saying that it is hazy outside, what might you expect to see when you open your front door?
   ____
3. Would an animal that is bellowing be using its voice?
   ____
4. Why would a person flinch if she came face to face with a tiger? Explain.
   ____
5. Explain what a person should do if his backpack becomes snagged on a doorknob.
   ____
6. If a strong, steady beam is coming from a lighthouse, is it correct to say that the light has a flicker?
   ____

Name ______________________________ Date ______________

"Snake on the Etowah" by David Bottoms
"Vanishing Species" by Bailey White

Reading Warm-up A

Read the following passage. Pay special attention to the underlined words. Then, read it again, and complete the activities. Use a separate sheet of paper for your written answers.

Jake and his parents were on a camping trip. They were staying in a three-sided wooden shelter at a campground. One afternoon, a ranger came around to alert everybody that a young bear had been sighted in the area. The ranger advised people to remove all food from their shelters and string it up in a tree.

Jake and his parents bundled their food into a backpack, tied the pack to a rope, and cast the rope up until it draped over a high tree branch. Then, they tied the rope tight so the backpack hung twelve feet in the air. They went to sleep feeling safe.

Just before dawn, they awoke to the sound of a bear pawing through a pile of clothes at the very edge of their shelter. The bear was less than a yard from Jake's feet.

He felt a shudder run through him. Other than that involuntary shivering movement, he managed to keep still. He heard faint sounds behind him as his parents eased their legs from their sleeping bags. Jake wasn't sure why they did that, for it was impossible to run away.

Scared as he was, Jake couldn't help thinking there was something majestic about the young bear. What was it that made even a small bear seem grand and impressive? It was because the bear was a wild creature that had to survive outdoors in all weather, without camping gear, groceries, or anything else humans depended on. The bear and its ancestors had been doing that for thousands of years.

Suddenly, it seemed to have found what it was looking for: Jake's T-shirt, which had a smear of peanut butter on it from yesterday's lunch. As usual, Jake had eaten at a picnic table, with napkins available, but had wiped his hands on his shirt.

Dragging the shirt, the bear left the shelter and vanished into the woods. Jake and his parents slumped against the walls in relief. After that, Jake never forgot to use a napkin to wipe his hands.

1. Underline the words that tell what was draped and where it hung. Describe something you have seen that is ***draped.***
2. Circle the words in a nearby sentence that have a meaning similar to shudder. Write down one other example of something that might make a person ***shudder.***
3. Underline the words that tell what was eased. Write down a word that has the opposite meaning of ***eased.***
4. Circle the words in a nearby sentence that have a meaning similar to majestic. Use ***majestic*** in a sentence.
5. Circle the words that describe the smear. What does ***smear*** mean?
6. Circle the word that tells what Jake and his parents felt when then slumped. Use ***slumped*** in a sentence.

Name ______________________________ Date ______________

"Snake on the Etowah" by David Bottoms
"Vanishing Species" by Bailey White

Reading Warm-up B

Read the following passage. Pay special attention to the underlined words. Then, read it again, and complete the activities. Use a separate sheet of paper for your written answers.

Imagine waking up to the bellowing of a pair of lions. Or the whooping morning calls of a family of gibbons. Many zoos now offer the opportunity to camp out overnight on their grounds. These popular programs have names like "Safari Sleepovers" or "Snore and Roar."

A zoo campout typically starts in the early evening, when regular visiting hours end. Guides often take campers on detailed tours of one exhibit: the zoo's collection of Amazon creatures, or its reptiles, or birds. Then, it may be time to break for a snack or put up tents. After that, campers may be offered a late-night tour of the zoo by flashlight.

It is a good idea to install fresh batteries in a flashlight before taking one of these tours. There will then be less of a chance the light could give off a wobbly flicker or go out. Some zoo paths are dark and unlit. A steady light will help prevent tripping or having your clothes snagged by a bush.

An overnight at the zoo is not appropriate for young children who might be spooked by the dark. In fact, people of any age who are afraid of the dark, or who might flinch at the sound of a nighttime screech, are probably better off visiting during the day.

But for those who do spend the night, waking up the next morning can be one of the best parts of the program. Plenty of interesting animal sounds can be heard very early in the morning before the zoo opens. Many animals are quite vocal when they first wake up to greet the day. If the weather is foggy or misty, and the air is hazy, it would not take much to imagine what it is like to hear some of these sounds in the wild.

Most zoo overnights end with breakfast and a crafts project or early-morning tour. Then, it is time to go home and tell everybody what an educational experience it can be to spend a night at the zoo.

1. Underline the words that tell which animals are bellowing. What other animals might make a *bellowing* sound?
2. Circle the word that gives you a clue to flicker. Write a sentence about something you have seen that has a *flicker.*
3. Circle the words that describe where the tent fabric might become snagged. Write a sentence using *snagged.*
4. Circle the words that explain what young children might get spooked by. Use *spooked* in a sentence.
5. Underline the words that give an example of what might make a person flinch. Write your own definition for *flinch.*
6. Underline the nearby words with a meaning similar to hazy. Describe a *hazy* view you have seen.

Name ______________________________ Date ______________

"Snake on the Etowah" by David Bottoms
"Vanishing Species" by Bailey White

Writing About the Big Question

THE BIG ?

What is the secret to reaching someone with words?

Big Question Vocabulary

benefit	connection	cultural	experience	express
feedback	individuality	inform	meaningful	media
misunderstand	relevant	sensory	significance	valid

A. *Use one or more words from the list above to complete each sentence.*

1. Animals are often able to ______________________ emotions without words.
2. Their gestures and movements form ______________________ messages.
3. Both Bottoms and White write about an ______________________ with animal communication.

B. *Follow the directions in responding to each of the items below.*

1. Write two sentences about ways to express yourself through different media.

   ____.

   ____.

2. Write about a meaningful experience you have had communicating with another person or animal. Use at least two of the Big Question vocabulary words.

   ____

   ____

C. *Complete the sentence below. Then, write a short paragraph in which you connect this idea to the Big Question.*

Sensory details can help make an experience real by ______________________

____

____

____

Name ______________________________ Date ______________

"Snake on the Etowah" by David Bottoms
"Vanishing Species" by Bailey White

Literary Analysis: Comparing Poetry and Prose

Literature comes in two major forms—prose and poetry.

- **Prose** is the ordinary form of written language. Prose is usually presented in paragraphs and runs continuously. It includes both fiction and nonfiction. Essays, stories, and novels are all forms of prose.
- **Poetry** is distinguished from prose by its use of precise words, deliberate line lengths, and sound devices such as rhyme and alliteration. Poetry is organized in stanzas and often uses line breaks to emphasize meaning. Poetry is abbreviated, so poets must choose precise words to express their ideas. Poems can rhyme, can be written in free verse, can be lyric, or can tell a story.

Though the two kinds of literature take different form, the writers of both often have the same task—to choose words and images that appeal to the reader and express precise meaning or emotion.

DIRECTIONS: *Use the following chart to identify the similarities and differences between the presentation of the poem "Snake on the Etowah" and that of "Vanishing Species."*

	Form	**Literary Techniques/ Language**	**Setting/Mood**	**Events**
"Snake on the Etowah"				
"Vanishing Species"				

DIRECTIONS: *Use the information from the chart to write a compare-and-contrast paragraph about the differences in the presentation of ideas in the poem and in the prose selection.*

Name ______________________________ Date ______________

"Snake on the Etowah" by David Bottoms
"Vanishing Species" by Bailey White

Vocabulary Builder

Word List

acquire extinction resurgence rituals sidling undulation

A. Directions: *Write a complete sentence to answer each question.*

1. If a plant or animal is facing *extinction,* what is likely to happen to it?

____

____

2. What happens if there is a *resurgence* of a fashion from a previous decade?

____

____

3. When you *acquire* something, what happens?

____

____

4. Where or when are you likely to participate in *rituals?*

____

____

5. What is a dog doing if it is *sidling* up to you?

____

____

6. Where might you witness an *undulation?*

____

____

B. Directions: *Circle* T *if the statement is true or* F *if the statement is false.*

T / F 1. If I want to *acquire* something, I will try to avoid it.

T / F 2. The child is *sidling* because he has just learned to walk.

T / F 3. *Rituals* are formed over many years.

T / F 4. *Resurgence* is the same as *extinction.*

T / F 5. *Undulations* are often violent.

Name ______________________ Date ______________

"Snake on the Etowah" by David Bottoms
"Vanishing Species" by Bailey White

Integrated Language Skills: Support for Writing to Compare Poetry and Prose

Before you write your essay comparing poetry and prose, use the graphic organizer below to jot down your ideas and answers to questions.

How do narrative and poetry differ?	
Narrative	Poetry

How are the two selections similar? List their common characteristics.	
"Snake on the Etowah"	"Vanishing Species"

How do the two selections differ? List their individual characteristics.	
"Snake on the Etowah"	"Vanishing Species"

What possibilities do the genres allow in expressing nature themes?	

Name ______________________________ Date ________________

"Snake on the Etowah" by David Bottoms
"Vanishing Species" by Bailey White

Open-Book Test

Short Answer *Write your responses to the questions in this section on the lines provided.*

1. What does the first phrase of "Snake on the Etowah" tell you about the speaker?

2. In "Snake on the Etowah," what does the speaker mean when he says, "I thought I knew how beauty could poison a moment with fear"?

3. The speaker in "Snake on the Etowah" finds the snake beautiful. Write one phrase from the poem that shows he feels this way.

4. In "Vanishing Species," how does the narrator's view of Mr. Linley change, and why? Explain using details from the story.

5. Near the middle of "Vanishing Species," the author writes: "We were impressed. Now we understood that nervous flicker in Mr. Linley's eyes and those quivering hands." What does she mean by the second sentence?

6. In "Vanishing Species," the alligator refuses to cooperate with Mr. Linley to make a second recording. Why do you think the alligator will not bellow this time? Support your answer with details from the story.

Name ______________________________ Date ______________

7. Both "Snake on the Etowah" and "Vanishing Species" feature a wild creature. In what way are these wild creatures alike?

____

____

8. Tell how Mr. Linley in "Vanishing Species" and the speaker in "Snake on the Etowah" are alike and different. Write one phrase in each section of the diagram. On the line provided, tell how both men feel about wildlife.

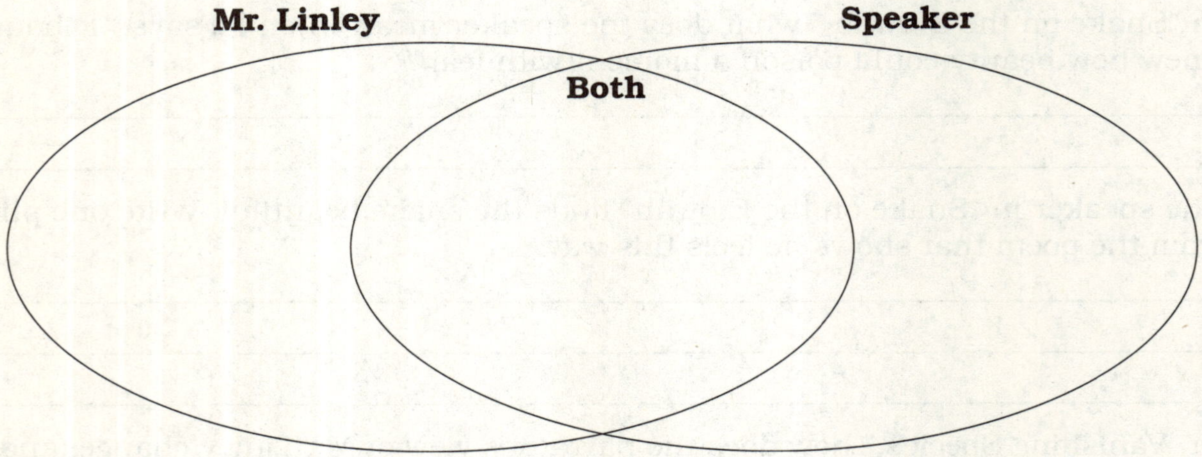

____

9. Reread paragraph 5 of "Vanishing Species." How is this paragraph similar to the poem "Snake on the Etowah"? How is it different?

____

____

____

10. How would "Snake on the Etowah" and "Vanishing Species" be helpful if the *extinction* of copperheads and alligators occurred? Base your response on the meaning of the word *extinction.*

____

____

____

Name ______________________ Date ______________

Essay

Write an extended response to the question of your choice or to the question or questions your teacher assigns you.

11. "Snake on the Etowah" is a poem, and "Vanishing Species" is a nonfiction essay. However, both describe a meeting between a human being and a wild creature. Which presentation did you enjoy more? Write a brief essay explaining your choice. Consider at least two of the following: characters, setting, colorful details, events.

12. The theme of a work of literature is the central idea its author wants to communicate. In an essay, identify a theme of each work related to the topic of *wild creatures*. Next, explain how each author uses details or events to convey this theme. Finally, evaluate the success of each work. In your view, which presents its theme most effectively? How so?

13. The tone of a literary work is the attitude the author takes toward his or her subject. For example, the tone of a work might be respectful, playful, or angry. In an essay, identify the tone of "Snake on the Etowah" and the tone of "Vanishing Species." Then, explain how the form of each work helps the author create this tone. Why do you think Bottoms chose the poem as his form? Why do you think White chose the narrative essay?

14. **Thinking About the Big Question: What is the secret to reaching someone with words?** "Snake on the Etowah" and "Vanishing Species" both use words to communicate a message about wildlife, but they do it in different ways. In which of the two works did the message come across more strongly to you? Explain why you think this work was so successful in reaching you. Cite specific words and phrases that had a strong effect.

Oral Response

15. Go back to question 2, 6, or 7 or to the question your teacher assigns you. Take a few minutes to expand your answer and prepare an oral response. Find additional details in the relevant text that will support your points. If necessary, make notes to guide your response.

Name ______________________________ Date ______________

"Snake on the Etowah" by David Bottoms
"Vanishing Species" by Bailey White

Selection Test A

Critical Reading *Identify the letter of the choice that best answers the question.*

____ **1.** What does the word *several* refer to in these first two lines of David Bottoms' poem?

Kicking through woods and fields, I'd spooked several
and once stepped on a coachwhip among gravestones,

A. animals **B.** snakes **C.** people **D.** ghosts

____ **2.** How does the speaker present his attitude toward the garter and cottonmouth in the first stanza of "Snake on the Etowah"?

A. He uses comparisons that make the snakes seem harmless.
B. He talks about the snakes as if they are friends.
C. He shows his fear of the snakes by his word choice.
D. He uses meter and rhythm to bring the snakes to life.

____ **3.** How does the author bring the concept of beauty to life in these lines from the poem?

I thought I knew how beauty could poison
a moment with fear,

A. He exalts beauty and its power.
B. He assigns a human quality to beauty.
C. He connects beauty to fear.
D. He describes something beautiful.

____ **4.** What is the tone, or attitude, the author of "Vanishing Species" takes toward the subject?

A. serious **C.** humorous
B. respectful **D.** satirical

____ **5.** How does the author of "Vanishing Species" express her feelings toward Mr. Linley?

A. She chooses words that make him appear somewhat fascinating yet ridiculous.
B. She describes his every move and his stupidity in going so close to the alligator.
C. She records the conversations between Mr. Linley, her aunt, and herself.
D. She uses literary techniques, such as alliteration, personification, and rhyme.

Name ______________________ Date ______________

___ 6. What is the point of Mr. Linley's work?

A. He hopes to document wildlife for his book.

B. He is a technical whiz and wants to show off his skills.

C. He likes to travel and has found a way to finance it.

D. He is fascinated with wildlife and wants to have recordings of it.

___ 7. What kind of mood or feeling does White hope to achieve with this sentence?

He [the alligator] ate everything that came out of the back of that truck.

A. fear

B. anger

C. humor

D. happiness

___ 8. What does White mean when she writes, "laws protecting alligators have resulted in a resurgence in their population"?

A. The number of alligators has increased because laws protect them.

B. No one is allowed to hunt alligators because it is against the law.

C. Alligators have come back in fashion in connection with new laws.

D. When people make new laws, animal populations grow quickly.

___ 9. Which of the following do "Snake on the Etowah" and "Vanishing Species" have in common?

A. observation of nature

B. humorous interaction

C. mocking attitude

D. extinct species

___ 10. What feeling do the authors of "Snake on the Etowah" and "Vanishing Species" seem to have in common?

A. a disregard for people

B. a respect for nature

C. a need to record information

D. a humorous perspective

___ 11. What is the difference in the word choice in "Snake on the Etowah" and "Vanishing Species"?

A. "Snake on the Etowah" uses formal language, whereas "Vanishing Species" includes figurative language to express ideas.

B. "Snake on the Etowah" uses general word choice, whereas "Vanishing Species" includes precise words and phrases.

C. "Snake on the Etowah" shows an appreciation for nature through word choice, whereas "Vanishing Species" uses bias to mock nature.

D. "Snake on the Etowah" paints a serene picture with sensory details, whereas "Vanishing Species" uses conversational language.

Name ______________________________ Date ______________

___ 12. Which idea is expressed in both "Snake on the Etowah" and "Vanishing Species"?

A. the infiltration of technology

B. a need to possess nature

C. an appreciation of nature

D. the effects of humans on nature

Vocabulary

___ 13. Which would be the most appropriate word to replace *acquire* in the following sentence from "Vanishing Species"?

He was on a quest to acquire and preserve amazing and unusual natural sounds from all over the world.

A. come by B. buy C. attain D. purchase

___ 14. Which word means the same as the word *resurgence*?

A. denial B. revival C. request D. emerge

___ 15. In which sentence is the word *extinction* used correctly?

A. I tried to *extinction* the fire before bed.

B. It was *extinction* that made the rabbit run.

C. The *extinction* on her face was telling.

D. Some rare species face *extinction*.

Essay

16. Both "Snake on the Etowah" and "Vanishing Species" share the same general setting. In an essay, compare and contrast the ways the authors present the setting. How do the authors make you feel about the setting? What emotions do they try to create?

17. What theme do "Snake on the Etowah" and "Vanishing Species" share? How do the authors present the theme differently? In an essay, identify the common theme of the selections and compare its presentation through the different writing forms.

18. **Thinking About the Big Question: What is the secret to reaching someone with words?** "Snake on the Etowah" and "Vanishing Species" both use words to say something about wildlife, but they do it in different ways. In which of the two works did the message come across more strongly to you? In an essay, explain why you think this work reached you with its message. Support your answer by giving examples of specific words and phrases that had a strong effect on you.

Name ______________________________ Date ______________

"Snake on the Etowah" by David Bottoms
"Vanishing Species" by Bailey White

Selection Test B

Critical Reading *Identify the letter of the choice that best completes the statement or answers the question.*

____ 1. In "Snake on the Etowah," what do the comparisons "like a bow" and "like a boot-lace" say about the speaker's attitude toward the snakes?
A. He feels that the snakes are dangerous.
B. He respects the snakes deeply.
C. He sees the snakes as nonthreatening.
D. He thinks the snakes are like string.

____ 2. Which line from the poem contains an example of personification, or assigning a human quality to a nonhuman thing?
A. under ivy in my yard
B. wiped dew from my eyes and found
C. I though I knew how beauty could poison
D. I felt something brush my thigh

____ 3. How does the mood or feeling shift in the second stanza of "Snake on the Etowah"?
A. The feeling changes from benign observation to being tinged with fear.
B. The feeling changes from observation of to interaction with nature.
C. The feeling changes from awe to humor to appreciation of beauty.
D. The feeling changes from one of fear to one of appreciation.

____ 4. What does the poet describe in the last stanza of "Snake on the Etowah"?
A. an encounter with a snake in the woods
B. his feelings about interacting with snakes
C. a day he spent fishing on the river
D. an encounter with a copperhead in the water

____ 5. Which is an example of alliteration from "Snake on the Etowah"?
A. Kicking through woods and fields
B. Wiped dew from my eyes and found
C. snagged on the sun
D. the head following upriver

____ 6. How does White feel about Mr. Linley in "Vanishing Species"?
A. She finds him invasive and rude.
B. She finds him intriguing and yet amusing.
C. She finds him intelligent and resourceful.
D. She finds him insightful and friendly.

____ 7. What does White mean by "alligators had been hunted to the brink of extinction"?
A. Alligators were nearly gone because of overhunting.
B. Alligators had been pushed over cliffs to kill them.
C. Hunters were not allowed to hunt alligators anymore.
D. Hunters sought alligators because they were so rare.

Name ______________________ Date ______________

____ 8. What purpose do the underlined sentences serve?

Aunt Belle revved the engine a few more times then shut it off. A quail bird whistled. The hot engine ticked. Then we saw the alligator swell up.

A. They help readers imagine how the alligator looked.
B. They paint a picture of the danger Mr. Linley faced.
C. They fill space between events.
D. They provide suspense as Mr. Linley approaches.

____ 9. What does White suggest about the alligator when she says "He just lay silent in the mud and glared at Mr. Linley"?

A. The alligator is not actually trained to bellow.
B. The alligator does not like Mr. Linley.
C. The alligator wants them to leave.
D. The alligator is bored with the trick.

____ 10. What does the author indicate when she says Mr. Linley "bid us a desultory good-bye"?

A. He is sad to leave Aunt Belle's house.
B. He is excited to have recorded the dog.
C. He is disappointed and somewhat aimless.
D. He is happy to get onto his next project.

____ 11. How do the authors of "Snake on the Etowah" and "Vanishing Species" show their respect for nature?

A. They observe animals and respect their power and beauty.
B. They express their fear of snakes and alligators.
C. They tell about experiences they have had with nature.
D. They use figurative language and sound devices.

____ 12. How do the subjects of "Snake on the Etowah" and "Vanishing Species" compare?

A. They focus on human interactions and reactions.
B. They positively address events concerning deadly animals.
C. They discuss the problems that wild creatures face today.
D. They show how people can help and protect nature and animals.

____ 13. How do the presentations of ideas differ in "Snake on the Etowah" and "Vanishing Species"?

A. The poem presents a feeling resulting from observation, whereas the nonfiction tells a story.
B. The poem uses direct descriptions, whereas the nonfiction uses imagery and figurative language.
C. Though they both tell a story, the poem gives a humorous presentation while the nonfiction is serious.
D. The poem details an experience, whereas the nonfiction reflects the author's impressions of a person.

Name ______________________ Date ______________

____ 14. Which best describes the way the authors perceive their subjects of nature?
A. Nature can be dominated by people.
B. People do not show enough respect for nature.
C. More people should write about their experiences with nature.
D. Nature, in the end, goes on with or without people.

Vocabulary

____ 15. In which sentence is the word *undulation* used correctly?
A. The *undulation* of the ocean waters lulled Jesse to sleep.
B. The clock's loud *undulation* scared the quiet child.
C. Kareem could not keep up with the *undulation* of the score.
D. Nancy's *undulation* was overcooked.

____ 16. An appropriate word to describe the movement of a snake is
A. resurgence.
B. sidling.
C. extinction.
D. acquire.

____ 17. Which of the following is an example of a *ritual*?
A. a trip to the zoo
B. buying a snack
C. a graduation ceremony
D. going to bed at a different time

Essay

18. Though "Snake on the Etowah" is a poem and "Vanishing Species" is nonfiction, they use some of the same literary techniques. For example, they both use sensory language and imagery to bring the scene and events to life. In an essay, compare how the poem and the nonfiction essay use word choice and imagery in order to express meaning and emotion, though the outcome is different.

19. Both "Snake of the Etowah" and "Vanishing Species" record and present a personal experience involving nature. In an essay, compare and contrast the attitudes toward nature that are expressed in these two works-

20. **Thinking About the Big Question: What is the secret to reaching someone with words?** "Snake on the Etowah" and "Vanishing Species" both use words to communicate a message about wildlife, but they do it in different ways. In which of the two works did the message come across more strongly to you? Explain why you think this work was so successful in reaching you. Cite specific words and phrases that had a strong effect.

Name ______________________ Date ______________

Writing Workshop—Unit 4, Part 1

Exposition: Problem-and-Solution Essay

Prewriting: Finding a Topic

Think about the following sentence starters to help you brainstorm for problems to solve.

Our community should fix . . .
I really wish people would . . .
Our school would be better if. . .
I get so annoyed when. . .

Then use this cluster diagram to help you brainstorm for topics. Write your favorite sentence starter in the center circle. Write your endings for that sentence starter in the circles around it. Finally, draw a box around the ending you like best.

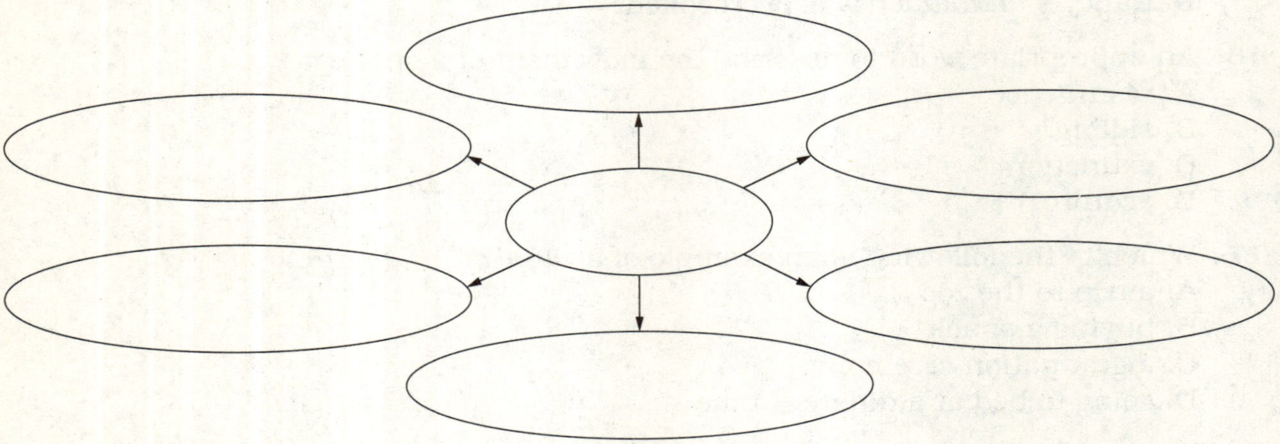

Drafting: Organizing and Supporting Your Ideas

To develop your problem-and-solution essay; fill in the boxes below.

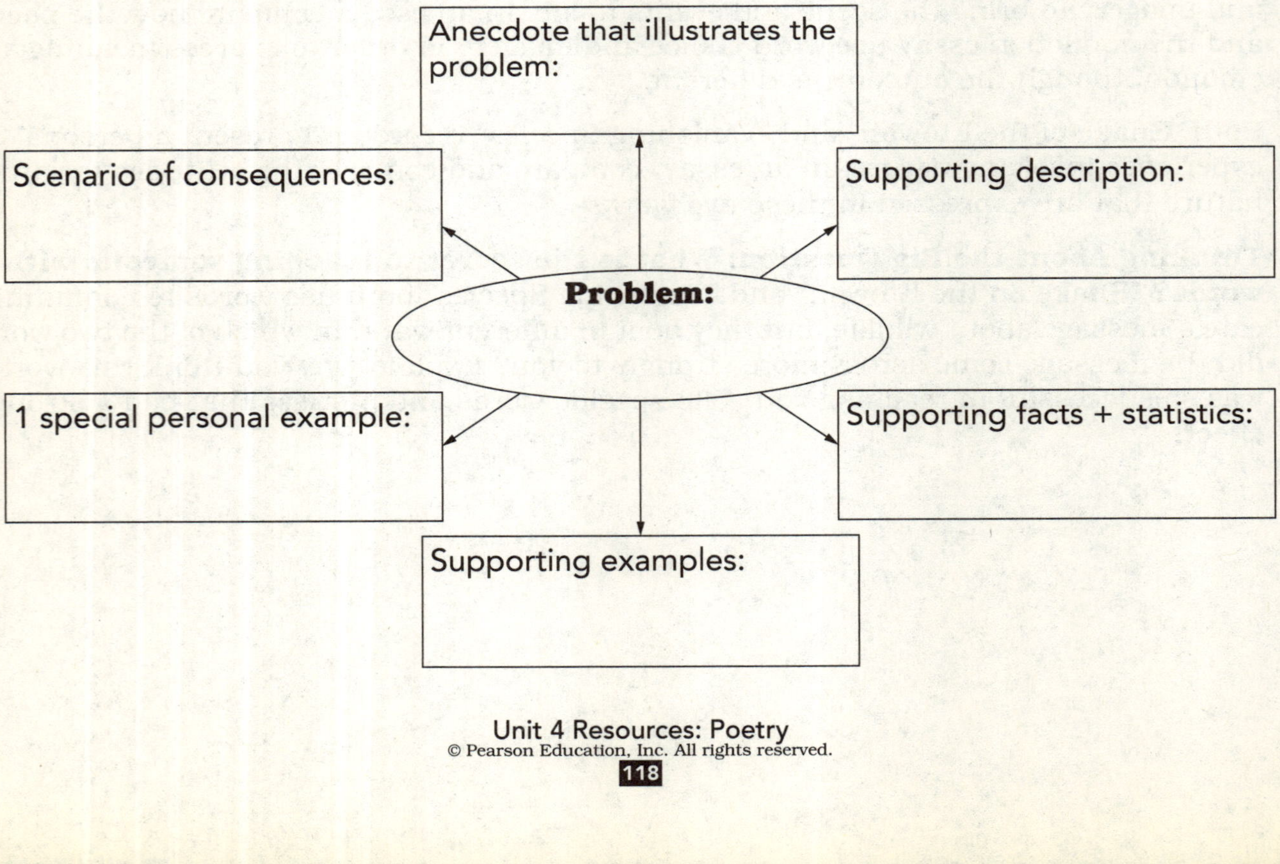

Name ______________________________ Date ______________

Writing Workshop—Unit 4, Part 1

Writing for Assessment: Integrating Grammar Skills

Choosing Between Active and Passive Voice

A verb is in the **active voice** when the subject performs the action. A verb is in the **passive voice** when its subject does not perform the action. Writing is stronger when most sentences use the active voice, but the passive voice may be used to stress the action or when the performer of the action is unknown.

Active Voice	Passive Voice
Lightning **struck** the barn. My family **is painting** the house.	The barn **was struck** by lightning. The house **is being painted** by my family. **Performer Unknown:** The office was closed. **To stress action:** The goal was exceeded.

Identifying Active and Passive Voice

A. Directions: *On the line before each sentence, write* active *or* passive *to identify the voice.*

________________ **1.** Fire broke out in the dry preserve area.

________________ **2.** Sparks were carried by the wind.

________________ **3.** A passing motorist called 9-1-1 from her car phone.

________________ **4.** Before the fire engines arrived, nearby houses were threatened.

Revising Active and Passive Voice

B. Directions: *On the lines provided, rewrite these sentences to make them active voice.*

1. Energy is released by a flash of lightning.

____

2. Thunder is produced by rapid heating of the air.

____

3. Lightning rods are used by owners of buildings.

____

4. Lightning is attracted by the metal in an umbrella.

____

Name ______________________ Date ______________

Unit 4: Poetry
Benchmark Test 7

MULTIPLE CHOICE

Reading Skill: Context Clues *Read the selection, and then answer the questions that follow.*

Be still, sad heart! and cease repining;
Behind the clouds is the sun still shining;
Thy fate is the common fate of all,
Into each life some rain must fall,
Some days must be dark and dreary.

—from "The Rainy Day" by Henry Wadsworth Longfellow

1. Which of these is a possible meaning for the word *repining* in the poem?
   A. expressing uncertainty
   B. expressing determination
   C. expressing happiness
   D. expressing discontent

2. In the poem, what type of context clue for *repining* is the word *shining*?
   A. explanation
   B. definition
   C. synonym
   D. antonym

3. What is the probable meaning of *dreary* in the poem?
   A. gloomy
   B. cheerful
   C. dry
   D. windy

4. Which words most clearly help you determine the meaning of *dreary*?
   A. *sad, rain* and *dark*
   B. *clouds, sun,* and *fate*
   C. *fate, life,* and *rain*
   D. *still, sad,* and *shining*

Read the selection from the poem. Then, answer the questions.

THE RIVER calmly flows,
Through shining banks, through lonely glen,
Where the owl shrieks, though ne'er the cheer of men
Has stirred its mute repose,
Still if you should walk there, you would go there again.

—from "Boat Song" by Ralph Waldo Emerson

5. What is the probable meaning of *glen* in the poem?
   A. a type of tree
   B. a small stream
   C. a narrow valley
   D. a farmer's house

6. Which phrase most clearly helps determine the meaning of *glen*?
   A. The river calmly flows, through
   B. Through shining banks
   C. Where the owl shrieks
   D. stirred its mute repose

Name ______________________________ Date ______________

Reading Skill: Compare and Contrast Features of Consumer Materials

Read the selection from a recipe. Then, answer the questions that follow.

Whisk together the flour and eggs until they are thoroughly mixed. Gradually add the milk and water, stirring to combine. Add the salt and butter, and beat until smooth. Then, heat a lightly oiled frying pan over medium-high heat. Pour the batter into the pan. Cook the crepe for about 2 minutes. Then, loosen the crepe with a spatula, turn, and cook the other side.

7. Which statement about the first 3 sentences of the recipe is true?
- **A.** They all make a suggestion for how to best cook the crepe.
- **B.** They all say how fast or slowly you should do each step.
- **C.** They all name an object used to cook the crepe.
- **D.** They all involve combining ingredients.

8. Which statement about the last 3 sentences of the recipe its true?
- **A.** They tell you how to cook the crepe.
- **B.** They tell you what to do before you start cooking the crepe.
- **C.** They tell you how to serve the crepe after you have cooked it.
- **D.** They tell you what equipment you will need to cook the crepe.

9. Based on the recipe, which of the following would be the correct thing to do?
- **A.** Add salt and sugar to the flour and eggs.
- **B.** Cook the crepe for about 2 minutes.
- **C.** Use a deep pot to cook the batter.
- **D.** Turn the crepe over with a fork.

10. Based on the context in which it is used, what is the most likely meaning of *spatula*?
- **A.** a tool for heating food
- **B.** a tool for frying food
- **C.** a tool for mixing food
- **D.** a tool for lifting food

Literary Analysis: Sound Devices

11. What type of sound device is used in the following lines of poetry?

A tapering turret overtops the work,

- **A.** alliteration
- **B.** onomatopoeia
- **C.** rhyme
- **D.** rhythm

12. Which sound device uses words to imitate sounds?
- **A.** rhythm
- **B.** onomatopoeia
- **C.** alliteration
- **D.** rhyme

Name ______________________________ Date ______________

13. Which of these is the best example of the use of rhythm as a sound device?
   A. A snail trail streamed across the summer porch.
   B. The water in the hot pan hissed and sputtered.
   C. When I wished upon a star, the star winked back at me.
   D. Four farmers toiled tirelessly in their fields.

Literary Analysis: Figurative Language

14. Which of these is an example of the use of figurative language?
   A. The breeze rustled the leaves of the tall elms.
   B. The grain stalks bowed to one another in the breeze.
   C. A sudden breeze cooled our hot faces as we worked.
   D. The wind chimes dinged and clanged in the breeze.

15. Which choice contains a simile?
   A. The sheriff was a hearty, loud-talking fellow.
   B. Her curiosity led her to learn a great deal.
   C. The stream gurgled its way over the rocks.
   D. Pynchon's Pond was as smooth as glass.

16. Which of the following is an example of personification?
   A. A rusted stove crouched in the corner.
   B. In the race, Evan ran like a gazelle.
   C. The trail bent left, toward the creek.
   D. She sat sleepily, nodding her head.

17. Which of these best defines the use of personification in making comparisons?
   A. Two unlike things are compared using *like* or *as*.
   B. Two unlike things are compared by saying that one is the other.
   C. A nonhuman subject is given human characteristics.
   D. Human behavior is described in terms of animal behavior.

Literary Analysis: Comparing Poetry and Prose

18. Which of the following is not a prose form?
   A. a novel
   B. a short story
   C. an essay
   D. a poem

Name ______________________________ Date ______________

Read the poem and answer the questions that follow.

19. What is the mood of the poem?
    - A. humorous
    - B. hopeful
    - C. angry
    - D. disappointed

20. Which of these poetic technique is most evident in "Casey at the Bat"?
    - A. alliteration
    - B. figurative language
    - C. rhyme
    - D. vivid setting

Vocabulary: Prefixes and Suffixes

21. In which pair of words does the prefix *im-* have the same meaning?
    - A. *impossible* and *implicate*
    - B. *immune* and *impale*
    - C. *improbable* and *immoral*
    - D. *imagination* and *imbecile*

22. What is the definition of *ponderous* in the following sentence?

    I was fascinated by the ponderous elephants as they lumbered around the circus tent.
    - A. unimportant
    - B. weighty
    - C. confusing
    - D. difficult to remember

23. What does the prefix *im-* mean in the word *imprison*?
    - A. in
    - B. not
    - C. out
    - D. big

24. Words that end with the suffix *-ive* are usually what part of speech?
    - A. adverbs
    - B. verbs
    - C. nouns
    - D. adjectives

Name ______________________________ Date ______________

25. Which prefix has the same meaning of *im-* as it is used in the word *immoderate*?
   A. en-
   B. un-
   C. uni-
   D. mega-

26. What is the meaning of *active* in the following sentence?

   Henry is an active member of the theater club.

   A. selfish
   B. lazy
   C. busy
   D. generous

Grammar

27. Which sentence contains a predicate pronoun as a subject complement?
   A. We wondered what happened to him.
   B. The best person for the job is she.
   C. Are they coming to our play?
   D. He was the Poet Laureate in 2001.

28. Which sentence contains a predicate noun used as a subject complement?
   A. The walk through the tunnel was eerie.
   B. What nationality are you?
   C. My dog is master of the household.
   D. The ground is sloping and uneven.

29. Which statement is true?
   A. An indirect object answers the question *What*?
   B. A direct object answers the question *To what*?
   C. An indirect object answers the question *Whom*?
   D. A direct object answers the question *Whom*?

30. What is the direct object in the following sentence?

   Olivia fed a cracker to the gray mule in the pen.

   A. Olivia
   B. cracker
   C. mule
   D. pen

31. Which sentence contains an indirect object?
   A. Elyssa handed her dad the purple iris.
   B. Jack hung the lantern on the nail.
   C. Dad gave the horse's reins to me.
   D. That coat is too large for Marco.

Name ______________________ Date ______________

32. Which sentence contains a verb in the active voice?
   A. A loud screech was heard in the tree.
   B. Are the streets really paved in gold?
   C. The baby is sleeping soundly.
   D. The new park was finished at last.

33. Which sentence contains a verb is the active voice?
   A. He really plays the guitar well.
   B. The audience was entertained by the guitarist.
   C. The guitar has been played by someone famous.
   D. The guitar was played all night long.

ESSAY

Writing

34. Imagine that you have been asked to write an introduction for a favorite recorded song that you will play for other students. You want to draw students' attention especially to the words of the song and their effect on you. Jot down two or three ideas about how you will explain why the words of this song are important to you. Mention any use of sound devices such as alliteration, onomatopoeia, rhyme, or rhythm in the song.

35. Jot down notes for a study for a poem about a walk in the woods. Begin by listing some things you might see, hear, smell, touch, and taste in the woods. Then choose three things on your list and write phrases that make comparisons using one example each of a simile, a metaphor, and personification, such as *The tall pines looked like sharpened pencils.*

36. Write a brief essay describing a problem in your school, or local community. Then, propose two possible solutions to the problem. Be sure to give reasons that explain why you think each solution might work.

Name ____________ Starting Date ____________ Ending Date ____________

Unit 4: Poetry Skills Concept Map—2

What is the secret to reaching someone with words?

Words you can use to discuss the Big Question

____
____
____
____
____
____
____

Literary Analysis: Poetry

Basic Elements of Poetry

- Sensory Language
- Figurative Language
- Sound Devices

Forms of Poetry

- Narrative
- Ballads
- Free Verse
- Haiku
- Rhyming Couplets
- Limericks

Poetry includes **lyric and narrative poems** (demonstrated in this selection) Selection name:

and **imagery** (demonstrated in this selection) Selection name:

Reading Skills and Strategies: Paraphrase

You can **paraphrase** by **rereading to clarify meaning** and by reading **aloud fluently according to punctuation**

Comparing Literary Works: Description

in poetry presents **levels of meaning** including **literal** (actual) **meaning** and **figurative** (symbolic) **meaning**

(demonstrated in these selections)

Selection names:

1.

2.

Informational Text: Technical Directions

(demonstrated in this selection) Selection name:

To be sure you understand and can follow all the steps → **analyze technical directions**

Student Log

Complete this chart to track your assignments.

Writing	Extend Your Learning	Writing Workshop	Other Assignments

Vocabulary Warm-up Word Lists

Study these words from the poetry of Robert Hayden, William Shakespeare, and Ricardo Sánchez. Then, complete the activities that follow.

Word List A

aromas [uh ROH muhz] *n.* strong, pleasant smells
The aromas of cooking made my mouth water.

benefits [BEN uh fits] *n.* advantages or help that you get from something
The benefits of Grandma's visit were three great meals every day.

brethren [BRETH ruhn] *n.* brothers; comrades or fellows
Native Americans treated the early white settlers like brethren, as if they were family.

familial [fuh MIL yuhl] *adj.* having to do with a family
Jenna's familial duties included watching her little brother.

resolution [rez uh LOO shuhn] *n.* the quality of having strong beliefs and the desire to do something
Though painting the house was not easy work, he completed the task with resolution.

thicketed [THIK it ed] *adj.* covered with a thick growth of shrubs or small trees
The island was thicketed with berry-producing shrubs.

Word List B

bonanza [buh NAN zuh] *n., used here as adj.* a sudden gain of money or good luck
Lydia's long-lost, wealthy uncle left her a bonanza inheritance in his will.

dart [DAHRT] *v.* to move suddenly and quickly in a direction
When prairie dogs sense danger, they dart underground.

folly [FAHL ee] *n.* foolishness; a silly thing
When the first steamboat appeared, some people thought it was a folly.

shackles [SHAK uhlz] *n.* metal rings joined by chains put around the wrists or ankles to prevent escape
The prisoner arrived in court in shackles, along with two guards.

summoning [SUH muhn ing] *v., used here as n.* calling people together
When a meal on the ranch was ready, there came a summoning from the "dinner bell."

yonder [YAHN duhr] *adj.* being at a certain distance, usually within view
"Run to yonder shed and get the shears for me," said Pa.

Name ________________________________ Date ________________

Poetry Collection: Robert Hayden, William Shakespeare, Ricardo Sánchez

Vocabulary Warm-up Exercises

Exercise A *Fill in each blank in the paragraph below with an appropriate word from Word List A. Use each word only once.*

Claire was firm in her [1] ____________________ to become a great chef, so she went to cooking school for a summer. The school was deep in the country. It had a comfortable, [2] ____________________ feel, and Claire felt at home right away. One of the [3] ____________________ of being in the country was that there was plenty of room to grow fresh vegetables to use in recipes. The tomato and bean plants grew so well that they [4] ____________________ part of the garden. During the day, the young chefs worked in the big kitchens. Mouth-watering [5] ____________________ filled the air. Each evening, they all enjoyed a fine meal and the company of their cooking [6] ____________________.

Exercise B *Revise each sentence so that the underlined vocabulary word is used in a logical way. Be sure to keep the vocabulary word in your revision.*

1. The bonanza find did not produce any gold.

____

____

2. If it begins to rain at the party, you can dart out from under the canopy.

____

____

3. In modern times, believing that the Earth is round is sheer folly.

____

____

4. Wearing shackles, the animals ran gracefully through the meadow.

____

____

5. The awards assembly began hours before the summoning of all winners to the stage.

____

____

6. Pick peaches from yonder tree, the one on the other side of the hill.

____

____

Name ________________________________ Date ________________

Poetry Collection: Robert Hayden, William Shakespeare, Ricardo Sánchez

Reading Warm-up A

Read the following passage. Pay special attention to the underlined words. Then, read it again, and complete the activities. Use a separate sheet of paper for your written answers.

I was so excited when my parents told me that we were going to a family reunion! I had never been to one before. All I knew was that there would be more than 300 Santoros in one place at one time, and that all of us were related, all of us were brethren. I realized that I had more cousins than I had ever dreamed of.

We got on the road early on the morning of the reunion, and started on our way. The family had rented an entire campground by the seashore for the event. We drove on and on, past the city, past small towns, and then through an area that was thicketed with low shrubs and berry bushes. The air smelled salty. We were almost there.

Soon I saw lines of cars parked by the sand, all with signs that said "Santoro Family Reunion." Even the vehicles seemed to have a familial likeness—there were several that looked the same as ours, as if they were relatives. We parked and jumped out of the car to join in the party. Aromas of grilling meats and vegetables filled my nose, and those delicious smells made me hungry right away. I was given a T-shirt with the family name on it, and before I knew it, I was in the middle of a game of beach volleyball.

One of the benefits of having a big group is the advantage of having plenty of helping hands. As if by magic, big tables were set up, and heaping platters of food were appearing on them. As I ate, laughed, and chatted with Santoros of every shape and size, I realized what a great thing a big family is. I decided then and there, with complete determination and resolution, that I would stay in touch with everyone and that I would organize another family reunion when I was older.

1. Circle the words that explain the meaning of brethren. Then, give a synonym for ***brethren***.
2. Underline the words that tell what made the area thicketed. Describe a ***thicketed*** area that you know about.
3. Circle the words that give a clue about the meaning of familial. Are there ***familial*** resemblances in your family?
4. Underline the words that tell what is making the aromas. Name some of your favorite ***aromas***.
5. Underline the word that is similar to benefits. Tell about some ***benefits*** you have by being a member of a family, a club, or a team.
6. Circle the word that helps you understand the meaning of resolution. Tell about something you have done with ***resolution***.

Name ______________________________ Date ________________

Poetry Collection: Robert Hayden, William Shakespeare, Ricardo Sánchez

Reading Warm-up B

Read the following passage. Pay special attention to the underlined words. Then, read it again, and complete the activities. Use a separate sheet of paper for your written answers.

Stories of the Old West rarely include African Americans. Freed from the shackles of slavery, many blacks did make their way to the frontier in search of better lives. Even before the Civil War, black miners turned up to hunt for gold in California. Bonanza gold made some rich; others opened businesses and started newspapers or schools.

After the Civil War, many former slaves became homesteaders, buying land from the government for next to nothing. Life was hard out on the plains. The land was tough to plow, and the weather was often unkind.

Supplies were hard to come by, too. Parents couldn't say to their kids, "Go over to yonder store and buy some rope," for the nearest store might be hundreds of miles away.

Some freed slaves heeded the army's summoning of soldiers to fight Indians on the Great Plains. The Indians nicknamed them "buffalo soldiers." This name was given out of respect; the Native Americans held the buffalo in high regard since it fed, clothed, and sheltered them.

About one of four cowboys in the Old West was black, and Nat Love was one of the most famous. He rode well and shot well. When a bull would dart this way and that, trying to avoid being caught, Nat was ready to bring it down with his rope.

Mary Fields, a freed slave, was rough and tough, too. Making her way to Montana, she hauled supplies and did other "heavy" work. She was always ready with her fists to convince people who thought it was folly for her to do such work. Later in life, she mellowed and began delivering mail. She became known as Stagecoach Mary for her ability to ride her stagecoach through any kind of weather and still show up on time.

Nat and Mary are just two of the "characters" that were part of the westward movement of African Americans. Many more stories remain to be told.

1. Underline the words that help you figure out the meaning of shackles. Define two meanings of ***shackles*** as it is used in this passage.
2. Circle the two words that give a clue to the meaning of bonanza. Explain what ***bonanza*** means.
3. Circle the phrase in the next sentence that contrasts strongly with yonder. Write a sentence with ***yonder,*** using real locations in your life.
4. Rewrite the sentence that includes summoning, replacing it with a synonym. Tell about an experience in which you did or did not respond to a ***summoning.***
5. Underline the words that give a picture of what it means to dart. Describe something you know that can ***dart.***
6. Underline what Mary Fields did to convince people who thought her work was folly. Tell about something that you think is ***folly.***

Name ______________________________ Date ______________

Poetry Collection: Robert Hayden, William Shakespeare, Ricardo Sánchez

Writing About the Big Question

THE BIG ?

What is the secret to reaching someone with words?

Big Question Vocabulary

benefit	connection	cultural	experience	express
feedback	individuality	inform	meaningful	media
misunderstand	relevant	sensory	significance	valid

A. *Use one or more words from the list above to complete each sentence.*

1. "I have called this meeting to ______________________ you of our new dress code," said Principal McNut.
2. The community was a spectrum of different ______________________ influences reflected in the people and food from around the world.
3. One way Clarissa expressed her ______________________ was through her art and writing.

B. *Follow the directions in responding to each of the items below.*

1. What is the benefit of talking about meaningful experiences? Use at least two Big Question Vocabulary words in your answer.

____

____.

2. Write about a time when you received feedback that made you uncomfortable.

____

____

C. *Complete the sentence below. Then, write a short paragraph in which you connect this idea to the Big Question.*

Reading about other people's feelings and experiences may benefit people and help them ____

____

____

____

Name ______________________________ Date ______________

Poetry Collection: Robert Hayden, William Shakespeare, Ricardo Sánchez

Reading: Reread to Paraphrase

To make their poems more powerful and memorable, poets often use language that is rarely used in everyday speech. To understand a poem, it may therefore be helpful to paraphrase it in simple, everyday language. When you **paraphrase,** you restate text in your own words. First, **reread the poem to clarify** the writer's meaning. Identify the most basic information in each sentence or phrase—what is being done and who or what is doing it. Use a dictionary or text aids like footnotes, if provided, to help you with unfamiliar terms. Once you understand the poet's meaning, restate the sentences in everyday English. Eliminate repetition, use simpler synonyms, and put unusual sentence structures into a word order that is easier to understand.

Directions: *Use this chart to paraphrase the poems by Shakespeare and Sánchez in this collection. One example has been provided for you.*

Poem	Original Lines	Paraphrased Lines
"Blow, Blow, Thou Winter Wind"	Line 1: "Blow . . . wind."	Winter wind, go ahead and blow.
	Lines 2–3: "Thou . . . ingratitude."	
	Lines 4–6: "Thy . . . rude."	
	Line 7: "Heigh-ho! . . . holly."	
	Line 8: "Most . . . folly."	
	Lines 9–10: "Then . . . jolly."	
	Lines 11–13: "Freeze . . . forgot."	
	Lines 14–16: "Though . . . not."	
	Lines 17–20: "Heigh-ho . . . jolly."	
"Old Man"	Lines 1–6: "old . . . freely;"	
	Lines 7–14: "old . . . life . . ."	
	Lines 15–21: "you . . . albuquerque . . ."	
	Lines 22–28: "old . . . there:"	
	Lines 29–36: "some . . . painful . . ."	
	Lines 37–47: "old . . . you . . ."	

Name ______________________________ Date ______________

Poetry Collection: Robert Hayden, William Shakespeare, Ricardo Sánchez

Literary Analysis: Lyric and Narrative Poetry

A **lyric poem** expresses the thoughts and feelings of a single speaker and uses images and other details to create a single, unified impression. A **narrative poem** tells a story in verse and has all the elements of a short story, including plot, conflict, setting, characters, and theme.

DIRECTIONS: *Choose one lyric poem and one narrative poem in this collection. Write the title of each poem on the line provided, and then answer the questions about it.*

A. Lyric Poem Title: ______________________________

1. Why is this poem a lyric poem? ______________________________

2. What are two feelings or emotions that the speaker expresses? ______________________________

3. List two images that the speaker uses and the ideas they convey. ______________________________

4. What main impression would you say the poem conveys? ______________________________

B. Narrative Poem Title: ______________________________

1. Why is this poem a narrative poem? ______________________________

2. Summarize the plot in one or two sentences. ______________________________

3. What is the main conflict or struggle, and how is it resolved in the end?

4. As specifically as possible, identify the poem's main setting.

5. Who is the main character? What minor characters does the poem feature?

Name ______________________ Date ______________

Poetry Collection: Robert Hayden, William Shakespeare, Ricardo Sánchez

Vocabulary Builder

Word List

aromas beckoning ingratitude legacy shackles supple

A. DIRECTIONS: *Answer each question with a sentence that uses one of the Word List words. Use each Word List word only once.*

1. What might someone get from a rich relative when that relative dies?

____

____

2. How would you describe a person who fails to give thanks to those who help him or her?

____

____

3. How would you describe a light in the darkness?

____

____

4. What might you call the smells of different coffees?

____

____

5. How could you restrain a criminal?

____

____

6. How could you describe a person's muscular body?

____

____

B. WORD STUDY: *The prefix* in- *means "not" or "lacking." Use the context of the sentences and what you know about the prefix* in- *to explain your answer to each question.*

1. What might a student do if he were *incapable* of solving a problem?

____

____

2. Are *indefinite* plans fixed? Explain.

____

____

Name ______________________________ Date ______________

Poetry Collection: Robert Hayden, William Shakespeare, Ricardo Sánchez

Enrichment: Old Age and Harriet Tubman

In the past hundred years, advances in medicine and social policy have helped increase the number of Americans who are 65 years old or more. Social attitudes toward old age have also changed. Today, under federal law, workers in most jobs can no longer be forced to retire when they reach 65. Senior citizens remain more physically active than they did fifty years ago, and many enjoy good health well into their seventies and eighties.

A. Directions: *Society's attitudes toward the elderly are reflected in books and magazines, on television, and in other media. Using magazines in the library or available to you at home, explore how old age is represented in magazine advertisements. Make copies of at least three ads that feature elderly people. Then, answer these questions.*

Ad #1: What product or service is being sold? ______________________________

What are the elderly people doing? ______________________________

Ad #2: What product or service is being sold? ______________________________

What are the elderly people doing? ______________________________

Ad #3: What product or service is being sold? ______________________________

What are the elderly people doing? ______________________________

From these ads, what do you conclude about our society's attitude toward old age?

____

____

____

____

____

____

B. Directions: *Harriet Tubman, the heroine mentioned in "Runagate Runagate," was born into slavery about 1820 and lived to be about 93 years old. Do research online or in a printed reference source to find out some of Tubman's achievements in the later part of her life. List at least three on the lines below.*

____

____

____

____

____

____

Name ______________________ Date ______________

Poetry Collection: Robert Hayden, William Shakespeare, Ricardo Sánchez

Open-Book Test

Short Answer *Write your responses to the questions in this section on the lines provided.*

1. The setting is the time and place of a literary work. What is the setting of the narrative poem "Runagate Runagate"? What details from the poem reveal this setting?

2. When you paraphrase lines from a poem, you restate them in your own words. How would you paraphrase the following lines from "Runagate Runagate"?

   And before I'll be a slave

   I'll be buried in my grave.

3. In "Runagate Runagate," what does the North Star represent? How do you know?

4. A lyric poem expresses the thoughts and feelings of a single speaker. What main feeling does the lyric poem "Blow, Blow, Thou Winter Wind" express? Support your answer with details from the poem.

5. In "Blow, Blow, Thou Winter Wind," the speaker compares human beings with winter weather. Explain the comparison. What point does this comparison make about humans? Support your answer with some details from the poem.

6. In "Blow, Blow, Thou Winter Wind," the speaker feels that people are full of *ingratitude.*

Name ______________________ Date ______________

7. In the left column of the chart, you will find lines from "Blow, Blow, Thou Winter Wind." To complete the chart, write a paraphrase of each line in the right column. On the line provided, explain how paraphrasing helps you understand the poem better.

Thy tooth is not so keen	
Most friendship is feigning	
This life is most jolly	

____

____

8. The speaker of "Old Man" learned a lot from his grandfather at family gatherings. What was the most significant thing he learned? Support your answer with details from the poem.

____

____

____

9. In the lyric poem "Old Man," what main emotions does the speaker express for his grandfather? What details in the poem tell you how the speaker feels?

____

____

____

10. In "Old Man," the speaker's grandfather leaves him a *legacy*. What is his *legacy*? Focus on the meaning of *legacy* in your response.

____

____

____

Essay

Write an extended response to the question of your choice or to the question or questions your teacher assigns you.

11. In "Old Man," the speaker pays tribute to his grandfather. In a brief essay, describe the grandfather. Tell what he is like, what he has done for the speaker, and how the speaker feels about him. Support your response with examples from the poem.

12. In an essay, explain what a lyric poem is. Then, tell why "Blow, Blow, Thou Winter Wind" qualifies as a lyric poem. Use examples from the poem to illustrate your points.

13. A good narrative poem will often contain suspense—the feeling of tension or excitement that makes readers keep reading to learn what happens next. In an essay, discuss the details that help build suspense in the narrative poem "Runagate Runagate."

14. **Thinking About the Big Question: What is the secret to reaching someone with words?** In "Runagate Runagate," "Blow, Blow, Thou Winter Wind," and "Old Man," the speakers are trying to describe feelings to the reader. In an essay, explain what one of the speakers is feeling. Use words and phrases from the poem to explain how the speaker reaches readers with his or her feelings.

Oral Response

15. Go back to question 1, 4, or 10 or to the question your teacher assigns you. Take a few minutes to expand your answer and prepare an oral response. Find additional details in "Runagate Runagate," "Blow, Blow, Thou Winter Wind," and "Old Man" that will support your points. If necessary, make notes to guide your response.

Name ______________________________ Date ______________

Poetry Collection: Robert Hayden, William Shakespeare, Ricardo Sánchez

Selection Test A

Critical Reading *Identify the letter of the choice that best answers the question.*

____ 1. In "Blow, Blow, Thou Winter Wind," what does the speaker say is worse than the winter wind?

A. the summer rain
B. the freezing cold
C. human beings who behave unkindly
D. life without friends or family

____ 2. Which is the best paraphrase of this line from "Blow, Blow, Thou Winter Wind"?

Most friendship is feigning,

A. Most people only pretend to be a friend.
B. Most friends are true.
C. Most friends fawn over you.
D. Friendship is demanding and tiring.

____ 3. What main feeling does the speaker express in "Blow, Blow, Thou Winter Wind"?

A. friendship
B. admiration
C. annoyance
D. disappointment

____ 4. Which word best describes the mood of these lines from "Blow, Blow, Thou Winter Wind"?

Then, heigh-ho, the holly!
This life is most jolly.

A. embarrassed
B. disappointed
C. bitter
D. cheerful

____ 5. In "Old Man," what is the cultural heritage of the speaker and his grandfather?

A. Native American only
B. Native American and Spanish
C. Spanish only
D. Spanish and Portuguese

Name ______________________________ Date ______________

___ 6. What main feeling does the speaker in “Old Man” express for his grandfather?
A. sorrow
B. contempt
C. admiration
D. envy

___ 7. What was the most significant thing the speaker in “Old Man” learned from his grandfather at family gatherings?
A. pride in his heritage
B. patience
C. recipes for cooking with green chiles
D. distrust for modern ways

___ 8. What is the best paraphrase for these lines from “Old Man”?
some of our blood was here, . . .
before the coming of coronado
A. Some of us bled in the fight with Coronado.
B. Some of our ancestors were here before the Spaniard named Coronado came.
C. Some of us lost blood in battles fought long before Coronado came.
D. Some of our ancestors lost blood in the Coronado River.

___ 9. In the narrative poem “Runagate Runagate,” what is the story mainly about?
A. farm life in the South during the 1800s
B. the Civil War
C. escaping from slavery
D. the civil rights movement of the 1950s

___ 10. What do these lines show about the people running in “Runagate Runagate”?
Runs falls rises stumbles on from darkness into darkness
and the darkness thicketed with shapes of terror
and the hunters pursuing and the hounds pursuing
A. They have reason to feel frightened.
B. They are cowardly.
C. They are fine athletes.
D. They are running in circles.

___ 11. In “Runagate Runagate,” how do the wanted posters describe Harriet Tubman?
A. as a coward
B. as a foolish, misguided person
C. as a great heroine of her people
D. as an armed, dangerous criminal

Name ______________________________ Date ______________

____ 12. If you were paraphrasing the following line from "Runagate Runagate," what word or phrase would be best to use in place of *dart*?

They'll dart underground when you try to catch them

A. dig
B. dash
C. dare
D. pointy object

Vocabulary and Grammar

____ 13. Which word means the same as *legacy*?

A. contract
B. lawyer
C. stocking
D. inheritance

____ 14. Which word means the opposite of *beckoning*?

A. calling
B. commanding
C. drying
D. dismissing

____ 15. How many prepositional phrases does the following line contain?

No more auction block for me

A. none
B. one
C. two
D. three

Essay

16. Write a paraphrase of a part you remember from "Blow, Blow, Thou Winter Wind" or "Runagate Runagate." Your paraphrase should be in paragraph form.

17. Write an essay about the grandfather in "Old Man." Explain what he is like, what he has done for the speaker, and how the speaker feels about him.

18. **Thinking About the Big Question: What is the secret to reaching someone with words?** In "Runagate Runagate," "Blow, Blow, Thou Winter Wind," and "Old Man," the speakers are trying to describe feelings to the reader. In an essay, explain what one of the speakers is feeling. Use words and phrases from the poem to explain how the speaker reaches readers with his or her feelings.

Name ______________________________ Date ______________

Poetry Collection: Robert Hayden, William Shakespeare, Ricardo Sánchez

Selection Test B

Critical Reading *Identify the letter of the choice that best completes the statement or answers the question.*

____ 1. In "Blow, Blow, Thou Winter Wind," what can you infer about the speaker?
- **A.** He behaves cruelly to others.
- **B.** He has been treated unkindly by others.
- **C.** He loves warm weather.
- **D.** He loves cold weather.

____ 2. What main point does "Blow, Blow, Thou Winter Wind" make about the harshness of nature?
- **A.** It is not as bad as the harshness of humans toward one another.
- **B.** It is worse than the harshness of humans toward one another.
- **C.** It reflects the harshness of human relationships.
- **D.** It is caused by forces human beings cannot understand.

____ 3. Which is the best paraphrase of this line from "Blow, Blow, Thou Winter Wind"?

Thy tooth is not so keen,

- **A.** Your bite is not so sharp.
- **B.** Your appetite is not so hungry.
- **C.** Your attitude is not so enthusiastic.
- **D.** My imagination is not so vivid.

____ 4. What main emotion does the lyric poem "Blow, Blow, Thou Winter Wind" express?
- **A.** love for friends and family
- **B.** admiration for nature
- **C.** irritation with bad weather
- **D.** disappointment with human behavior

____ 5. In the lyric poem "Old Man," what main emotions does the speaker express for his grandfather?
- **A.** love but disappointment
- **B.** contempt and biting humor
- **C.** admiration and respect
- **D.** puzzlement and indifference

____ 6. What does the speaker in "Old Man" think about the past times of which his grandfather speaks?
- **A.** Those times are out of date and best forgotten.
- **B.** Life in those times was in some ways freer.
- **C.** Life in those times was full of pain and misery.
- **D.** No one today can understand or appreciate those times.

Name ______________________ Date ______________

____ 7. What is the main thing that the grandfather in "Old Man" teaches the speaker to value?
A. his cultural heritage
B. the family business in Albuquerque
C. nature
D. friendship

____ 8. Which is the best paraphrase for the term *pueblos* in "Old Man"?
A. small stones
B. large farms
C. Indian (Native American) communities
D. annual family gatherings in the Southwest

____ 9. What is the setting of the narrative poem "Runagate Runagate"?
A. a June evening just after World War I
B. a late afternoon in biblical times
C. a dark night before the Civil War
D. the morning of July 4, 1776

____ 10. What is the main conflict in the narrative poem "Runagate Runagate"?
A. the battle between North and South in the Civil War
B. the attempt by American slaves to escape using the Underground Railroad
C. Susyanna's struggle not to show her emotions
D. the struggle of the slaves to remain quiet as they escape to freedom

____ 11. What does the North Star represent in "Runagate Runagate"?
A. faith
B. freedom
C. brotherly love
D. old mysteries

____ 12. What are these lines from "Runagate Runagate"?

If you see my Pompey, 30 yrs of age,
new breeches, plain stockings, negro shoes;
if you see my Anna, likely young mulatto
branded E on the right cheek, R on the left

A. lyrics to old Negro spirituals that contain coded messages about slavery
B. letters from slaves hoping to learn the whereabouts of runaway slaves in their families
C. ads or posters from slave owners seeking the capture and return of runaway slaves
D. dialogue spoken by Harriet Tubman and other "conductors" on the Underground Railroad

____ 13. Which is the best paraphrase of these lines from "Runagate Runagate"?

and she's turned upon us, leveled pistol
glinting the moonlight

A. And she turned around, offering us her pistol, which sparkled in the moonlight.
B. And she turned toward us and raised her pistol, which shone in the moonlight.
C. And she rotated her pistol, trying to make it level with the shining moonlight.
D. And she pointed her pistol upward, trying to shoot the glowing rays of moonlight.

Name ______________________________ Date ______________

Vocabulary and Grammar

___ 14. Which of the following choices is a *legacy*?
A. a contract signed by two partners
B. a good grade in school
C. the origin of a word
D. a wedding ring passed down in a family

___ 15. Which sentence uses both underlined vocabulary words correctly?
A. She thanked us with ingratitude for offering help in a time of anguish.
B. She thanked us with anguish for offering help in a time of ingratitude.
C. Their ingratitude caused joy and anguish.
D. Their cruelty and ingratitude caused pain and anguish.

___ 16. How many prepositional phrases does this line contain?
They'll dart underground when you try to catch them
A. none
B. one
C. two
D. three

___ 17. In these lines from "Old Man," what sort of prepositional phrase is "of our blood"?
some of our blood was here,
he would say,
A. an adjective modifying the noun *blood*
B. an adjective modifying the pronoun *some*
C. an adverb modifying the verb *would say*
D. an adverb modifying the adverb *here*

Essay

18. Write a brief essay in which you explain what a lyric poem is and why "Blow, Blow, Thou Winter Wind" or "Old Man" qualifies as a lyric poem.

19. Like all good stories, good narrative poems often contain suspense—the feeling of tension or excitement that makes readers keep reading to learn what happens next and what happens in the end. In an essay, discuss the details that build suspense in the narrative poem "Runagate Runagate."

20. **Thinking About the Big Question: What is the secret to reaching someone with words?** In "Runagate Runagate," "Blow, Blow, Thou Winter Wind," and "Old Man," the speakers are trying to describe feelings to the reader. In an essay, explain what one of the speakers is feeling. Use words and phrases from the poem to explain how the speaker reaches readers with his or her feelings.

Vocabulary Warm-up Word Lists

Study these words from the poetry of Emma Lazarus, Henry Wadsworth Longfellow, and Paul Laurence Dunbar. Then, complete the activities that follow.

Word List A

cruelties [KROO uhl teez] *n.* actions that cause pain or suffering
The prisoners of war suffered many cruelties in prison.

defiance [di FY uhns] *n.* disobedience; standing up against
In defiance of the law, many northerners aided runaway slaves.

hovel [HUHV uhl] *n.* a small, dirty hut
The lovely cottage promised in the advertisement was really a hovel.

huddled [HUHD ld] *adj.* crowded or gathered together
The huddled crowd stood under the canopy until the rain stopped.

peril [PER uhl] *n.* great danger
In times of peril, the bell rang out a warning to the townsfolk.

refuse [REF yoos] *n.* the leftover part of something
Who could toss a fine painting in the garbage as if it were refuse?

Word List B

consciences [KAHN shuhns ez] *n.* the feelings that tell you whether what you are doing is right or wrong
The team members' consciences bothered them after they let their manager take the blame for their bad playing.

dread [DRED] *n.* great fear of something that may happen
Harold experienced a sense of dread before every math test.

masses [MAS ez] *n.* all the ordinary people
To be sure of victory, the candidates spent time meeting the masses.

steed [STEED] *n.* a horse, especially one with spirit used in war
The black steed had a will of its own but it was brave.

teeming [TEEM ing] *adj.* being full of people
On December 26, the mall was teeming with shoppers looking for sales.

transfigured [trans FIG yuhrd] *adj.* changed for the better, usually in ways that can be seen
The sculptor transfigured a pile of junk into an amazing work of art.

Name _______________________________ Date ________________

Poetry Collection: Emma Lazarus, Henry Wadsworth Longfellow, Paul Laurence Dunbar

Vocabulary Warm-up Exercises

Exercise A *Fill in each blank in the paragraph below with an appropriate word from Word List A. Use each word only once.*

Yesterday, in the city, I saw the [1] ________________ of protesters. They marched together in the cold, outside of a [2] ________________ where some homeless people [3] ________________ for warmth. As people passed, the protesters spoke out about the [4] ________________ of allowing people to live like [5] ________________ on the streets. The protesters were in [6] ________________ of being arrested, but their efforts paid off when a Red Cross van pulled up and took the homeless people to a shelter for food, clothing, and a warm place to sleep.

Exercise B *Write a complete sentence to answer each question. For each answer, use a word from Word List B to replace each underlined word or words without changing its meaning.*

1. Does going to the dentist fill you with fear?

____

____

2. Would you buy a horse with lots of spirit for a young child learning to ride?

____

____

3. After a long vacation, why do some people look greatly changed?

____

____

4. What times of day would you want to avoid crowded highways?

____

____

5. Why is it important for the ordinary people to vote in elections?

____

____

6. What happens when people do not listen to their senses of right and wrong?

____

____

Name ______________________________ Date ______________

Poetry Collection: Emma Lazarus, Henry Wadsworth Longfellow, Paul Laurence Dunbar

Reading Warm-up A

Read the following passage. Pay special attention to the underlined words. Then, read it again, and complete the activities. Use a separate sheet of paper for your written answers.

If I asked you to define the word *liberty*, you might say it means "freedom." Then, I might ask, "Freedom from what?" or "Freedom to do what?" You would probably have to stop and think before answering those questions.

Over the years, to different groups of people, *liberty* has meant different things. In early American colonial times, it meant freedom to practice one's own religion. Later, it came also to mean defiance of the taxes and other controls that the British put upon the colonists. Americans were not going to stand for any laws being forced on them!

When war broke out with the British, *liberty* mostly meant independence from Britain. After the American victory, it came to mean "citizenship for certain white males and a handful of free men of color."

Slaves brought over from Africa had no liberty. They arrived in this country huddled and chained together in the worst conditions one can imagine. Many of them died at sea. Those who survived often had to endure the cruelties of their masters. How could a slave owner enjoy his own "liberty" when there was none for the people he beat or sold? How could he enjoy living in a fine home while his slaves lived in a hovel? As you know, slavery ended in 1865. The freeing of slaves gave a new definition to *liberty*.

With the great number of immigrants entering the United States in the 1840s, *liberty* began to mean other things as well. It stood for freedom from peril at the hands of a cruel ruler's soldiers who knocked down your door and attacked you. It meant freedom from hunger. It meant freedom to earn a living at a job of one's choosing. It stood for *not* being treated like refuse by a government that regarded your beliefs as worthless garbage.

One might say that the meaning of *liberty* continues to change even today. Do you agree?

1. Underline a sentence that helps you understand defiance. Explain a time you have been in ***defiance*** of something you felt was unjust.
2. Circle the word that hints at the meaning of huddled. Describe a time you had to remain ***huddled*** for some reason.
3. Circle two cruelties mentioned. Describe ***cruelties*** that take place today.
4. Underline what the author contrasts with a hovel. Describe what a ***hovel*** might look like.
5. Underline the peril from which some immigrants were fleeing. Describe a time when someone you know or read about was in ***peril***.
6. Circle a synonym for refuse. Write a sentence that tells people what to do with their ***refuse***.

Name ______________________________ Date ______________

Poetry Collection: Emma Lazarus, Henry Wadsworth Longfellow, Paul Laurence Dunbar

Reading Warm-up B

Read the following passage. Pay special attention to the underlined words. Then, read it again, and complete the activities. Use a separate sheet of paper for your written answers.

Sitting atop his strong steed, Paul Revere looked across the Charles River on the night of his famous ride. He saw two lanterns hanging high up in the Old North Church. They were his signal to warn the people that the British were coming by sea, but they were also lights of freedom.

By 1775, Boston had already been a center for freedom for more than a hundred years. Puritans had settled in nearby Plymouth in 1620 for religious freedom. Ten years later, a number of them followed a preacher, William Blackstone, to an area now known as Boston.

Before long, this new colony became a booming community. In 1680, the British took control of the growing colony. In the 1760s, they began to tax Bostonians heavily without allowing them a voice in the British government. The people resented it. Not only the town's leaders but also its masses felt a growing desire to rise up against the British. In 1775, despite the dread of war against the much stronger British army, the colonists fired "the shot heard round the world." The American Revolution had begun.

After years of fighting, Americans won their freedom from the British. Boston was at peace. New buildings began rising up everywhere. Docks for ships stretched out into the sea. Slowly, Boston was being transfigured into a real city. Boston was a busy place, teeming with people and industry.

In the 1830s, Boston again became a light for freedom. Horace Mann, a former lawyer and strong supporter of education, helped shape the public school system of Massachusetts. More people now could learn to read and write. Publisher William Lloyd Garrison and writer Harriet Beecher Stowe stirred the people's consciences by attacking slavery in the United States. A growing number of people began to believe that freedom should extend to all, and eventually, it did.

1. Underline the words that help you figure out what a steed is. Describe what Revere's ***steed*** might have been like.

2. Circle the people whom the author contrasts with the masses. Give an example from history of rulers being cruel to the ***masses***.

3. Circle the words that tell you why the colonists had a dread of war. Describe a time when you had a ***dread*** of something.

4. Underline two sentences that describe a transfigured Boston. Describe a person or place you know that has been ***transfigured***.

5. Circle the two things with which Boston was teeming. Describe a ***teeming*** city.

6. Underline what people's consciences led them to believe. Describe a time you and your friends followed your ***consciences***.

Name ______________________________ Date ______________

Poetry Collection: Emma Lazarus, Henry Wadsworth Longfellow, Paul Laurence Dunbar

Writing About the Big Question

What is the secret to reaching someone with words?

Big Question Vocabulary

benefit	connection	cultural	experience	express
feedback	individuality	inform	meaningful	media
misunderstand	relevant	sensory	significance	valid

A. *Use one or more words from the list above to complete each sentence.*

1. Dunbar communicates the African American ______________________ experience through his poetry.
2. Lazarus understands that all people ______________________ a need for home.
3. Longfellow commemorates the ______________________ of a historical icon's brave deeds.
4. The ______________________ that Americans feel surpasses cultural differences.

B. *Follow the directions in responding to each of the items below.*

1. What do you include if you want to inform someone about a significant event?

   ____.

   ____.

2. What kind of feedback would you give one of the poets you have read? Use at least two of the Big Question vocabulary words.

   ____

   ____

C. *Complete the sentence below. Then, write a short paragraph in which you connect this idea to the Big Question.*

Someone who has contributed greatly to the history of our country is ______________

____

____

____

Name ______________________________ Date ______________

Poetry Collection: Emma Lazarus, Henry Wadsworth Longfellow, Paul Laurence Dunbar

Reading: Reread to Paraphrase

To understand a poem, it often helps to paraphrase it in simple, everyday language. When you **paraphrase,** you restate text in your own words. First, **reread the poem to clarify** the writer's meaning. Identify the most basic information in each sentence or phrase—what is being done and who or what is doing it. Use a dictionary or text aids like footnotes, if provided, to help you with unfamiliar terms. Once you understand the poet's meaning, restate the sentences in everyday English. Eliminate repetition, use simpler synonyms, and put unusual sentence structures into a word order that is easier to understand.

DIRECTIONS: *Use this chart to paraphrase the two shorter poems in this collection. An example has been provided for you.*

Poem	Original Lines	Paraphrased Lines
"The New Colossus"	Lines 1–2: "Not . . . land;"	Unlike the giant bronze statue on the Greek island of Rhodes, with its image of conquest,
	Lines 3–6: "Here . . . Exiles."	
	Lines 6–8: "From . . . frame."	
	Lines 9–10: "Keep . . . lips."	
	Lines 10–12: "Give . . . shore."	
	Lines 13–14: "Send . . . door!"	
"Harriet Beecher Stowe"	Lines 1–3: "She . . . alone."	
	Line 4: "She . . . slept:"	
	Lines 5–6: "Her message . . . throne."	
	Lines 7–8: "Command . . . leapt."	
	Lines 9–10: "Around . . . flame"	
	Lines 11–13: "Blest . . . priestess!"	
	Lines 13–14: "At . . . fame."	

Name ______________________________ Date ______________

Poetry Collection: Emma Lazarus, Henry Wadsworth Longfellow, Paul Laurence Dunbar

Literary Analysis: Lyric and Narrative Poetry

A **lyric poem** expresses the thoughts and feelings of a single speaker and uses images and other details to create a single, unified impression. A **narrative poem** tells a story in verse and has all the elements of a short story, including plot, conflict, setting, characters, and theme.

DIRECTIONS: *Choose one lyric poem and one narrative poem in this collection. Write the title of each poem on the line provided, and then answer the questions about it.*

A. Lyric Poem Title: ______________________________

1. Why is this poem a lyric poem? ______________________________

____

2. What are two feelings or emotions that the speaker expresses? ______________

____

3. List two images that the speaker uses and the ideas they convey. ______________

____

____

4. What main impression would you say the poem conveys? ______________

____

B. Narrative Poem Title: ______________________________

1. Why is this poem a narrative poem? ______________________________

____

2. Summarize the plot in one or two sentences. ______________

____

____

3. What is the main conflict or struggle, and how is it resolved in the end?

____

____

4. As specifically as possible, identify the poem's main setting.

____

____

5. Who is the main character? What minor characters does the poem feature?

____

____

Name ______________________ Date ______________

Poetry Collection: Emma Lazarus, Henry Wadsworth Longfellow, Paul Laurence Dunbar

Vocabulary Builder

Word List

defiance exiles peril somber transfigured yearning

A. DIRECTIONS: *Answer each question with a sentence that uses one of the Word List words. Use each Word List word only once.*

1. What is the mood at a funeral usually like?

____

____

2. What adjective describes a person who craves a piece of candy?

____

____

3. How can you describe danger?

____

____

4. What do you call people who are forced to leave their homelands?

____

____

5. How could you describe a child's refusing to listen to his or her parent?

____

____

6. If something is changed, what can it be said to be?

____

____

B. WORD STUDY: *The prefix* trans- *means "change." Use the context of the sentences and what you know about the prefix* trans- *to explain your answer to each question.*

1. What is a *translator's* job?

____

____

2. What might happen to someone who experiences *translocation*?

____

____

Name ______________________________ Date ______________

Poetry Collection: Emma Lazarus, Henry Wadsworth Longfellow, Paul Laurence Dunbar

Enrichment: American Heroes

Paul Revere is just one of a long list of American heroes. Heroes possess qualities that we admire. They are people whose actions inspire and help others. Our stories, poems, and films are filled with the deeds of heroes. They provide examples of noble behavior and lessons in how to overcome difficulties and rise to challenges. We also see heroes in our daily lives—the firefighter who risks his or her life to rescue someone from a burning building, the driver who stops to help people injured in a car accident, the surgeon who donates his skills to help cure a child in need. A closer look at our society's heroes reveals a lot about ourselves—about what we value, and why.

A. DIRECTIONS: *Use your own knowledge and experience to answer these questions.*

1. What are some character traits common to American heroes?

____

____

2. Why do you think there are more male than female heroes depicted in American history?

____

____

3. Do we have heroes who are artists, scholars, physicians, or scientists? Explain.

____

____

4. Do you think it is important for a society to have heroes? Why?

____

____

5. Do you think our idea of heroism will change in the next hundred years? Explain.

____

____

B. DIRECTIONS: *Think of someone you consider a hero. Your hero might be someone famous or a lesser-known person from your everyday life. Describe this person's heroic qualities.*

____

____

____

____

____

Name ______________________________ Date ______________

Poetry Collections: Robert Hayden, William Shakespeare, Ricardo Sánchez; Emma Lazarus, Henry Wadsworth Longfellow, Paul Laurence Dunbar

Integrated Language Skills: Grammar

Prepositions and Prepositional Phrases

A **preposition** is a word that relates a noun or pronoun to another word in the sentence. The noun or pronoun is called the **object of the preposition**. A **prepositional phrase** consists of a preposition, its object, and any words that modify the object. The entire phrase serves as an adjective or an adverb. Study this example:

The boy *with Mary* danced *around the empty room.*

The first preposition, *with,* relates its object, the noun *Mary,* to another word in the sentence, *boy.* The preposition and its object form the prepositional phrase *with Mary.* The phrase serves as an adjective, describing the noun *boy*—it tells you *which* boy. The second preposition, *around,* relates its object, the noun *room,* to another word in the sentence, *danced.* The preposition, its object, and the words *the* and *empty,* which modify the object, form the prepositional phrase *around the empty room.* The phrase serves as an adverb, describing the verb *danced*—it tells you *where* the boy danced.

The chart shows some words that are often used as prepositions.

Sequence	Location	Direction	Other Relationships
after before during until	above in near under	around down from up	about at for of

A. Practice: *Circle the prepositional phrase in each sentence, labeling the preposition* P *and its object* OP. *Draw an arrow to the word that the phrase modifies. On the line before the sentence, indicate whether the phrase serves as an* adjective *or an* adverb.

______________ 1. The study of poetry is not always easy.

______________ 2. To understand a poem, you often read between the lines.

______________ 3. I enjoyed that poem by an African American poet.

______________ 4. He wrote poetry after the Civil War.

______________ 5. Read it with me as I recite it aloud.

B. Writing Application: *Expand each sentence by adding a prepositional phrase to describe the underlined word. Write the new sentence on the line.*

1. The dog barked all night. ______________________________
2. The moonlight streamed. ______________________________
3. We sat together. ______________________________

Name ______________________________ Date ______________

Poetry Collections: Robert Hayden, William Shakespeare, Ricardo Sãnchez; Emma Lazarus, Henry Wadsworth Longfellow, Paul Laurence Dunbar

Integrated Language Skills: Support for Writing a Lyric or Narrative Poem

Use this sheet to jot down your notes for your lyric or narrative poem. If you plan to write a lyric poem, fill in the information called for on the first chart. If you plan to write a narrative poem, fill in the information called for on the second chart.

Lyric Poem
Person:
Qualities:
Achievements:

Narrative Poem
Events:
Characters:
Details of Setting:

Name ______________________________ Date ______________

Poetry Collections: Robert Hayden, William Shakespeare, Ricardo Sánchez; Emma Lazarus, Henry Wadsworth Longfellow, Paul Laurence Dunbar

Integrated Language Skills: Support for Extend Your Learning

Listening and Speaking: Robert Hayden, William Shakespeare, Ricardo Sánchez

Create your evaluation form using the chart below. Add at least two more qualities to the first column. Decide on a scale for scoring—for example, a four-point scale with *1* being "poor" and *4* being "outstanding." Then, photocopy the form, or copy it by hand, and use it to evaluate each person's reading of a poem in the collection.

Title:		
Qualities	**Score**	**Comments**
Varied Tone		
Proper Pauses		
Clear Reading		

Listening and Speaking: Emma Lazarus, Henry Wadsworth Longfellow, Paul Laurence Dunbar

Create your evaluation form using the chart below. Add at least two more qualities to the first column. Decide on a scale for scoring—for example, a four-point scale with *1* being "poor" and *4* being "outstanding." Then, photocopy the form, or copy it by hand, and use it to evaluate each person's reading of a poem in the collection.

Title:		
Qualities	**Score**	**Comments**
Varied Tone		
Proper Pauses		
Clear Reading		

Name ______________________________ Date ______________

Poetry Collection: Emma Lazarus, Henry Wadsworth Longfellow, Paul Laurence Dunbar

Open-Book Test

Short Answer *Write your responses to the questions in this section on the lines provided.*

1. In "The New Colossus," the Statue of Liberty speaks. What is her main message? What details make the message clear?

___

___

___

2. A lyric poem uses images and details to create a single, unified impression. What makes "The New Colossus" a lyric poem? Include specific images and details in your answer.

___

___

___

3. In "The New Colossus," people in other countries are said to be "yearning to breathe free." Why might they feel such a *yearning*? Focus on the meaning of *yearning* in your response.

___

___

___

4. At the end of "The New Colossus," the statue says, "I lift my lamp beside the golden door!" What is the "golden door"? Explain.

___

___

___

5. What is the time setting of "Paul Revere's Ride"? What details from the poem reveal this setting?

___

___

___

6. When you paraphrase a poem, you restate it in your own words. How would you paraphrase the line "Hang a lantern aloft in the belfry arch" from "Paul Revere's Ride"?

___

___

Name ______________________________ Date ______________

7. Like a short story, a narrative poem has characters, a conflict, and a plot. Fill in the chart below with these elements for "Paul Revere's Ride." Cite a detail from the poem to support each answer. Then, on the line provided, tell which element you feel is most important in the poem, and why.

	Characters	**Conflict**	**Plot**
Description			
Detail from Poem			

____

____

8. Paraphrasing means restating something in your own words. How would you paraphrase the line "She spoke to the consciences that long had slept" from "Harriet Beecher Stowe"?

____

____

9. What main emotion does the speaker in "Harriet Beecher Stowe" express toward the subject? Include details from the poem to support your answer.

____

____

____

____

10. In "Harriet Beecher Stowe," the speaker talks about "two peoples" who are transfigured. Who are the "two peoples," and how are they changed?

____

____

____

____

Name ______________________ Date ______________

Essay

Write an extended response to the question of your choice or to the question or questions your teacher assigns you.

11. A narrative poem tells a story in verse and has the elements of a short story. In an essay, explain why "Paul Revere's Ride" is a narrative poem. Sum up the events, tell where and when they take place, and explain who the characters are. Include details from the poem to support your response.
12. Choose one of the lyric poems, "The New Colossus" or "Harriet Beecher Stowe." In an essay, explain why your choice is a lyric poem. Use examples from the poem to illustrate your response.
13. The Statue of Liberty, Paul Revere, and Harriet Beecher Stowe are all figures or symbols important to America's heritage. Choose one, and explain its significance in an essay. Use details from the poem to illustrate your points.
14. **Thinking About the Big Question: What is the secret to reaching someone with words?** Each of the three poems—"The New Colossus," "Paul Revere's Ride," and "Harriet Beecher Stowe"—seeks to use words to give an important message about freedom to its readers. In an essay, choose one of the poems and explain its message about freedom. Use words and phrases from the poem to show how the poet communicates his or her idea.

Oral Response

15. Go back to question 3, 5, or 10 or to the question your teacher assigns you. Take a few minutes to expand your answer and prepare an oral response. Find additional details in "The New Colossus," "Paul Revere's Ride," and "Harriet Beecher Stowe" that will support your points. If necessary, make notes to guide your response.

Name ______________________________ Date ______________

Poetry Collection: Emma Lazarus, Henry Wadsworth Longfellow, Paul Laurence Dunbar

Selection Test A

Critical Reading *Identify the letter of the choice that best answers the question.*

____ 1. In "The New Colossus," what or who is "the brazen giant of Greek fame"?

A. the Statue of Liberty

B. an ancient Greek statue, to which the Statue of Liberty is compared

C. the United States of America

D. Emma Lazarus, who wrote the poem, which is very popular in Greece

____ 2. Which is the best paraphrase of this line from "The New Colossus"?

"Keep, ancient lands, your storied pomp!" cries she

A. "Old nations, keep your stuffy elegance that we read about in stories," she cries.

B. "Old Europeans, stay where you live, and do not come here," she cries.

C. "Old countries, build your tall castles with their many floors," she cries.

D. "Own up to the truth, old countries, instead of telling tales," she cries.

____ 3. What is the main message of the words that the Statue of Liberty speaks in "The New Colossus"?

A. I am a tired, old woman, but I am still strong.

B. Welcome to needy immigrants in search of a new home.

C. America is a beacon of knowledge and education.

D. It is better to light one candle than curse the darkness.

____ 4. What makes "The New Colossus" a lyric poem?

A. It has fourteen lines.

B. It has a complex rhyme scheme.

C. It refers to ancient Greece.

D. It gives a speaker's thoughts and feelings.

____ 5. In "Harriet Beecher Stowe," what does the speaker most admire about Stowe?

A. her kindness

B. her fame

C. her help in the struggle for freedom

D. her style of writing

____ **6.** Which is the best paraphrase of this line from "Harriet Beecher Stowe"?

And from its sheath the sword of justice leapt.

A. And from its pages the pen of justice jumped to the public's attention.
B. And from its case the sword of justice jumped.
C. Justice burst out of a tight dress and became a deadly weapon.
D. Stowe's book proves that the pen is mightier than the sword.

____ **7.** What do the details in "Harriet Beecher Stowe" suggest about the influence of Stowe's novel, *Uncle Tom's Cabin*?

A. It had little impact on America.
B. It had a strong impact on America.
C. It had a strong impact on white Americans, but no impact on African Americans.
D. It had a strong impact on black Americans, but no impact on white Americans.

____ **8.** Why is "Harriet Beecher Stowe" *not* a narrative poem?

A. It does not focus on telling a story.
B. It does not contain dialogue.
C. It has no theme.
D. Stowe was a real person.

____ **9.** When does the narrative poem "Paul Revere's Ride" take place?

A. on the night of April 18, 1775
B. on the evening of July 4, 1776
C. on a night in the middle of winter
D. on the morning of December 7, 1941

____ **10.** What is Paul Revere's mission in "Paul Revere's Ride"?

A. to fight the British troops until reinforcements arrive
B. to carry a secret message to the British troops
C. to carry a secret message from the British troops
D. to warn the other colonists of the movements of the British troops

____ **11.** What main qualities does Paul Revere display in "Paul Revere's Ride"?

A. recklessness and foolishness
B. daring and patriotism
C. anger and jealousy
D. patriotism and ambition

Name ______________________ Date ______________

____ **12.** Which is the best paraphrase of this line from "Paul Revere's Ride"?

Hang a lantern aloft in the belfry arch

A. Put a light in the hayloft, which is shaped like an arch in a church.
B. Send an arc of light out of the small lamp located on the church's roof.
C. Put a small glass lamp high in the church tower.
D. Ring the bells in the church tower as loudly as you can.

Vocabulary and Grammar

____ **13.** Which word is most nearly *opposite* in meaning to the word *aghast*?

A. calm
B. surprised
C. amazed
D. breathless

____ **14.** To which of the following would you apply the adjective *complacent*?

A. to someone who never worries and is always satisfied
B. to someone who always worries and is never satisfied
C. to someone who never yells and is always shy
D. to someone who always yells and is never shy

____ **15.** How many prepositional phrases do these lines contain?

It was one by the village clock,
When he galloped into Lexington.

A. one
B. two
C. three
D. none

Essay

16. Write a brief essay in which you show that "Paul Revere's Ride" is a narrative poem. Sum up the events, tell where they take place, and tell who the characters are.

17. Paul Revere and Harriet Beecher Stowe both made a mark on American history. Choose one of them, and write a short essay explaining why he or she is considered an American hero. Use details from the poem by Longfellow or the poem by Dunbar to support your ideas.

18. **Thinking About the Big Question: What is the secret to reaching someone with words?** Each poem in this section—"The New Colossus," "Paul Revere's Ride," and "Harriet Beecher Stowe"—tries to say something important about freedom. Choose one of the poems, and then write a brief essay in which you explain its message about freedom. Support your answer with specific words and phrases from the poem.

Name ______________________ Date ______________

Poetry Collection: Emma Lazarus, Henry Wadsworth Longfellow, Paul Laurence Dunbar

Selection Test B

Critical Reading *Identify the letter of the choice that best completes the statement or answers the question.*

____ 1. At the end of "The New Colossus," the statue says, "I lift my lamp beside the golden door!" What is "the golden door"?
- **A.** a door that lets tourists climb to the top of the Statue of Liberty
- **B.** the gate of heaven, to which the statue's raised arm points
- **C.** the gangplank of the ship bringing immigrants to America
- **D.** New York harbor, doorway to America

____ 2. In "The New Colossus," what does the speaker point out about the old Colossus of Rhodes?
- **A.** The Colossus of Rhodes was small.
- **B.** The Colossus of Rhodes was the model for the Statue of Liberty.
- **C.** The Colossus of Rhodes represented power and conquest.
- **D.** The Colossus of Rhodes cast bolts of lightning at ships that passed by.

____ 3. Which is the best paraphrase of this line from "The New Colossus"?

The wretched refuse of your teeming shore.

- **A.** the miserable outcasts of a crowded continent
- **B.** the awful litter on crowded beaches
- **C.** the miserable people who insist on leaving a crowded land
- **D.** the selfish people who spurn people from slums

____ 4. What main emotion does the speaker in "The New Colossus" express?
- **A.** the speaker's feelings about the Statue of Liberty and immigration to America
- **B.** the speaker's feelings about the Colossus of Rhodes and ancient Greece
- **C.** the Statue of Liberty's joy about holding lightning in her torch
- **D.** the Statue of Liberty's angry feelings toward her children

____ 5. Which is the best paraphrase of these lines from "Harriet Beecher Stowe"?

Her message, Freedom's clear reveille, swept
From heedless hovel to complacent throne.

- **A.** Stowe's message of freedom was ignored in both rich and poor households.
- **B.** Stowe's message awoke rich and poor alike to the cause of freedom.
- **C.** Stowe's message about freedom turned poor hovels into glorious mansions.
- **D.** Reveille inspired Stowe to write her sweeping message, which affects us all.

____ 6. In "Harriet Beecher Stowe," who are the "two peoples" that the speaker says were transfigured?
- **A.** African Americans and white Americans
- **B.** slaves and their descendants
- **C.** Americans and Europeans
- **D.** Northerners and Southerners

Name ______________________________ Date ________________

____ 7. In "Harriet Beecher Stowe," what is it the speaker assumes you know about the subject of the poem?
A. that Stowe fought in the Civil War
B. that Stowe was related to Dunbar
C. that Stowe exposed the horrors of slavery
D. that Stowe was a descendant of slaves

____ 8. What main emotion does the speaker in "Harriet Beecher Stowe" express toward the subject?
A. admiration
B. anger
C. amazement
D. sorrow

____ 9. What is the main conflict in the poem "Paul Revere's Ride"?
A. Paul Revere's struggle to stay on his horse
B. the British troops' struggle to arrest Paul Revere and put him on trial for treason
C. Paul Revere's internal struggle about whether or not to betray Britain
D. Paul Revere's struggle to warn the colonists of the advancing British troops

____ 10. What is the setting of the poem "Paul Revere's Ride"?
A. the start of the American Revolution
B. the War of 1812
C. the first Thanksgiving
D. the Civil War

____ 11. What is the meaning of "One, if by land, and two, if by sea" in "Paul Revere's Ride"?
A. One man will signal if the troops come by land, and two will signal if they come by sea.
B. There will be one hour's notice if the troops come by land and two if they come by sea.
C. One spy will hide among the British troops on land and two on a ship off the coast.
D. If the British come by land, one lantern will glow; if they come by sea, two will glow.

____ 12. Which is the best paraphrase of these lines from "Paul Revere's Ride"?

And the spark struck out by that steed in his flight,
Kindled the land into flame with its heat.

A. Sparks from Paul Revere's horse started a brush fire.
B. Paul Revere's horse sparked fear in everyone who saw it riding across the land.
C. Paul Revere wiped out the spark of victory in the British troops.
D. Paul Revere's ride helped ignite a rebellion across the colonies.

____ 13. *Lyric* describes which of the poems in this collection?
A. "The New Colossus" only
B. "Harriet Beecher Stowe" only
C. "The New Colossus" and "Harriet Beecher Stowe"
D. "Paul Revere's Ride" and "Harriet Beecher Stowe"

Name ______________________________ Date ____________

Vocabulary and Grammar

____ 14. Which sentence uses its underlined vocabulary word correctly?
A. Their laughter was loud and somber.
B. The car aghast smelled peculiar.
C. The children, yearning to run around, felt cooped up in the classroom.
D. She is a complacent customer, always demanding top service or a refund.

____ 15. How many prepositional phrases do these lines contain?

Creeping along from tent to tent,
And seeming to whisper, "All is well!"

A. one in the first line; one in the second
B. two in the first line; none in the second
C. two in the first line; one in the second
D. two in the first line; two in the second

____ 16. What does *complacent* mean in the following sentence?

Before reading *Uncle Tom's Cabin*, many people felt *complacent* regarding slavery.

A. satisfied
B. resentful
C. gloomy
D. horrified

____ 17. In these lines, what sort of prepositional phrase is "at our sea-washed, sunset gates"?

Here at our sea-washed, sunset gates shall stand
A mighty woman with a torch. . . .

A. an adjective that modifies *gates*
B. an adjective that modifies *woman*
C. an adverb that modifies *mighty*
D. an adverb that modifies *Here*

Essay

18. Write a brief essay in which you identify a work that is a lyric poem and explain why it qualifies as one. Select from "The New Colossus," "Harriet Beecher Stowe," and "Paul Revere's Ride."

19. Paul Revere, Harriet Beecher Stowe, and the Statue of Liberty are all figures or symbols important to America's heritage. Choose two, and explain their significance in a brief essay. Use details from the poems to illustrate your points.

20. **Thinking About the Big Question: What is the secret to reaching someone with words?** Each of these poems—"The New Colossus," "Paul Revere's Ride," and "Harriet Beecher Stowe"—seeks to use words to give an important message about freedom to its readers. In an essay, choose one of the poems, and then explain its message about freedom. Use words and phrases from the poem to show how the poet communicates his or her idea.

Vocabulary Warm-up Word Lists

Study these words from the poetry of John Updike, N. Scott Momaday, and Alice Walker. Then, complete the activities that follow.

Word List A

continent [KAHN tuh nuhnt] *n.* one of the large land masses on Earth
My aunt has visited every continent except Antarctica.

dusk [DUSK] *n.* the time before it gets dark, just after sunset
Mom says that she has trouble seeing when she drives at dusk.

planes [PLAYNZ] *n.* flat surfaces
A simple box has six different planes.

shimmer [SHIM er] *v.* to shine with a soft light that seems to shake a bit
When the moon is full, I see its reflection shimmer on the lake.

swarm [SWAWRM] *n.* a large group of insects that move together
They say that a swarm of killer bees can take down a large animal.

withdraw [with DRAW] *v.* to go away or leave
Since the room was full of noisy five-year-olds, I decided to withdraw from it.

Word List B

accents [AK sents] *n.* the different ways people pronounce words because of where they were born or live
Traveling through the South, I heard about a dozen different accents.

behold [bi HOHLD] *v.* to look at or to see something
Fans, behold how incredible his guitar-picking skills are!

cedars [SEE derz] *n.* evergreen trees with red, sweet-smelling wood
As we walked through the forest of tall cedars, I felt very small.

parkas [PAR kuhz] *n.* thick, warm coats with hoods
The warmest parkas are filled with soft feathers, called down.

radiator [RAY dee ay tuhr] *n.* a heating unit in a room
I loved the hissing sound the old radiator made as it heated the cold room.

stiffen [STI fuhn] *v.* to become difficult to move
Grandpa's knee would stiffen at the first sign of any bad weather.

Name ______________________________ Date ______________

Poetry Collection: John Updike, N. Scott Momaday, Alice Walker

Vocabulary Warm-up Exercises

Exercise A *Fill in each blank in the paragraph below with an appropriate word from Word List A. Use each word only once.*

On the huge [1] ____________ of North America, there is a great variety of weather. For example, May can be hot in some places and cool in others. People in the Central American countries may stay indoors in May, to avoid fighting off a [2] ____________ of annoying insects in the heat. At the same time, people around the Great Lakes are enjoying the outdoors. They might sit peacefully in the afternoon, watching the sun [3] ____________ on the water. In the western part of North America, beautiful sunsets bring the calm of [4] ____________, a time just to sit quietly. In the far northeast, chilly weather makes people [5] ____________ from the night air. All over North America, clear days of May make the [6] ____________ of objects seem to stand out more sharply.

Exercise B *Answer the questions with complete explanations.*

1. Would you use a radiator in a place where the temperature averages ninety degrees all year?

____

____

2. What emotion might cause a person to stiffen his or her whole body?

____

____

3. During which sports might athletes wear parkas?

____

____

4. When might you tell someone to behold something?

____

____

5. Which accents can you recognize as being from a particular place?

____

____

6. Why is the wood from cedars often used to build chests in which clothes are stored?

____

____

Name ______________________________ Date ______________

Poetry Collection: John Updike, N. Scott Momaday, Alice Walker

Reading Warm-up A

Read the following passage. Pay special attention to the underlined words. Then, read it again, and complete the activities. Use a separate sheet of paper for your written answers.

People around the world listen to rock music today. Yet, this popular form of music had its beginnings right here on our own continent. It began in the 1950s. At this time, three unique American musical styles came together. These were pop, rhythm and blues, and country and western.

Elvis Presley was the first huge star to put it all together. His rock-and-roll music was incredibly popular among American teenagers. His voice was great. The beat of his music was strong, fast, and exciting.

Presley also put on quite a show. He was famous for his way of dancing and for wearing fancy clothes and flashy jewelry that would shimmer under the spotlights. Presley was also very good-looking. He had dazzling eyes and cheekbones that looked like chiseled planes. Girls swooned over Presley and followed him everywhere like a swarm of bees.

Because rock and roll really appealed to the young, many stars would withdraw from the main stage as they aged. Plenty of young musicians were always waiting in the wings to take their place. Today, however, some successful, older rock stars perform to audience of all ages.

Perhaps the biggest force for change in the American rock-and-roll generation came from England. A group of four young British lads named the Beatles stormed the United States. In 1964, people went wild when they heard the Beatles' music for the first time.

New influences have always kept rock music fresh and surprising. Folk, soul, disco, heavy metal, punk, hip hop, rap . . . you can hear bits of all of it in rock music. Chances are, if you walk down the street on any summer day at dusk, you will hear rock-and-roll music coming from someone's open window. Its energy, messages for young and old alike, and inclusion of different styles will always keep it popular.

1. Underline the word in the paragraph that gives a clue about which continent is "our own." Then, list the name of each *continent*.
2. Circle the words describing what would shimmer under the lights. Then, explain what *shimmer* means.
3. Underline the word in the previous sentence that tells what dazzling eyes and cheekbones like chiseled planes add up to. Then, explain why cheekbones might look like *planes*.
4. Circle the word defining the type of swarm the girls resembled. Then, describe a time when you have seen a *swarm* of people.
5. Underline the words telling when rock stars would withdraw from the action. Then, tell about a time when you had to *withdraw* from somewhere.
6. Circle the words telling when you might hear rock music at dusk. Explain why people would be home listening to music at *dusk*.

Name ______________________________ Date ______________

Poetry Collection: John Updike, N. Scott Momaday, Alice Walker

Reading Warm-up B

Read the following passage. Pay special attention to the underlined words. Then, read it again, and complete the activities. Use a separate sheet of paper for your written answers.

I had always wanted to visit Boston. In my mind, I pictured myself walking through Boston Common, going to a Red Sox game, and feeling excited to behold the historical places along the Freedom Trail. I knew I would stiffen as I saw the spot where the Boston Massacre occurred, frozen in awe to see such an important part of our country's fight for freedom.

I always imagined these events happening during the summer months. Yet, my first visit to Boston occurred in the dead of winter, in January. It was a time when I did not like to leave the quiet, snow-covered cedars in the woods behind our house. My friends and I loved to don parkas and walk on snowshoes through the forest. With our ice skates slung over our shoulders, we would reach our own frozen pond and play hockey for hours. These were great days for me, and I hated to miss them. Nevertheless, I could not turn down an opportunity to see Boston.

My father, who had to go there on business, took me with him for a long weekend. We stayed in a famous old hotel right downtown. An old-fashioned hissing radiator heated the room, and the furniture, I think, dated back to the time of Paul Revere's ride.

The weather was bitter cold, so Dad and I stuck to indoor activities. We rode an elevator to the top of the tallest building to see the splendid city spread out before us. We went to the brightly lit shops and restaurants of historic Faneuil Hall. There, I enjoyed listening to the accents of the Bostonians who were chatting with shopkeepers and friends. We also visited the Museum of Fine Arts and Harvard University in Cambridge.

The highlight of the trip for me, however, was not the history or the culture. It was sports! We got tickets to a Celtics basketball game. Now, what could be more exciting than that?

1. Underline the words naming what the writer would behold along the Freedom Trail. Then, explain what ***behold*** means.
2. Circle a word in the sentence that gives a clue about the meaning of stiffen. Then, explain how someone who would ***stiffen*** might move.
3. Underline the words telling where the cedars are located. Then, describe what ***cedars*** look like.
4. Circle the word naming something besides parkas that the narrator and his or her friends would wear. Then, explain why they would wear ***parkas***.
5. Underline the words that tell what a radiator does. Then, write a sentence using ***radiator***.
6. Circle the word naming whose accents the writer heard. Then, list three types of ***accents*** that you have heard.

Name ______________________________ Date ____________________

Poetry Collection: John Updike, N. Scott Momaday, Alice Walker

Writing About the Big Question

What is the secret to reaching someone with words?

Big Question Vocabulary

benefit	connection	cultural	experience	express
feedback	individuality	inform	meaningful	media
misunderstand	relevant	sensory	significance	valid

A. *Use one or more words from the list above to complete each sentence.*

1. In his poem "January," Updike uses ____________________ details to appeal to sight and feeling.
2. In Alice Walker's poem, she expresses the ____________________ experiences she had with her sister.
3. N. Scott Momaday examines the ____________________ between man and nature in "New World."

B. *Follow the directions in responding to each of the items below.*

1. Write two sentences about the benefit of observing nature. Consider how observation affects your life.

   ____.

   ____.

2. Write about a significant experience you had at a particular time of the year. Use at least two of the Big Question vocabulary words.

   ____

   ____

C. *Complete the sentence below. Then, write a short paragraph in which you connect this idea to the Big Question.*

Poetry written about nature helps us discover ____________________

____

____

____

Name ______________________________ Date ______________

Poetry Collection: John Updike, N. Scott Momaday, Alice Walker

Reading: Read According to Punctuation to Paraphrase

When you **paraphrase** a poem, you restate it in your own words. First, read the poem through carefully and try to determine the complete thoughts it contains. **Use the punctuation** on the page—as well as the words themselves—to help you identify complete thoughts. Next, restate the meaning of each complete thought in your own words. Eliminate unneeded repetition. Mentally fill in any missing words to complete thoughts that are not fully stated. If the vocabulary is difficult, use simpler synonyms. Put unusual sentence structures into a word order that is easier to understand.

DIRECTIONS: *Use this chart to paraphrase the first two parts of "New World" by N. Scott Momaday. An example has been provided for you.*

Complete Thoughts	Paraphrased Lines
Lines 1–2: "First Man, behold:"	Look, First Man
Lines 3–5: "the earth . . . leaves;"	
Lines 6–8: "the sky . . . rain."	
Lines 9–15: "Pollen . . . mountains."	
Lines 16–19: "Cedars . . . pines."	
Lines 20–28: "At . . . pools."	
Lines 29–31: "Grasses . . . shine."	
Lines 32–36: "Shadows . . . smoke."	

Name ______________________________ Date ______________

Poetry Collection: John Updike, N. Scott Momaday, Alice Walker

Literary Analysis: Imagery

Poetry often makes use of **imagery,** language that appeals to one or more of the five senses. Each instance of imagery is called an **image**. If you take note of the images as you read a poem, you will often understand it better. As you read, imagine that you are actually seeing, smelling, hearing, tasting, or touching the things described by the poet. Put yourself at the scene mentally, and experience the images.

Directions: *Use this chart to help you focus on the imagery in the three poems in this collection. From each poem, list words or phrases that appeal to the senses in the corresponding boxes. Remember that many images appeal to more than one sense.*

	Sight	Sound	Touch	Smell	Taste
"January"					
"New World"					
"For My Sister Molly . . ."					

Name ______________________________________ Date ____________________

Poetry Collection: John Updike, N. Scott Momaday, Alice Walker

Vocabulary Builder

Word List

extinguished inexpressible pollen recede remote wearisome

A. Directions: *Circle* T *if the statement is true or* F *if the statement is false.* Then, explain your answer.

T / F 1. After a wave comes up on the shore, it begins to recede.

____

T / F 2. A remote land is close by.

____

T / F 3. A wearisome task is easily completed.

____

T / F 4. Flowers produce pollen.

____

T / F 5. An extinguished fire is no longer a danger.

____

T / F 6. An inexpressible emotion cannot be described.

____

B. Word Study: *The roots* -cede- *and* -ceed- *mean "go" or "yield." Use the context of the sentences and what you know about the* roots -cede- and -ceed- *to explain your answer to each question.*

1. If a line *proceeds* quickly, what happens?

____

____

2. If someone *exceeds* expectations at work, what will likely happen?

____

____

C. Directions: *Circle the letter of the word that is closest in meaning to the Word List word in CAPITAL LETTERS.*

1. RECEDE
   A. triumph B. grow C. retreat D. increase
2. REMOTE
   A. distant B. near C. connected D. clear
3. EXTINGUISHED
   A. forgotten B. empty C. extinct D. alive
4. WEARISOME
   A. old B. tiring C. soothing D. fashionable

Name ______________________________ Date ______________

Poetry Collection: John Updike, N. Scott Momaday, Alice Walker

Enrichment: The Pulitzer Prize

All three writers in this collection are past winners of the Pulitzer Prize. Pulitzers have been given since 1917 for achievements in American journalism, letters, drama, and music. *Letters* means fiction, history, poetry, biography or autobiography, and general nonfiction. N. Scott Momaday and Alice Walker won their prizes for poetry; John Updike won his for fiction. Although these awards have little financial value in themselves, it is a great honor to receive them.

The Pulitzer Prizes were the idea of Joseph Pulitzer, an American newspaper publisher. Pulitzer was born in Hungary and immigrated to the United States in 1847. In 1878, he became the owner and publisher of the *St. Louis Post-Dispatch*, a newspaper that, under his guidance, became a success. In 1883, he bought the *New York World* and made that a success, too. People liked his use of cartoons and other illustrations, bold news coverage and news stunts, and crusades against corruption.

In 1890, Pulitzer suffered partial blindness, but he continued to direct his newspapers. He gave money to establish the Pulitzer Prizes and what is now the Columbia School of Journalism, which administers the Pulitzer Prizes.

Directions: *Refer to the information in the passage above to answer these questions.*

1. How do you think Joseph Pulitzer felt about his adoptive country? Why do you think so?

____

____

2. Why do you think Pulitzer established what is now the Columbia School of Journalism?

____

____

3. How might winning a Pulitzer Prize help a writer's career?

____

____

4. Can a writer for a British newspaper win a Pulitzer Prize? Why?

____

____

Name ______________________________ Date ________________

Poetry Collection: John Updike, N. Scott Momaday, Alice Walker

Open-Book Test

Short Answer *Write your responses to the questions in this section on the lines provided.*

1. Paraphrasing is restating something in your own words. Look at the second stanza of "January." How would you paraphrase these lines?

2. In "January," the image "The trees' black lace" appeals to the sense of sight. What thing is the poet describing with this image? Explain using details from the poem.

3. From where does the speaker make his observations in "January"? Support your answer with details from the poem.

4. In "New World," the speaker says the sky "glistens with rain." What is another thing in nature that *glistens*? Explain.

5. In "New World," the speaker says, "Pollen/is borne/on winds/that low/and lean/upon/mountains." How would you paraphrase those lines?

6. Imagery is language that appeals to the senses. To which senses do these lines from "New World" appeal most strongly? Explain.
   At noon/turtles/enter/slowly/into/the warm/dark loam.

Name ______________________ Date ______________

7. In "New World," how does N. Scott Momaday create a sense of the unity and completeness of nature? Explain using details from the poem.

8. For each poem, "January," "New World," and "For My Sister Molly . . . ," fill in one example of imagery and tell the sense to which it appeals. On the line provided, tell which image you think is most powerful, and explain why.

	"January"	**"New World"**	**"For My Sister Molly . . ."**
Imagery			
Sense			

9. In "For My Sister Molly . . . ," how does the speaker feel about her sister? Explain your answer using details from the poem.

10. In "For My Sister Molly . . . ," what does Molly teach the speaker? Explain using details from the poem.

Essay

Write an extended response to the question of your choice or to the question or questions your teacher assigns you.

11. Do you think John Updike got his description of January right? In an essay, describe what January is like for you. Compare and contrast your impression of January with the images Updike creates in his poem.

Name ______________________ Date ______________

12. In "New World," the images the poet creates change from the beginning to the end. In an essay, describe how the images change. Use examples from the poem to support your response.

13. Each of the three poems—"January," "New World," and "For My Sister Molly . . . "—uses imagery to express feelings. In an essay, discuss the use of imagery in one of the poems. Examine the ways in which the poem uses images to show the emotions or thoughts of the speaker.

14. **Thinking About the Big Question: What is the secret to reaching someone with words?** In "January," "New World," and "For My Sister Molly . . . ," the poets create a world with words. Which world would you rather inhabit? Why? Use words from the poem you choose to illustrate your response.

Oral Response

15. Go back to question 4, 7, or 9 or to the question your teacher assigns you. Take a few minutes to expand your answer and prepare an oral response. Find additional details in "January," "New World," and "For My Sister Molly . . . " that will support your points. If necessary, make notes to guide your response.

Name ______________________________ Date ______________

Poetry Collection: John Updike, N. Scott Momaday, Alice Walker

Selection Test A

Critical Reading *Identify the letter of the choice that best answers the question.*

____ 1. What does the speaker describe in "January"?
A. a cold time of year
B. a typical school day
C. a winter holiday
D. a summer day in South America

____ 2. To what senses does this image from "January" appeal most?

The radiator
　Purrs all day.

A. sight, sound, touch
B. sight, taste, smell
C. touch and taste
D. sight and smell

____ 3. Which is the best paraphrase of these lines from "January"?

And parkas pile up
　Near the door.

A. And cars crash near the front door.
B. And we get lots of visitors parking near the door.
C. And warm jackets form a heap near the door.
D. And animals form a pile trying to get in the door.

____ 4. In "New World," what seems to be the speaker's relationship with the world of nature?
A. He dislikes it and prefers city life.
B. He likes it but knows very little about it.
C. He admires it and observes it carefully.
D. He considers it harsh and cruel to most living things.

____ 5. What three specific times does "New World" describe?
A. yesterday, today, and tomorrow
B. dawn, noon, and dusk
C. spring, summer, and fall
D. the past, the present, and the future

Name ______________________ Date ______________

____ 6. Which is the best paraphrase of these lines from "New World"?

eagles / hie and / hover / above / the plain

A. Eagles hurry and hang above the flatland.
B. Eagles hang in midair and wave their wings.
C. Eagles race and rush in an ugly way.
D. Eagles soar and swoop in a simple, everyday way.

____ 7. To which senses do these lines from "New World" appeal most strongly?

At noon / turtles / enter / slowly / into / the warm / dark loam.

A. sight and sound
B. sight and touch
C. touch and taste
D. sound and smell

____ 8. Which is the best paraphrase of these lines from "For My Sister Molly Who . . ."?

For my sister Molly who in the fifties
Knew Hamlet well . . .

A. for my sister Molly who, by the time she was fifty, knew Shakespeare's play *Hamlet* well
B. for my sister Molly who met a man named Hamlet when they were both in their fifties
C. for my sister whom Molly knew in the 1950s in a small village
D. for my sister Molly who in the 1950s understood Hamlet, a character in Shakespeare

____ 9. In "For My Sister Molly Who . . . ," how does the speaker feel about her sister?
A. She is jealous of her sister.
B. She barely knows her sister.
C. She admires her sister.
D. She thinks her sister is very foolish.

____ 10. In "For My Sister Molly Who . . . ," to which senses do these lines appeal most?

Who walked among the flowers
And brought them inside the house
And smelled as good as they
And looked as bright.

A. smell and sight
B. smell and sound
C. taste and smell
D. sight and sound

Name ______________________________ Date ______________

Vocabulary and Grammar

____ **11.** Which word is *closest* in meaning to the word "remote" in the following sentence?

The remote village lie atop the horizon.

A. dead
B. high
C. far away
D. identified

____ **12.** What does *glistens* mean in these lines?

the sky
glistens
with rain.

A. thickens
B. moistens
C. hears
D. shines

____ **13.** What is the infinitive phrase in the following sentence?

To read poetry aloud is something new to me.

A. to read
B. to read poetry aloud
C. to read poetry aloud is something new
D. to me

Essay

14. Write a composition in which you paraphrase "New World" or "For My Sister Molly Who in the Fifties." Your paraphrase should be in paragraph form, not line for line.

15. Do you think John Updike got his description of January right? In a short essay, explain what January is like for you, and compare and contrast it with Updike's description in the poem.

16. **Thinking About the Big Question: What is the secret to reaching someone with words?** In "January," "New World," and "For My Sister Molly Who in the Fifties," the poets create a world with words. Which of these worlds appeals to you the most? Why? Explain your answer in an essay that gives examples from the poem you choose.

Name ______________________ Date ______________

Poetry Collection: John Updike, N. Scott Momaday, Alice Walker

Selection Test B

Critical Reading *Identify the letter of the choice that best completes the statement or answers the question.*

____ 1. What is the landscape that the speaker describes in "January"?
A. a snowy place
B. a tropical climate
C. Antarctica
D. Montana

____ 2. Which word or phrase best describes how the speaker feels in "January"?
A. frightened
B. sad to be home
C. exhausted
D. glad to be home

____ 3. In the following stanza of "January," what does the image "trees' black lace" capture?

The river is
A frozen place
Held still beneath
The trees' black lace.

A. on the tree branches, the tiny leafless twigs that form a dark lace pattern
B. on the trees, the green leaves that form a leaf pattern often seen on lace
C. on the trees, the dark thin branches that wave in the wind like black shoelaces
D. the shadow of the trees interlaced with the dark frozen river

____ 4. In "January," what does the speaker mean by the image in the following lines?

The sun a spark
Hung thin between
The dark and dark.

A. The sun barely shows behind the dark clouds.
B. The sun sends off thin sparks in the night.
C. The sun appears for only a short time between the long winter nights.
D. The sun is unable to relieve the depression of winter.

____ 5. Which is the best paraphrase of these lines from "January"?

Fat snowy footsteps
Track the floor,

A. Thick snowy footprints show where animals walked.
B. Thick snowy outlines of feet mark the floor.
C. Large snow boots lie on the floor of the house.
D. A fat snowy creature followed us into the house.

____ 6. Which word best describes the speaker's feeling about the scene in "New World"?
A. fear
B. wonder
C. pride
D. sorrow

Name ______________________________ Date ______________

___ 7. What do these lines from "New World" describe?

Shadows / withdraw / and lie / away / like smoke.

A. a forest fire
B. a magic trick
C. the end of the speaker's depression
D. the sun lighting up the morn

___ 8. Which of these images from "New World" most strongly appeals to the sense of touch?
A. the earth glittering with leaves
B. light gathering in pools
C. gray foxes stiffening in the cold
D. rivers following the moon

___ 9. Which is the best paraphrase of these lines from "New World"?

Pollen / is borne / on winds / that low / and lean / upon / mountains.

A. The Roman god of plants is swept up on winds blowing between the mountains.
B. Small flower cells carried by low-blowing winds help make the mountains fertile.
C. The wind carries dustlike flower grains that drop onto the mountains.
D. Flower powder is carried on winds that moan and press on the mountains.

___ 10. In "For My Sister Molly Who . . . ," how did Molly treat the speaker in the fifties?
A. She treated her as a complete equal.
B. She was a devoted older sister, entertaining and teaching the speaker.
C. She was a spoiled girl who usually ignored the speaker but was sometimes kind.
D. She was an opinionated older sister who bossed around the speaker.

___ 11. Which is the best paraphrase of these lines from "For My Sister Molly . . ."?

Waking up the story buds
Like fruit.

A. whetting our appetite for stories
B. picking stories out of the air like buds and fruit off trees
C. telling stories about morning in a garden
D. making stories more flowery and appealing by adding details

___ 12. From the details in "For My Sister Molly . . .," what did Molly teach the speaker?
A. literature
B. creativity
C. their heritage
D. all the above

___ 13. How do the quotation marks in these lines from "For My Sister Molly . . . " help you understand and paraphrase the lines?

And taught me not to say us for we
No matter what "Sonny said." . . .

A. They indicate that the speaker is not sure Sonny said *us*.
B. They indicate that "Sonny said" is a lie.
C. They indicate that a reader should say the two words slowly.
D. They indicate that the speaker had claimed that Sonny spoke well.

Name ______________________ Date ______________

Vocabulary and Grammar

____ 14. Which word is most nearly *opposite* in meaning to the word *recede*?
A. enter
B. lead
C. win
D. fail

____ 15. Which of these things usually *glistens*?
A. a headache
B. a song
C. a new dime
D. an old hat

____ 16. How many infinitive phrases do these lines contain?

Who had been to school
And knew (and told us too) that certain
Words were no longer good
And taught me not to say us for we

A. none
B. one
C. two
D. three

____ 17. Identify the infinitive phrase and its function in the following line.

And loved to read "Sam McGee from Tennessee"

A. *To read* is an adjective modifying "Sam McGee from Tennessee."
B. *To read* is a noun, the direct object of the verb *loved.*
C. *To read "Sam McGee from Tennessee"* is an adverb modifying *loved.*
D. *To read "Sam McGee from Tennessee"* is the direct object of the verb *loved.*

Essay

18. Based on the poem "For My Sister Molly Who in the Fifties," write a short essay in which you identify the conclusions you draw about Molly's personality, background, attitudes, and talents.

19. Write a brief essay discussing the use of imagery in one of the poems—"January," "New World," or "For My Sister Molly Who in the Fifties." Examine the ways in which the poem uses images to convey the emotions or thoughts of its speaker.

20. **Thinking About the Big Question: What is the secret to reaching someone with words?** In "January," "New World," and "For My Sister Molly . . . ," the poets create a world with words. Which world would you rather inhabit? Why? Use words from the poem you choose to illustrate your response.

Vocabulary Warm-up Word Lists

Study these words from the poetry of Amy Ling, Wendy Rose, and E. E. Cummings. Then, complete the activities that follow.

Word List A

century [SEN chuh ree] *n.* a period of one hundred years
A century ago, there was no television or Internet.

delicious [di LISH uhs] *adj.* delightful
My grandfather described ballet as a delicious treat for his eyes.

eldest [EL dist] *adj.* oldest
My eldest brother is four years older than me and two years older than my other brother.

image [IM ij] *n.* a representation; a likeness
People in our family often say that I am the perfect image of my Aunt Caroline.

perch [PERCH] *v.* to sit or stand on the top or edge of something
I wish my cat would not perch on the upstairs windowsills when the windows are open.

twinkling [TWING kling] *v.* sparkling; shining with quick flashes
In the country, the stars were twinkling brightly.

Word List B

aqua [AH kwuh] *adj.* bluish-green in color
The cool, aqua water of the pool looked so inviting!

exquisite [EK skwiz it] *adj.* beautiful
For fancy occasions, my mother wears an exquisite ruby necklace.

humorous [HYOO mer uhs] *adj.* funny and enjoyable
We went to a humorous play put on by the local junior college.

jostling [JAHS ling] *n.* the act of pushing or bumping into others
I often feel upset by the jostling that I experience when riding the subway.

slippered [SLIP uhrd] *adj.* wearing soft, light shoes
My little sister's slippered feet made her walk as quiet as a mouse.

woodpecker [WOOD pek er] *n.* a tree-climbing bird that pecks holes in trees to get insects
I like watching the red head of that woodpecker, but I don't like listening to its racket.

Name ______________________________ Date ____________________

Poetry Collection: Amy Ling, Wendy Rose, E. E. Cummings

Vocabulary Warm-up Exercises

Exercise A *Fill in each blank in the paragraph below with an appropriate word from Word List A. Use each word only once.*

In our small town, we have had a Fourth of July parade every year for more than a [1] ____________________. The [2] ____________________ person in town always leads off the parade, seated in a fancy car. We eat [3] ____________________ hot dogs while watching parade participants like the marching band, fancy floats, dancers and jugglers, and funny clowns. Bringing up the rear is someone dressed to be the exact [4] ____________________ of Uncle Sam. It's amazing what a likeness to the cartoons this costume has. Usually, the whole town turns out for the parade. Chairs line the streets, and some people [5] ____________________ high up on rooftops so as to get a bird's-eye view. The town's good feelings last until the evening's fireworks outshine the stars that are [6] ____________________ in the sky.

Exercise B *Circle* T *if the statement is true or* F *if the statement is false. Then, explain your answer.*

1. You are likely to see a <u>woodpecker</u> in the treeless areas of the Great Plains.
   T / F ____
2. Shopping during quiet weekday mornings can help you avoid the crowds and their <u>jostling</u>.
   T / F ____
3. You can expect to see many <u>slippered</u> feet on a hike.
   T / F ____
4. Mother Nature gives us <u>exquisite</u> gifts such as earthquakes.
   T / F ____
5. The sky, the ocean, and some people's eyes all can be described as <u>aqua</u>.
   T / F ____
6. A <u>humorous</u> line that you read in a book can cause you to laugh aloud.
   T / F ____

Name ______________________ Date ______________

Poetry Collection: Amy Ling, Wendy Rose, E. E. Cummings

Reading Warm-up A

Read the following passage. Pay special attention to the underlined words. Then, read it again, and complete the activities. Use a separate sheet of paper for your written answers.

My name is Amazing. At least, that is what people always say when they see me: "He is 'Amazing!'" They yell these words from the decks of small boats and big ships, as they watch me swimming in the ocean. Some of them pay money just to go out to sea, hoping for a glimpse of me.

It is a delicious feeling for me, to be so admired just for doing what a giant sea turtle does best. I try to think about why my image is so impressive.

I suppose it is my size, but what these people should find really incredible is my age. I know that seeing a three-hundred-pound turtle might be shocking, but these people should imagine how it feels to be swimming around at my age. I wish I could stop and rest sometimes. Think about the birds, for example. They get to quit flying and perch on something for a nice long nap whenever they feel like it.

I believe that I am the eldest sea turtle in the world. I have lived more than eighty years, outliving three of my own children. Each year, I have seen the fireworks that are twinkling in the sky as people around the world welcome a new year. I even saw the world usher in a new century a phenomenon that occurs only once every hundred years!

During my years on Earth, I have watched the ocean waters grow more and more polluted. I have seen people pull more and more of my food out of the seas. As I near the end of my life, I hope that people who see me, who call me "Amazing," will make some changes so that giant sea turtles will thrive in this world. I hope humans know that what they really should call us is "Endangered."

1. Underline the words describing what the turtle finds delicious. Then, tell about something other than a food or drink that is ***delicious*** to you.
2. Circle a word in the next sentence that names what the turtle believes is impressive about its image. Then, explain what ***image*** means.
3. Underline the word telling what birds are doing before they perch on something. Then, describe a good place for a bird to ***perch***.
4. Circle the words in the paragraph naming how long the eldest turtle has lived. Then, tell about the ***eldest*** member of your family.
5. Underline the word naming what was twinkling in the sky. Then, tell about something else you have seen that was ***twinkling*** in the sky.
6. Circle the word in the previous sentences that hints at the meaning of century. If the turtle is speaking today, what new ***century*** did it see the world celebrate?

Name ______________________________ Date ________________

Poetry Collection: Amy Ling, Wendy Rose, E. E. Cummings

Reading Warm-up B

Read the following passage. Pay special attention to the underlined words. Then, read it again, and complete the activities. Use a separate sheet of paper for your written answers.

Nonverbal communication is vital to expressing people's true thoughts and feelings. We watch how others move and stand when they speak. We hear the tone of their voice and notice their facial expressions and body language. All of this information is extremely important. Just think about it—has a person's exquisite smile ever meant more to you than a hundred words that this individual might have spoken?

Signing is another critical form of communication. For those who can neither hear nor communicate verbally, signing is a powerful tool for listening and speaking. Many parents today are teaching their very young children to sign so that they can communicate before they are able to talk.

Going beyond these forms of daily nonverbal communication are art forms created to speak to us without words. For example, the ancient art of drumming is considered a universal form of communication. As you listen to people playing in a drum circle, for example, you can feel their emotions. A drumbeat can sound serious or humorous, powerful or lighthearted. Drummers can tell entire stories. A drumbeat can take you to the top of a mountain or to the depths of the brilliant aqua ocean.

Other art forms work wordlessly, too. Rather than hearing a message, you see it. For example, a mime is a person who acts out complete scenes without speaking a word. Often appearing in slippered feet, mimes try to avoid creating any sounds. Even when a scene calls for jostling or other usually noisy encounters, a mime succeeds in showing the action quietly. Watching a mime perform is like seeing a woodpecker at work through a soundproof window. You can hear what is happening but only in your mind. Through the silence, you can think more deeply about the action you see.

1. Underline the word naming something exquisite. Then, describe an ***exquisite*** nonverbal communication you have seen.

2. Circle the word that means the opposite of humorous. Then, describe something ***humorous*** you have heard lately.

3. Underline the word naming something aqua. Then, explain what ***aqua*** means.

4. Circle the words explaining why mimes often have slippered feet. Then, describe how your feet look when they are ***slippered***.

5. Circle the word that tells what calls for jostling. Explain why ***jostling*** might be described as a noisy action.

6. Underline what the writer compares to watching a woodpecker through a soundproof window. Then, explain the work of a ***woodpecker***.

Name ______________________________ Date ______________

Poetry Collection: Amy Ling, Wendy Rose, E. E. Cummings

Writing About the Big Question

What is the secret to reaching someone with words?

Big Question Vocabulary

benefit	connection	cultural	experience	express
feedback	individuality	inform	meaningful	media
misunderstand	relevant	sensory	significance	valid

A. *Use one or more words from the list above to complete each sentence.*

1. Karl hoped to ______________________ from his practice in speech class.
2. Jasmine realized too late the ______________________ of the harsh words she spoke.
3. "Make sure you include only ______________________ details in your essay," Ms. Brennan said.

B. *Follow the directions in responding to each of the items below.*

1. Express your ideas about a relevant issue in your school or community. Use at least two Big Question vocabulary words.

   ____.

   ____.

2. Make a connection between literature and life, referring to a poem, story, or novel you have read recently.

   ____

   ____

C. *Complete the sentence below. Then, write a short paragraph in which you connect this idea to the Big Question.*

Stimulating the senses with familiar smells can stir up memories of ______________

____

____

____

Name ______________________________ Date ______________

Poetry Collection: Amy Ling, Wendy Rose, E. E. Cummings

Reading: Read According to Punctuation to Paraphrase

When you **paraphrase** a poem, you restate it in your own words. First, read the poem through carefully and try to determine the complete thoughts it contains. **Use the punctuation** on the page—as well as the words themselves—to help you identify complete thoughts. Next, restate the meaning of each complete thought in your own words. Eliminate unneeded repetition. Mentally fill in any missing words to complete thoughts that are not fully stated. If the vocabulary is difficult, use simpler synonyms. Put unusual sentence structures into a word order that is easier to understand.

DIRECTIONS: *Because the poem "your little voice" does not use standard punctuation or capitalization to make complete thoughts clear, try to figure them out from the poem's words and the spacing of the words on the page. On the chart below, list your paraphrase on the right. An example has been provided for you.*

Complete Thoughts	Paraphrased Lines
Lines 1–2: "your . . . leaping"	I heard your little voice over the telephone.
Lines 3–4: "and . . . dizzy"	
Lines 5–10: "With . . . faces"	
Line 11: "floating . . . me"	
Lines 12–17: "I . . . moon"	
Lines 18–19: "dear . . . crazy"	
Lines 19–24: "how . . . voice"	

Name ______________________________ Date ______________

Poetry Collection: Amy Ling, Wendy Rose, E. E. Cummings

Literary Analysis: Imagery

Poetry often makes use of **imagery,** language that appeals to one or more of the five senses. Each instance of imagery is called an **image.** If you take note of the images as you read a poem, you will often understand it better. As you read, imagine that you are actually seeing, smelling, hearing, tasting, or touching the things described by the poet. Put yourself at the scene mentally, and experience the images.

DIRECTIONS: *Use this chart to help you focus on the imagery in the three poems in this collection. From each poem, list words or phrases that appeal to the senses in the corresponding boxes. Remember that many images appeal to more than one sense.*

	Sight	Sound	Touch	Smell	Taste
"Grandma Ling"					
"Drum Song"					
"your little voice"					

Name ______________________________ Date ______________

Poetry Collection: Amy Ling, Wendy Rose, E. E. Cummings

Vocabulary Builder

Word List

burrow exquisite impertinently jostling tongue vertical

A. Directions: *Circle* T *if the statement is true or* F *if the statement is false. Then, explain your answer.*

T / F 1. An animal that makes its home in a passage underground lives in a burrow.

____

T / F 2. Most teachers like students who speak impertinently.

____

T / F 3. A jostling ride is comfortable.

____

T / F 4. If you hold your tongue, you don't speak.

____

T / F 5. An exquisite diamond will be really expensive.

____

B. Word Study: *The root* -vert- *means "turn." Use the context of the sentences and what you know about the root* -vert- *to explain your answer to each question.*

1. What happens to a person who suffers *vertigo*?

____

____

2. What function do *vertebrae* play in your spinal column?

____

____

C. Directions: *Circle the letter of the word that is closest in meaning to the Word List word in capital letters.*

1. VERTICAL
   A. normal B. upright C. green D. horizontal
2. BURROW
   A. hole B. whole C. lend D. donkey
3. IMPERTINENTLY
   A. relevantly B. intelligently C. rudely D. eagerly

Name ________________________________ Date ________________

Poetry Collection: Amy Ling, Wendy Rose, E. E. Cummings

Enrichment: The Telegraph and the Telephone

Before the 1840s, messages had to be physically transported from one place to another. The invention of the telegraph changed all that. By using electrical wires, the telegraph enabled people to send messages over great distances in a short time. However, these messages were sent one letter of the alphabet at a time in a code made up of long and short sounds. The sender at point A would give a message to a telegraph operator, who would put the message into code and send it over the wires to another telegraph operator at point B. The second operator would translate the coded message back into letters of the alphabet and get it to the person the sender wanted to reach near point B.

By the 1870s, two American inventors working to improve the telegraph separately came up with a way of using electrical wires to transmit actual human voices. Their names were Alexander Graham Bell and Elisha Gray. Because Bell reached the patent office a few hours ahead of Elisha Gray, he got the credit for the invention of the telephone. It took decades, however, before telephones became everyday objects in American homes. The poem "your little voice" was first published in 1923, when having a telephone was still a fairly new experience for many Americans.

A. DIRECTIONS: *Answer these questions based on the information in the passage above and your own knowledge, including your understanding of the poem "your little voice."*

1. How did the telegraph improve communications?

____

____

2. How is the telephone an improvement over the telegraph?

____

____

3. How do you think people reacted to telephones when the first ones began to appear?

____

____

4. What details in "your little voice" suggest that the telephone was still fairly new?

____

____

B. DIRECTIONS: *On the lines below, or on a separate sheet of paper, describe the effects of the cell phone or another recent invention. Your description may be in the form of a poem.*

____

____

____

Name ______________________________ Date ______________

Poetry Collections: John Updike, N. Scott Momaday, Alice Walker;
Amy Ling, Wendy Rose, E. E. Cummings

Integrated Language Skills: Grammar

Infinitives and Infinitive Phrases

An **infinitive** is the form of a verb that includes the word *to* and acts as a noun, an adjective, or an adverb. Each of these sentences contains the infinitive *to dance.*

Noun: *To dance* is difficult for some people. [serves as the subject of the sentence]

Noun: Many people love *to dance.* [serves as the direct object of the verb *love*]

Adjective: That catchy music is an invitation *to dance.* [modifies the noun *invitation*]

Adverb: It is easy *to dance* to that music. [modifies the adjective *easy*]

An **infinitive phrase** is an infinitive with modifiers or a complement. The entire phrase acts as a single part of speech. The following sentences show some ways in which infinitives are expanded into infinitive phrases. In each sentence, the infinitive phrase is in italics.

With Adverb: I would love *to dance well.* [phrase serves as noun (direct object)]

With Direct Object: He gave me an invitation *to dance a mambo.* [phrase serves as adjective (modifies *invitation*)]

With Prepositional Phrase: I find it easy *to dance to that music.* [phrase serves as adverb (modifies *easy*)]

A. Practice: *Circle the infinitive phrase in each sentence. On the line after the sentence, indicate whether the phrase serves as a* noun, *an* adjective, *or an* adverb. *If it serves as a noun, tell whether it is a subject, a direct object, or another part of the sentence. If it serves as an adjective or an adverb, tell what it modifies.*

1. I like to read poetry aloud. ______________________________
2. It is easiest to recite poetry with a strong rhythm. ______________________________
3. We had an assignment to do a poetry reading. ______________________________
4. To set the poem to music was difficult. ______________________________
5. We were able to rehearse twice. ______________________________

B. Writing Application: *Complete each sentence by adding an infinitive phrase on the line.*

1. I really want ______________________________
2. It is fun ______________________________
3. My cousin gave me tips ______________________________

Name ______________________________ Date ______________

Poetry Collections: John Updike, N. Scott Momaday, Alice Walker;
Amy Ling, Wendy Rose, E. E. Cummings

Integrated Language Skills: Support for Writing a Review of Poetry

Use this chart to help you evaluate the poems in Collection 7 or 8. To rate each element, use *A+, A, A-, B+, B,* and so on. Consider *C* a passing grade and *F* failure. In the third column, include examples as well as your general comments. Then, use the information on the chart to help you write your review.

Poem Title:		
Element	**Rating**	**Details**
sound		
word choice		
imagery		

Poem Title:		
Element	**Rating**	**Details**
sound		
word choice		
imagery		

Poem Title:		
Element	**Rating**	**Details**
sound		
word choice		
imagery		

Name ______________________________ Date ______________

Poetry Collections: John Updike, N. Scott Momaday, Alice Walker;
Amy Ling, Wendy Rose, E. E. Cummings

Integrated Language Skills: Support for Extend Your Learning

Research and Technology: John Updike, N. Scott Momaday, Alice Walker

Use this modified timeline to record important events in the life of the poet you investigate. Include information on the author's birth date, education, employment, changes of residence, publications, awards, and death date, if relevant.

Poet: ______________________________

Year	Important Event	Source of Information

Research and Technology: Amy Ling, Wendy Rose, E.E. Cummings

Use this modified timeline to record important events in the life of the poet you investigate. Include information on the author's birth date, education, employment, changes of residence, publications, awards, and death date, if relevant.

Poet: ______________________________

Year	Important Event	Source of Information

Name ______________________________ Date ______________

Poetry Collection: Amy Ling, Wendy Rose, E.E. Cummings

Open-Book Test

Short Answer *Write your responses to the questions in this section on the lines provided.*

1. The imagery in lines 8–10 of "Grandma Ling" appeals to the sense of hearing. What specific words create the imagery? What feeling do you get from these words? Explain.

2. In "Grandma Ling," the speaker says, "my image stood before me,/acted on by fifty years." How would you paraphrase these lines?

3. In "Grandma Ling," the speaker does not meet her grandmother for many years. How does she feel toward Grandma Ling when they finally meet? Support your answer with details from the poem.

4. Each stanza of "Drum Song" uses imagery, or language that appeals to the senses. Look at the first stanza. To what sense does the imagery appeal? Support your answer with details from the poem.

5. The snowhare in "Drum Song" lives in a *burrow.* What other animal might have a *burrow*? Explain.

6. In "Drum Song," the speaker gives many details about animals. Based on these details, what conclusion can you draw about the speaker's experiences with animals? Include some examples to support your answer.

Name ______________________________ Date ______________

7. How does the subject of the last stanza of "Drum Song" differ from the subjects in the first three stanzas? What do you think the writer is trying to say by including this subject? Explain your answer using details from the poem.

____

____

____

____

8. The full title of the E. E. Cummings poem is "your little voice/Over the wires came leaping." How would you paraphrase, or restate, this title?

____

____

9. The chart below has two examples of imagery from "your little voice." For each one, put a checkmark under each sense to which that imagery appeals. Then, choose one of the examples and, on the line provided, tell what emotional effect it has.

Imagery	**Sight**	**Touch**	**Hearing**
"the jostling and shouting of merry flowers"			
"floating hands were laid upon me"			

____

10. In "your little voice," the speaker has strong feelings about the person whose voice he hears. How does he feel? What details from the poem reveal these feelings?

____

____

____

Essay

Write an extended response to the question of your choice or to the question or questions your teacher assigns you.

11. In an essay, describe the speaker's situation in either "Grandma Ling" or "your little voice." If you write about "Grandma Ling," be sure to explain how the speaker feels about her grandmother. If you write about "your little voice," be sure to explain how the speaker feels about the person who has the little voice. Use details from the poem you choose to support your response.

Name ______________________ Date ______________

12. In an essay, explain the view of nature presented in "Drum Song." Cite details from the poem to support your general comments about its theme.
13. Both "Grandma Ling" and "your little voice" use imagery to convey the emotions or attitudes of the speakers. Choose one of these poems. In an essay, discuss how the poet uses imagery to present the speaker's feelings. Support your response with details from the poem.
14. **Thinking About the Big Question: What is the secret to reaching someone with words?** "Grandma Ling," "Drum Song," and "your little voice" all use words to describe women. Which poem most successfully reaches you with its description? Which woman or women do you find most interesting, and why? Support your ideas with details from the poem.

Oral Response

15. Go back to question 3, 5, or 7 or to the question your teacher assigns you. Take a few minutes to expand your answer and prepare an oral response. Find additional details in "Grandma Ling," "Drum Song," and "your little voice" that will support your points. If necessary, make notes to guide your response.

Name ______________________________ Date ______________

Poetry Collection: Amy Ling, Wendy Rose, E. E. Cummings

Selection Test A

Critical Reading *Identify the letter of the choice that best answers the question.*

____ 1. According to "Grandma Ling," where does the speaker first meet Grandma Ling?

A. Pennsylvania

B. Taiwan

C. in her backyard

D. in a mirror

____ 2. Which word best describes the speaker's feelings toward Grandma Ling when they met?

A. frightened

B. shy

C. warm

D. bored

____ 3. To what senses does this image from "Grandma Ling" appeal most strongly?

Before she came to view, I heard
her slippered feet softly measure
the tatami floor with even step;

A. sound and touch

B. sight and touch

C. touch and taste

D. sight and smell

____ 4. Which is the best paraphrase of these lines from "Grandma Ling"?

and there I faced
my five foot height, sturdy legs and feet,

A. And there I saw someone the same height as me, with strong legs and feet.

B. And there I stood as tall as I could on strong legs and feet to face someone much shorter.

C. And there I accepted that I was five feet tall, with thick legs and feet.

D. And there I observed someone else who was five feet tall, with slim legs and feet.

____ 5. In "Drum Song," what or whom does the speaker describe?

A. animals and children

B. animals, men, women, and children

C. children only

D. animals and women

Name ______________________ Date ______________

___ 6. In "Drum Song," to what sense does the first line of each stanza appeal?
A. With the command "Speak," it appeals to the sense of sound.
B. With the command "Watch," it appeals to the sense of sight.
C. With the command "Look," it appeals to the sense of sight.
D. With the command "Listen," it appeals to the sense of sound.

___ 7. Which is the best paraphrase of these lines in "Drum Song"?

. . . Snowhare . . .
your whiskers dance
bush to burrow

A. Your whiskers move as you dig under a bush.
B. Your whiskers shake as you move from a bush to your hole.
C. Your dance whisks you from a bush to a hole in the ground.
D. You tell lies as you look for a bush to dig up.

___ 8. Which of these attitudes does "Drum Song" express?
A. a positive attitude toward nature
B. a negative attitude toward nature
C. a positive attitude toward science
D. a negative attitude toward people

___ 9. In "your little voice," where does the speaker hear the voice?
A. in a garden
B. at a dance
C. on an airplane
D. on the phone

___ 10. In "your little voice," how does the speaker feel about the person whose voice he hears?
A. angry
B. loving
C. confused
D. jealous

___ 11. Which is the best paraphrase of this line from "your little voice"?

With the jostling and shouting of merry flowers . . .

A. with the pushing and shouting of happy flowers
B. with the shoving and shouting of angry flowers
C. with the pushing and shouting, I was reminded of jolly flowers
D. with the joking and cheering of happy flowers

Name ______________________________ Date ______________

____ 12. To which sense does this image from "your little voice" appeal most strongly?

I was whirled and tossed into delicious dancing

A. smell
B. touch
C. taste
D. sound

Vocabulary and Grammar

____ 13. Which word is most nearly *opposite* in meaning to the word *impertinently*?

A. politely
B. unnecessarily
C. thoughtlessly
D. strongly

____ 14. What does *burrow* mean in this sentence?

The woodchuck went into its burrow.

A. fur
B. period of sleep in winter
C. hole providing shelter
D. to dig in the ground

____ 15. Identify the infinitive phrase in the following sentence.

I went to the stadium because I like to watch baseball games.

A. to the stadium
B. because I like
C. to watch
D. to watch baseball games

Essay

16. Write a composition in which you paraphrase the four stanzas of the poem "Drum Song" by Wendy Rose. Present your paraphrase in paragraph form, not as a poem.

17. Write a brief essay about the speaker's situation in either "Grandma Ling" or "your little voice." If you write about "Grandma Ling," be sure to explain how the speaker feels about her grandmother. If you write about "your little voice," be sure to explain how the speaker feels about the person who has the little voice.

18. **Thinking About the Big Question: What is the secret to reaching someone with words?** "Grandma Ling," "Drum Song," and "your little voice" all use words to describe women. Which description did you like best? Which woman or women do you find most interesting, and why? Support your ideas with details from the poem.

Name ______________________________ Date ______________

Poetry Collection: Amy Ling, Wendy Rose, E. E. Cummings

Selection Test B

Critical Reading *Identify the letter of the choice that best completes the statement or answers the question.*

____ 1. In "Grandma Ling," how does the speaker meet her grandmother?
- **A.** She leaves China and joins her grandmother in Pennsylvania.
- **B.** She travels to Taiwan and meets her grandmother there.
- **C.** She meets her every time she looks in a mirror, since the resemblance is so strong.
- **D.** She "digs a hole to China" and meets her grandmother in the world of imagination.

____ 2. Which is the best paraphrase of these lines from "Grandma Ling"?

my image stood before me,
acted on by fifty years.

- **A.** A photograph of me had faded over time.
- **B.** Something in a fifty-year-old mirror stood before me.
- **C.** I saw someone who looked like me but fifty years older.
- **D.** I saw something I had not seen in fifty years.

____ 3. In "Grandma Ling," how do the speaker and her grandmother communicate?
- **A.** in English
- **B.** in Chinese
- **C.** through an interpreter
- **D.** with smiles and hugs

____ 4. Which of these images from "Grandma Ling" most strongly appeals to the senses of sight, sound, and touch?
- **A.** the hole dug deep enough to reach China
- **B.** the slippered feet softly measuring the tatami floor
- **C.** the aqua paper-covered door sliding open
- **D.** the grandmother's square forehead, high cheeks, and wide-set eyes

____ 5. Each stanza in "Drum Song" begins "Listen," and then presents an image—of a turtle, woodpecker, snowhare, and women. Together, what do these images imply?
- **A.** Human beings are part of nature.
- **B.** Human beings have conquered nature.
- **C.** Modern life is no longer close to nature.
- **D.** Nature is cruel to animals and humans.

____ 6. From the details in "Drum Song," what can you conclude about the speaker?
- **A.** The speaker has observed animals in the wild.
- **B.** The speaker has a lot of pets.
- **C.** The speaker would like to have a turtle as a pet.
- **D.** all of the above

Name ______________________________ Date ______________

____ 7. Which is the best paraphrase of these lines from "Drum Song"?

. . . perch
on vertical earth
of tree bark and
branch.

A. sit on a fallen log
B. squat on bark-covered ground
C. sit in or on a living tree
D. dive between the trees

____ 8. In "Drum Song," what might the image "your tongues melt" mean?
A. The women are working in desert heat.
B. The snow on the mountains melts.
C. The drum speaks.
D. Women unfreeze their tongues and talk.

____ 9. How does the speaker in "your little voice" feel about hearing the voice?
A. delighted
B. puzzled
C. angry
D. gloomy

____ 10. What seems to be the relationship between the speaker in "your little voice" and the person with the "little voice"?
A. co-workers
B. couple in love
C. parent-child
D. teacher-pupil

____ 11. In "your little voice," what is the purpose of the image of the merry flowers skipping?
A. to show that the people in the poem are part of nature
B. to help us picture the garden where the poem takes place
C. to capture the sound and rhythm of the little voice
D. to convey the speaker's happiness on hearing the little voice

____ 12. Which of these images from "your little voice" most strongly appeals to the sense of touch?
A. pale important stars
B. i felt suddenly dizzy
C. skipping high-heeled flames
D. floating hands were laid upon me

____ 13. Which is the best paraphrase of these lines from "your little voice"?

Looked up
with impertinently exquisite faces

A. admired the beautiful though irrelevant appearance
B. looked up with boldly beautiful faces
C. looked up at the bold, beautiful sky
D. admired the rude beauty that could not be met

Name ______________________________ Date ______________

Vocabulary and Grammar

____ 14. Which of the following people is behaving *impertinently*?
A. a doctor saving lives
B. a student answering a teacher rudely
C. an actress whose hair is blown by wind
D. a farmer carefully planting a crop of corn

____ 15. Which sentence uses the underlined vocabulary word correctly?
A. Draw a straight line from left to right; then, draw a vertical line that crosses it.
B. A car should not cross double vertical lines painted down the center of the highway.
C. A person needs to be completely vertical when he or she sleeps.
D. Climbing the tall mountain gave me vertical.

____ 16. How many infinitive phrases do these lines contain?

go slow, go steady,
from rock to water
to land to rock to
water.

A. none B. one C. two D. five

____ 17. Identify the infinitive phrase and in its function in these lines.

She smiled, stretched her arms
to take to heart the eldest daughter

A. The infinitive phrase *to take* serves as an adjective modifying *heart.*
B. The infinitive phrase *to take to heart* serves as an adjective modifying *daughter.*
C. The infinitive phrase *to take to heart* is a noun, the object of the verb *stretched.*
D. The infinitive phrase *to take to heart* is an adverb modifying *stretched.*

Essay

18. Write a brief essay about the view of nature presented in "Drum Song." Cite details from the poem to support your general comments about its theme.

19. Write a brief essay discussing the use of imagery in both "Grandma Ling" and "your little voice." Examine the ways in which each poem uses images to convey the emotions or attitudes of its speaker.

20. **Thinking About the Big Question: What is the secret to reaching someone with words?** "Grandma Ling," "Drum Song," and "your little voice" all use words to describe women. Which poem most successfully reaches you with its description? Which woman or women do you find most interesting, and why? Support your ideas with details from the poem.

"The Road Not Taken" by Robert Frost
"O Captain! My Captain!" by Walt Whitman

Vocabulary Warm-up Word Lists

Study these words from the poetry of Robert Frost and Walt Whitman. Then, complete the activities that follow.

Word List A

fearful [FEER fuhl] *adj.* terrible; bad
The fearful mudslides luckily did not reach our house.

flung [FLUHNG] *v.* thrown suddenly with force
When our team won, many hats were flung happily into the air.

grim [GRIM] *adj.* gloomy and depressing
The house, closed up for years, had a grim, unloved appearance.

swaying [SWAY ing] *v., used here as adj.* moving slowly from side to side
The swaying crowd chanted loudly in support of the home team.

trodden [TRAHD n] *v.* walked or stepped on
The hunters have trodden a path into the deep woods.

victor [VIK tuhr] *adj.* being the winner in a struggle or battle (old-fashioned form of *victorious*)
The victor team celebrated by going out to dinner.

Word List B

bouquets [boo KAYZ] *n.* bunches of flowers
We arranged six bouquets of fresh flowers to place on the tables.

claim [KLAYM] *n.* a right to have or do something
The farmer said he had a claim on all the land up to the fence.

hence [HENS] *adv.* from this time on; from this point on
From that happy day hence, they never had to work again.

mournful [MAWRN fuhl] *adj.* very sad; full of sorrow
Her beautiful but mournful voice brought us all to tears.

trills [TRILZ] *v.* makes a sound in music by quickly repeating two notes that are similar
The flute player trills the same two notes throughout the first four measures of the song.

undergrowth [UN der grohth] *n.* bushes and small trees that grow around and beneath larger trees
The rabbit hopped across the lawn and disappeared in the undergrowth.

Name ______________________________ Date ______________

"The Road Not Taken" by Robert Frost
"O Captain! My Captain!" by Walt Whitman

Vocabulary Warm-up Exercises

Exercise A *Fill in each blank in the paragraph below with an appropriate word from Word List A. Use each word only once.*

Our backpacks are [1] ____________ over our shoulders and tightened. James has a [2] ____________ expression on his face. "Come on. Cheer up," I tell him. "It's not a real survival test, only a game." Still, James, feeling scared, eyes the thick, dark, [3] ____________ woods as if his life depends on getting through them safely. We start out along a path through the trees where leaves lie just as they fell. No one has [4] ____________ there recently. High, thin, [5] ____________ branches shift with the breeze, but the thicker, lower ones don't move a hair. The only sounds are our footsteps and our breathing. James cares a lot more about being the [6] ____________ than I do. I'm just happy to be outdoors, using my compass and my wits to get through the woods.

Exercise B *Circle* T *if the statement is true or* F *if the statement is false. Then, explain your answer.*

1. On Valentine's Day, people sometimes send <u>bouquets</u> to their loved ones.
   T / F ______________________________
2. You might be annoyed if a bird <u>trills</u> outside your window at 5:00 A.M.
   T / F ______________________________
3. You will find a lot of <u>undergrowth</u> in a desert.
   T / F ______________________________
4. When you are feeling sad, you can be cheered up by <u>mournful</u> music.
   T / F ______________________________
5. Starting today you have an eleven o'clock curfew, <u>hence</u> you should be home before that hour.
   T / F ______________________________
6. If you are babysitting two children, only one has a <u>claim</u> on your attention.
   T / F ______________________________

Name ______________________________ Date ______________

"The Road Not Taken" by Robert Frost
"O Captain! My Captain!" by Walt Whitman

Reading Warm-up A

Read the following passage. Pay special attention to the underlined words. Then, read it again, and complete the activities. Use a separate sheet of paper for your written answers.

The weather looked grim. The snow had been coming down for hours, and now the winds had reached blizzard speed. The best thing to do in such harsh, gloomy conditions was to stay indoors, warm and safe.

Doreen knew, however, that her mother was out there somewhere. In such weather, even a strong, capable woman driving a reliable van could get into trouble. Risking her own safety, Maureen bundled up, grabbed a shovel, and headed out into the fearful storm.

Doreen wrapped her scarf—which she usually flung over her shoulder—tightly around her face. Only her eyes peeked out.

For some reason, the phrase "the road not taken" suddenly popped into her mind. Why was she thinking of the title of a poem at a time like this? She considered it a moment. Then, she realized that she was indeed taking an unusual road by going to look for her mother.

Doreen walked along the shoulder of the road through snow that no one else had trodden. She stopped every few seconds to scan the distance for her mother, but she couldn't see far. Bare, swaying trees caught in the wind and occasional headlights were her only company.

There was a side road just about where Doreen was now standing—or there would have been, had it not been covered in one continuous snow bank. "The road not taken" crept into her mind again. She knew it meant something different this time, something literal. She quickly turned onto the side road.

For a second, Doreen imagined herself part of a victor team, having saved the most travelers stranded in the blizzard. However, there was just one traveler she wanted to save now. Suddenly, she could hear a motor grinding and wheels rocking on the slick snow. She sighed as she recognized her mother's van.

1. Circle the two words in the paragraph that define grim. Write about something you have seen or read that was *grim*.
2. Underline the sentence in the first paragraph that tells what made the storm fearful. Tell about a *fearful* storm you've been in or heard about.
3. Circle the word that tells that Doreen's scarf was not flung over her shoulder. Tell what would happen to a glass bowl that was *flung*.
4. Circle a word that is close in meaning to trodden. Rewrite the sentence with *trodden*, replacing the word with a synonym.
5. Circle what causes swaying trees. Describe another *swaying* object.
6. Underline the part of the sentence that explains what a victor team would have done. Write about a time that you were a *victor*.

Name ______________________________ Date ______________

"The Road Not Taken" by Robert Frost
"O Captain! My Captain!" by Walt Whitman

Reading Warm-up B

Read the following passage. Pay special attention to the underlined words. Then, read it again, and complete the activities. Use a separate sheet of paper for your written answers.

April 1865 was a fateful month for Abraham Lincoln. The Confederate government abandoned its capital of Richmond, Virginia. On the fourth, President Lincoln walked through its streets. On the ninth, General Lee surrendered to General Grant, and the Civil War was over. On the fourteenth, however, while Lincoln was watching a play at the Ford Theater in Washington, D.C., John Wilkes Booth shot and killed him.

Although the country needed Lincoln to help heal its wounds, death had the stronger claim. A week later, Mr. Lincoln's funeral train left Washington. It traced most of the route he had taken to greet the people after his election, before he took office. Its destination was Springfield, Illinois, which Lincoln thought of as his hometown.

The train steamed slowly toward Philadelphia and on to New York. Mournful crowds stood by the tracks wherever the train passed. In rural areas, people stood in the undergrowth beneath towering trees. When the train stopped in major cities, hundreds of thousands of people waited in lines for hours to view President Lincoln's body. Some brought bouquets of spring flowers and other tokens of their love for the fallen leader.

At Albany, the train turned west and traveled across New York State. It went through Ohio and Indiana. It entered Chicago, where it stopped, and then it steamed on to Springfield.

When an important leader dies these days, many a bugle trills with the sad notes of "Taps," a tune that always sends sorrow through the crowd. Perhaps the most touching aspect of Lincoln's arrival in Springfield, however, was the attendance of his horse, Old Bob, and his dog, Fido. They were silently led in to see their master one last time.

The nation had lost its leader. Now, it was more important than ever for people to put aside differences and help the country heal. However, it would be a long time hence before that healing would begin.

1. Circle the two things that had a claim on President Lincoln. Write about two things that both have a ***claim*** on you now.
2. Underline two words in the previous paragraph that give clues to what mournful means. Write about an event in which crowds would be the opposite of ***mournful***.
3. Circle the phrase that gives a clue to the meaning of undergrowth. Describe what you might find in ***undergrowth***.
4. Underline the words that help you figure out the meaning of bouquets. Describe another event when people might bring ***bouquets***.
5. Circle the words that tell you that trills has something to do with music. Write about a creature that ***trills***.
6. Circle the word that hints at the meaning of hence. Rewrite the sentence with ***hence***, replacing the word with a phrase that has the same meaning.

Name ______________________________ Date ______________

"The Road Not Taken" by Robert Frost
"O Captain! My Captain!" by Walt Whitman

Writing About the Big Question

What is the secret to reaching someone with words?

Big Question Vocabulary

benefit	connection	cultural	experience	express
feedback	individuality	inform	meaningful	media
misunderstand	relevant	sensory	significance	valid

A. *Use one or more words from the list above to complete each sentence.*

1. Whitman makes a ______________________ between a ship and the government of the country.
2. Whitman expresses the ______________________ of the history of our country in his poem.
3. Frost examines a ______________________ experience that reflects the choices we make in life.

B. *Follow the directions in responding to each of the items below.*

1. How would you best express your opinion of the choices you have made thus far in life?

   ____.

   ____.

2. Who has reached you with his or her words? Write two sentences explaining the experience. Use at least two of the Big Question vocabulary words.

   ____

   ____

C. *Complete the sentence below. Then, write a short paragraph in which you connect this idea to the Big Question.*

Choosing words carefully when we write helps us to ______________________

____

____

____

Name ______________________________ Date ______________________

"The Road Not Taken" by Robert Frost
"O Captain! My Captain!" by Walt Whitman

Literary Analysis: Comparing Types of Description

Descriptive writing paints word pictures for readers. A variety of descriptions can be used in poetry to present **levels of meaning.**

- **Literal meaning** is the actual, everyday meaning of words.
- **Figurative meaning** relies on figures of speech and the symbolic nature of language.

An **analogy** is a figurative description that compares two or more things that are similar in some ways, but otherwise unalike. For example, a poem that literally describes the ocean also can be read as an analogy: It may compare the ocean to life because both are vast, deep, and ever-changing. The poem, therefore, has two levels of meaning—one literal and one figurative.

DIRECTIONS: *On the following chart, for each quotation from a poem, note words and images that give you clues about its figurative meaning. The first one is done for you.*

Passages from "The Road Not Taken"	Which words and images give you clues about the figurative meaning of the passage?
1. "Two roads diverged in a yellow wood,"	Two roads = choices; yellow wood = life
2. "Then took the other, as just as fair, / And having perhaps the better claim, / Because it was grassy and wanted wear;"	

Passages from "O Captain! My Captain!"	Which words and images give you clues about the figurative meaning of the passage?
3. "O Captain! my Captain! our fearful trip is done, / The ship has weather'd every rack, the prize we sought is won,"	
4. "My Captain does not answer, his lips are pale and still, / My father does not feel my arm, he has no pulse nor will."	

Name ______________________ Date ______________

"The Road Not Taken" by Robert Frost
"O Captain! My Captain!" by Walt Whitman

Vocabulary Builder

Word List

diverged   exulting

A. Directions: *Complete the following word map by filling in the appropriate information.*

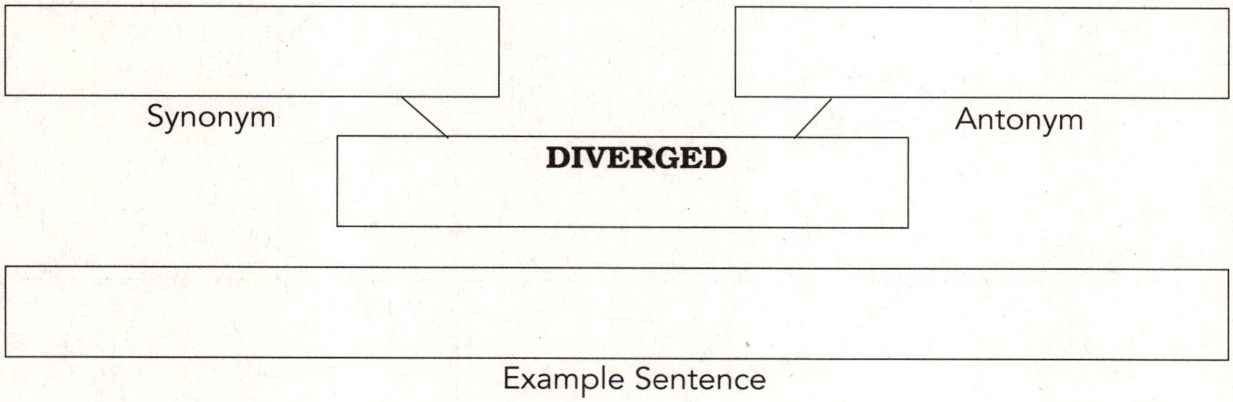

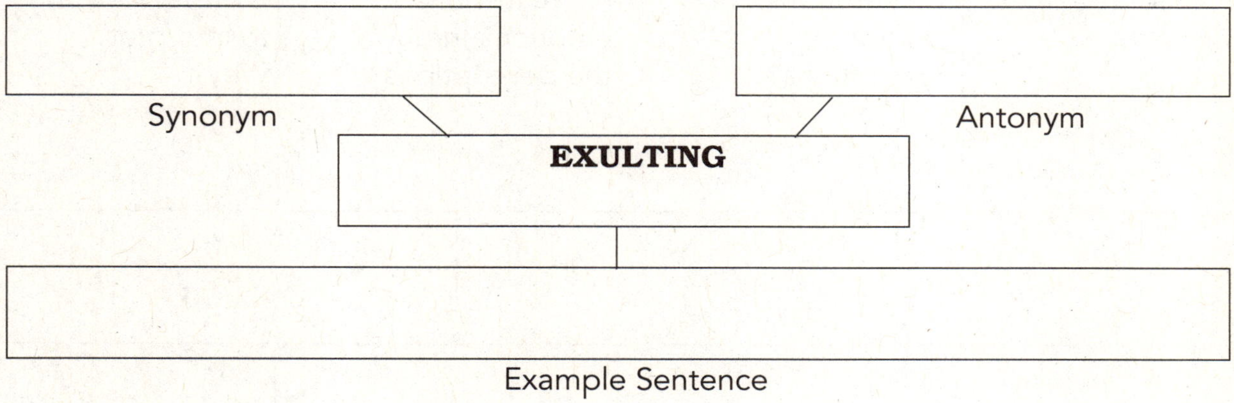

B. Directions: *Circle the letter of the pair that best expresses a relationship similar to that expressed in the pair in CAPITAL LETTERS.*

1. DIVERGED : SEPARATED ::
   - **A.** converged : split
   - **B.** removed : extracted
   - **C.** weighed : calculated
   - **D.** dressed : appeared

2. EXULTING : LAMENTING ::
   - **A.** talk : converse
   - **B.** barrel : basket
   - **C.** seldom : often
   - **D.** dwindle : decrease

Name ______________________________ Date ______________

"The Road Not Taken" by Robert Frost
"O Captain! My Captain!" by Walt Whitman

Integrated Language Skills: Support for Writing to Compare Description in Literary Works

Before you write your essay, use the graphic organizer below to list ideas about each poem.

"The Road Not Taken"

↑	↑	↑	↑
How common are the experiences the poets describe?	How universal are the emotions that prompt the descriptions?	Which poet better expresses his emotions through the descriptions? Why?	Which message is easier for you to interpret? Why?
↓	↓	↓	↓

"O Captain! My Captain!"

Now, use your notes to write your essay comparing the descriptions in "The Road Not Taken" and "O Captain! My Captain!"

Name ______________________________ Date ______________

Poetry by Robert Frost and Walt Whitman

Open-Book Test

Short Answer *Write your responses to the questions in this section on the lines provided.*

1. In "The Road Not Taken," the speaker tells of two roads that *diverged.* How would his life be different if the roads had not diverged? Focus on the meaning of in your response.

____

____

____

2. In "The Road Not Taken," the speaker says, "And sorry I could not travel both/And be one traveler . . ." What does he mean by this statement?

____

____

____

3. In "The Road Not Taken," the two roads ". . . that morning equally lay/In leaves no step had trodden black." What is meant by these lines?

____

____

4. In a poem's figurative meaning, one thing represents another thing. What do the "two roads" represent in "The Road Not Taken"? Explain your answer using details from the poem.

____

____

5. What are the speaker's feelings at the end of "The Road Not Taken"? Support your answer with details from the poem.

____

____

____

____

6. "O Captain! My Captain!" is an analogy, or a figurative comparison between two unlike things. With whom is the Captain being compared in this analogy? Explain using details from the poem.

____

____

____

Name ______________________ Date ______________

7. In "O Captain! My Captain!" what is the figurative meaning of "our fearful trip"? That is, what does the trip represent, or symbolize?

8. What does the speaker mean in this line from "O Captain! My Captain!"?

   The ship has weather'd every rack, the prize we sought is won.

9. What does the ship represent in "O Captain! My Captain!"? Explain using details from the poem.

10. In the chart below, sum up the literal and figurative meanings of "The Road Not Taken" and "O Captain! My Captain!" On the lines provided, tell why it is important to understand the figurative meaning.

Poem	Literal Meaning	Figurative Meaning
"The Road Not Taken"		
"O Captain! My Captain!"		

Essay

Write an extended response to the question of your choice or to the question or questions your teacher assigns you.

11. The poems "The Road Not Taken" and "O Captain! My Captain!" present images with a literal meaning. In an essay, compare the literal meaning of the images in each poem. First, explain "literal meaning." Describe the literal meaning of the images in "The Road Not Taken" and summarize what happens. Then, describe the literal meaning of the images in "O Captain! My Captain!" and tell what happens in the poem.

12. Both "The Road Not Taken" and "O Captain! My Captain!" address the personal feelings of the speakers. In an essay, compare and contrast the speakers in the two poems. What does each speaker say about his subject? How does each speaker feel about his subject? Support your ideas using details from the poems.

13. Both "The Road Not Taken" and "O Captain! My Captain!" are analogies. Write an essay comparing the poets' use of analogy in their poems. Explain how each poet uses analogy in his poem. Then, tell which poem you feel uses analogies more effectively, and why. Finally, explain why each of these analogy poems has become so famous. Support your ideas using details from the poems.

14. **Thinking About the Big Question: What is the secret to reaching someone with words?** Both "The Road Not Taken" and "O Captain! My Captain!" use words to communicate a message to readers. In an essay, explain the poems' messages, and then tell which poem reached you most strongly with its message. Cite words and phrases that helped get the message across.

Oral Response

15. Go back to question 3, 4, or 6 or to the question your teacher assigns you. Take a few minutes to expand your answer and prepare an oral response. Find additional details in "The Road Not Taken" and "O Captain! My Captain!" that will support your points. If necessary, make notes to guide your response.

Name ______________________ Date ______________

"The Road Not Taken" by Robert Frost
"O Captain! My Captain!" by Walt Whitman

Selection Test A

Critical Reading *Identify the letter of the choice that best answers the question.*

____ **1.** At the beginning of "The Road Not Taken," what decision does the speaker face?
A. which road to take
B. where to eat lunch
C. whether to go forward or go back
D. whether to keep walking or stop and rest

____ **2.** What do the following lines from "The Road Not Taken" mean?

And sorry I could not travel both
And be one traveler,

A. He thinks both paths are equally good.
B. He is only one man and cannot go down two roads at the same time.
C. He wishes that he were traveling with someone, so they could each explore a path.
D. He regrets not taking the other road as he looks back.

____ **3.** What is the difference between the two roads in "The Road Not Taken"?
A. One road is wider.
B. One road has a better view.
C. One road is less traveled.
D. One road is rockier.

____ **4.** What does the speaker mean in these lines from "The Road Not Taken"?

Oh, I kept the first for another day!
Yet knowing how way leads on to way,
I doubted if I should ever come back.

A. After walking the first road, he will come back and go down the road he did not take.
B. He does not like to travel in the same part of the woods over and over again.
C. He likes to walk in the woods by himself and knows the way very well.
D. He wants to take the other path later, but realizes he will probably never have that chance.

____ **5.** Whom does the speaker in "The Road Not Taken" stand for?
A. someone lost in the woods
B. a person who made a decision
C. a person now standing at a fork
D. a person who likes a well-beaten path

Name ______________________________ Date ________________

____ 6. What do the "two roads" represent in "The Road Not Taken"?
A. significant people who impact our lives
B. paths that fate leads us to
C. the beginnings of new phases in life
D. important decisions made in life

____ 7. On the surface, "The Road Not Taken" is about a walk in the woods. What is the meaning of the poem on a deeper level?
A. It is about traveling through life with others to help you make decisions.
B. It is about loving and protecting nature by not disturbing natural habitats.
C. It is about what to do when faced with life's important decisions.
D. It is about the importance of exercise and enjoying the outdoors.

____ 8. Who is the Captain in "O Captain! My Captain!"?
A. Walt Whitman
B. General McClellan
C. a ship's captain
D. President Lincoln

____ 9. In "O Captain! My Captain!" which historical event is the poet mourning?
A. the defeat of the Confederacy
B. the victory of the Union
C. the assassination of President Lincoln
D. the death of Walt Whitman's father

____ 10. In the following lines from "O Captain! My Captain!" what does the *ship* represent?
The ship has weather'd every rack,
the prize we sought is won.
A. the United States
B. the North
C. the South
D. the presidency

____ 11. Why does the speaker of "O Captain! My Captain!" say the following lines?
It is some dream that on the deck,
You've fallen cold and dead.
A. He dreamt the president had died.
B. He wishes the president were not dead.
C. He dreamt while sleeping on the deck.
D. He is afraid of dying on a ship.

Name ______________________________ Date ______________

___ 12. What do the following lines from “O Captain! My Captain!” mean?

My Captain does not answer, his lips are pale
and still,

A. The Captain is dead.
B. The Captain is too cold to talk.
C. The Captain is mad.
D. The Captain is sleeping.

___ 13. In “O Captain! My Captain!” what does “fearful trip” refer to when the speaker says, “From fearful trip the victor ship comes in”?

A. the Civil War
B. a fierce storm at sea
C. the presidency
D. Lincoln's life

Vocabulary and Grammar

___ 14. Which would be an appropriate word to replace *diverged*?

A. divided
B. presented
C. conformed
D. unequaled

___ 15. In which of the following instances would you most likely find someone *exulting*?

A. at a funeral
B. during a test
C. after a dental appointment
D. after winning a game

Essay

16. The poems “The Road Not Taken” and “O Captain! My Captain!” present images with a literal meaning. In an essay, compare the literal meaning of the images in each poem. What is a “literal meaning”? What is the literal meaning of the images in “The Road Not Taken”? How would you summarize what happens on the surface of the poem? What is the literal meaning of the images in “O Captain! My Captain!”? How would you summarize what happens on the surface of the poem?

17. The images in “The Road Not Taken” and “O Captain! My Captain!” have figurative meanings. Write an essay comparing the figurative descriptions in the two poems. What is a “figurative meaning”? What is the figurative meaning of “The Road Not Taken”? What is the figurative meaning of “O Captain! My Captain!”?

18. **Thinking About the Big Question: What is the secret to reaching someone with words?** Both “The Road Not Taken” and “O Captain! My Captain!” use words to get a message across to readers. In an essay, explain the poems' messages, and then tell which poem reached you most strongly with its message. Cite words and phrases that helped get the message across.

Name ______________________________ Date ______________

"The Road Not Taken" by Robert Frost
"O Captain! My Captain!" by Walt Whitman

Selection Test B

Critical Reading *Identify the letter of the choice that best completes the statement or answers the question.*

____ 1. The speaker in "The Road Not Taken" is a person who
- **A.** is lost in the woods.
- **B.** remembers making a decision.
- **C.** is currently standing at a fork in the road.
- **D.** likes to walk on a well-beaten path.

____ 2. In "The Road Not Taken," the description of the wood as yellow
- **A.** tells us the wood is very young, not yet full grown.
- **B.** makes the setting seem churchlike.
- **C.** tells us the scene is taking place at noon.
- **D.** helps us see the scene as autumnal.

____ 3. Which is the best restatement of these lines from "The Road Not Taken"?

And sorry I could not travel both
And be one traveler, . . .

- **A.** I regret I couldn't take both roads.
- **B.** I regret I am only one person.
- **C.** I regret that I am traveling alone.
- **D.** I am sorry to be far from home.

____ 4. In "The Road Not Taken," when Frost says two roads ". . . that morning equally lay / In leaves no step had trodden black," he means that
- **A.** both roads were covered in yellow leaves.
- **B.** both roads were wet with dew.
- **C.** neither road led to a place the speaker wanted to go.
- **D.** neither road had been walked on yet that morning.

____ 5. Which line or lines from "The Road Not Taken" describe the setting?

I. I shall be telling this with a sigh / Somewhere ages and ages hence:
II. Yet knowing how way leads on to way, / I doubted if I should ever come back.
III. Though as for that, the passing there / Had worn them really about the same.

- **A.** I
- **B.** II
- **C.** III
- **D.** I, II, and III

____ 6. What is "The Road Not Taken" about below its surface meaning?
- **A.** It closely observes the impact of humans on the woods.
- **B.** It urges readers to take chances.
- **C.** It raises questions of choice and decision making.
- **D.** It urges readers to exercise and enjoy the outdoors.

Name ______________________________ Date ______________

____ **7.** In "O Captain! My Captain!" the poet is mourning
A. the defeat of the Confederacy.
B. the victory of the Union.
C. the assassination of President Lincoln.
D. the endlessness of war.

____ **8.** The Captain in "O Captain! My Captain"
A. represents Walt Whitman.
B. is buried at sea.
C. is a ship's captain.
D. represents President Lincoln.

____ **9.** In the first line from "O Captain! My Captain!" what does "our fearful trip" refer to?
A. the Civil War
B. the battle at Antietam Creek
C. the presidency
D. Lincoln's life

____ **10.** Which statement best expresses the underlying meaning of this line from "O Captain! My Captain!"?

The ship has weather'd every rack, the prize we
sought is won.

A. Despite its hardships, the North will now be richer than the South.
B. The Union has survived great difficulties and won the war.
C. The Union has been greatly weakened by the war.
D. The ship has withstood every peril and returns home safely.

____ **11.** In "O Captain! My Captain!" what is the underlying meaning of this line?

The port is near, the bells I hear, the people all
exulting.

A. Many Americans will greet the ship and pay their respects to President Lincoln.
B. The goal of keeping America one country is within reach, and people are joyous.
C. I am glad to be approaching victory and returning to my church and my people.
D. We're are not quite home yet. We still have to quell riots.

____ **12.** Why are the people acting as they are in the following lines of "O Captain! My Captain!"?

For you bouquets and ribbon'd wreaths—for you
the shores a-crowding,
For you they call, the swaying mass, their eager
faces turning:

A. They are paying tribute to Lincoln because he has died.
B. They are welcoming the general who won many battles, but died in the last one.
C. They are celebrating Lincoln's election to a second term.
D. They are paying tribute to a great sailor who is bringing them wealth.

Name ______________________________ Date ______________

____ 13. What does the *ship* represent in this line from "O Captain! My Captain!"?

The ship is anchor'd safe and sound, its voyage
closed and done,

A. the North
B. the South
C. the United States
D. the war

Vocabulary

____ 14. In which sentence is *diverged* used correctly?
A. Where the two roads *diverged* into one road, the traffic became backed up.
B. The river flowed south and then *diverged* to the southeast and the southwest.
C. The crowd was happy to be *diverged* into the waterpark.
D. When it started to rain, we *diverged* and canceled the picnic.

____ 15. Which word is most *opposite* in meaning to *diverged*?
A. divided
B. presented
C. converged
D. unequaled

____ 16. In which sentence is *exulting* used correctly?
A. We enjoyed the wedding, *exulting* in the love of the happy couple.
B. The tribal people, *exulting* the hunter with fire power, thought he was a god.
C. The *exulting* rain was pleasant to walk in, even if it made us wet.
D. When the guest of honor arrived late, the *exulting* group got up and left.

Essay

17. Both "The Road Not Taken" and "O Captain! My Captain!" address personal feelings. In an essay, compare and contrast the speakers in the two poems. What does each speaker say about his subject? How does each speaker feel about his subject?

18. Both "The Road Not Taken" and "O Captain! My Captain!" are analogies. Write an essay comparing the authors' use of analogy. What is analogy? How does Frost use analogy in his poem? How does Whitman use analogy in his poem? Why has each of these analogy poems become so famous?

19. **Thinking About the Big Question: What is the secret to reaching someone with words?** Both "The Road Not Taken" and "O Captain! My Captain!" use words to communicate a message to readers. In an essay, explain the poems' messages, and then tell which poem reached you most strongly with its message. Cite words and phrases that helped get the message across.

Name ______________________________ Date ______________

Writing Workshop—Unit 4, Part 2

Comparison-and-Contrast Essay

Prewriting: Gathering Details

Use the Venn diagram below to list ideas and details about your two subjects. Use the center section to record similarities and the outer sections of each circle to record differences.

Subject: ______________ **Subject:** ______________

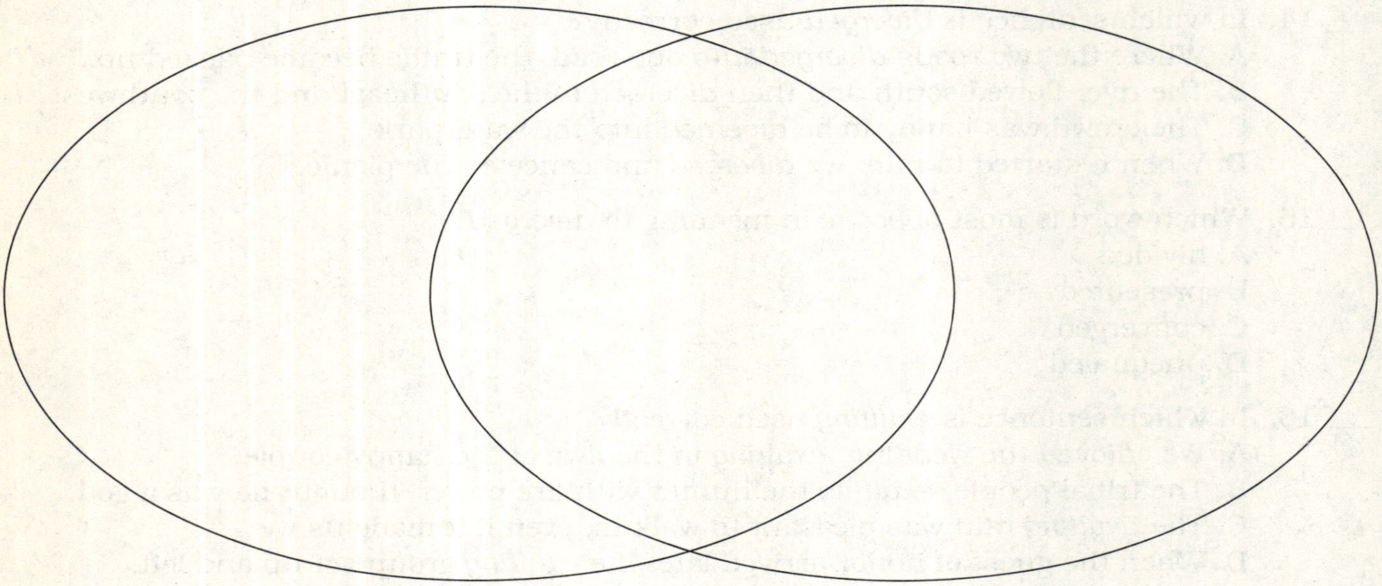

Drafting: Providing Elaboration

Use the chart below to develop the main point of each supporting paragraph in your essay.

Paragraphs	First Paragraph	Second Paragraph
State the topic of each paragraph.		
Extend the idea by restating it in a new way, applying it to a particular case, or contrasting it with another point.		
Elaborate with specific examples, facts, statistics, explanations, or quotations.		

Name ______________________________ Date ______________

Writing Workshop—Unit 4, Part 2

Comparison-and-Contrast Essay: Integrating Grammar Skills

Revising to Vary Sentence Patterns

Keep your writing lively by avoiding repetitious sentence patterns. First, identify a repetitive pattern. Then, mix up your sentence structure.

Use a variety of sentence beginnings to spruce up your writing.

Start with a noun:	The diner, tapping impatiently, called for the check.
Start with an adjective:	Surprised, the waiter rushed over.
Start with a prepositional phrase:	After a brief apology, the waiter delivered the bill.

Pack information into your sentences using appositives and appositive phrases.

Appositive: The diner, a theatergoer, needed to leave the restaurant quickly.

Appositive phrase: The waiter, an experienced theatergoer himself, understood the rush.

Identifying Sentence Patterns

A. Directions: *Read the paragraph below. Draw a triangle around each noun that starts a sentence. Draw a box around each adjective that starts a sentence. Draw a circle around each prepositional phrase that starts a sentence. Underline each appositive.*

In ancient Egypt, pharaohs built pyramids. The pyramids, tombs of the pharaohs, held immense treasures. Enormous and grand, the pyramids are exciting for archaeologists. During an expedition, archaeologists found a sealed door within a pyramid. Excited, they entered a room filled with ancient treasure.

____

____

____

Fixing Repetitive Sentence Patterns

B. Directions: *Read the paragraph below. On the lines provided, rewrite the paragraph to vary the sentence patterns. Be sure to change the sentence beginnings and use at least one appositive.*

The mummy of King Tutankhamen was in the tomb. King Tutankhamen was an Egyptian ruler. The body was preserved by Egypt's dry climate and was in excellent condition. King Tut was wearing a mask of solid gold, and he looked magnificent! Archaeologists found many objects to study in King Tut's tomb.

Name ______________________________ Date ______________

Unit 4 Vocabulary Workshop—1
Idioms

Idioms are so much a part of our language that sometimes we don't even realize we are using them.

Directions: *Complete the crossword puzzle by filling in the missing words of the idioms.*

Across

1. A watched pot never ____________.
3. beat a ____________ horse
4. ____________ in the sky
6. dime a ____________
7. ____________ the music

Down

1. ____________ in the woods
2. safe and ____________
3. beauty is only skin ____________
5. bat an ____________
7. drag your ____________

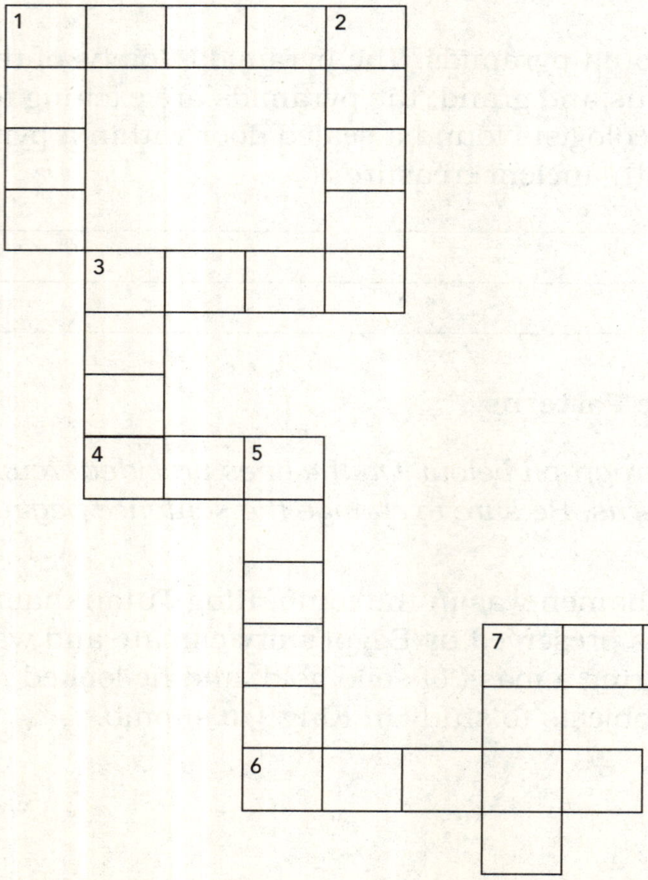

Name ______________________________ Date ____________________

Unit 4 Vocabulary Workshop—2
Idioms

People who are not native English speakers can be easily confused by idioms because the words are not meant to be taken literally.

Directions: *Translate the following idioms for a nonnative, English-speaking friend, but first, write or draw the image your friend gets when s/he hears the idiom for the first time. Have fun with this!*

Name ______________________________ Date ______________

Communications Workshop—Unit 4

Evaluating Media Messages

After choosing your commercial, fill out the following chart to evaluate the content and techniques of what you see.

Title of commercial: ______________________________

What are some of the images presented in the commercial?
What is the message behind them?
What mood is created by key words, music, or sound effects?
What media techniques are used to persuade you to agree with this meassage?
How would you rate the credibility of this message?

Name ______________________________ Date ______________

Unit 4: Poetry

Benchmark Test 8

MULTIPLE CHOICE

Reading Skill: Paraphrase *Read the selection, and then answer the questions that follow.*

Announced by all the trumpets of the sky,
Arrives the snow, and, driving o'er the fields,
Seems nowhere to alight: the whited air
Hides hill and woods, the river, and the heaven,
And veils the farmhouse at the garden's end.

—from "The Snowstorm" by Ralph Waldo Emerson

1. What is the best paraphrase of lines 1 through 3, up to the colon?
   A. The sky is full of wonder, and trumpets blow everywhere.
   B. While we were driving over the fields, the snow started.
   C. The snow comes, blown about with great force by the wind.
   D. The wind is blowing hard and sounds like trumpets.

2. Which best restates the clause in lines 3 through 5 beginning "the whited air"?
   A. The snow falls softly on the land.
   B. The snow blots out everything.
   C. Snow falls but does not stick.
   D. The weather is cold and gloomy.

Read the selection from a poem by John Masefield. Then, answer the questions that follow.

I must go down to the seas again, for the call of the running tide
Is a wild call and a clear call that may not be denied;
And all I ask is a windy day with the white clouds flying,
And the flung spray and the blown spume, and the sea-gulls crying.

I must go down to the seas again, to the vagrant gypsy life,
To the gull's way and the whale's way where the wind's like a whetted knife;
And all I ask is a merry yarn from a laughing fellow-rover,
And quiet sleep and a sweet dream when the long trick's over.

—from "Sea Fever" by John Masefield

3. Which is the best paraphrase of the excerpt from Masefield's poem?
   A. I love the wind and the salt spray when I am near the sea.
   B. I cannot resist the call of the wild, free life on the seas.
   C. I love to sail the sea on a clear, windy day.
   D. I envy the wild, free life of seagulls and whales.

Name ______________________________ Date ______________

Reading Skill: Analyze Technical Directions

Read the selection from a computer manual. Then, answer the questions that follow.

Try these steps if your computer display goes blank or if your system freezes:

1. Unplug all external devices that are connected to your computer except the power adapter.
2. Simultaneously depress the Command and Control keys, as well as the Power button, to reactivate the system.
3. Allow the battery to charge at least ten percent before plugging in any external devices.

4. What problem does this part of the manual address?
   - A. the battery losing its charge
   - B. the power adapter failing
   - C. the system freezing
   - D. the external devices not working
5. Which statement about steps 1 and 3 is true?
   - A. They both involve the power adapter.
   - B. Step 1 mentions external devices; step 3 does not.
   - C. Step 1 deals with the computer's plug; step 3 does not.
   - D. They address the beginning and end of the repair process.
6. What will depressing the Command, Control, and Power buttons do?
   - A. charge the battery
   - B. reactivate the system
   - C. shut down the external devices
   - D. make the computer display go blank

Literary Analysis *Read the selections, and then answer the questions that follow.*

Shall I compare thee to a summer's day?
Thou art more lovely and more temperate.
Rough winds do shake the darling buds of May,
And summer's lease hath all too short a date.

—from "Sonnet 18" by William Shakespeare

The tide rises, the tide falls,
The twilight darkens, the curfew calls;
Along the sea-sands damp and brown
The traveller hastens toward the town,
And the tide rises, the tide falls.

—from "The Tide Rises, the Tide Falls" by Henry Wadsworth Longfellow

7. What form of poetry are the lines by William Shakespeare?
   - A. lyric poetry
   - B. humorous poetry
   - C. concrete poetry
   - D. narrative poetry
8. What is a poet trying to do in a lyric poem?
   - A. tell a story
   - B. express thoughts and feelings
   - C. describe a setting
   - D. entertain the reader with humor

Name ______________________________ Date ________________

9. Identify the level of meaning is used in the following sentence?

Adolfo whirled through the house, a cyclone destroying everything in its path.

A. descriptive meaning
B. figurative meaning
C. literal meaning
D. actual meaning

10. What is the main purpose of a narrative poem?

A. to express a feeling
B. to tell a story
C. to describe a character
D. to describe a setting

11. Which imagery from Longfellow's poem appeals to the senses of touch and sight?

A. the tide rises, the tide falls
B. the twilight darkens
C. the traveller hastens
D. the sea-sands damp and brown

12. Which of these best defines imagery in poetry?

A. pictures that accompany poetry
B. comparison of one thing to another
C. language that appeals to the senses
D. imagination in poetry

13. Which of these is an example of the use of imagery?

A. The icy snow crunched underfoot.
B. Jack filled his plate with food.
C. Two chimneys rose from the house.
D. His mind was busily at work.

14. Which of these reflects the actual meaning of words?

A. a description using metaphor
B. a description using analogy
C. a figurative description
D. a literal description

15. Which of these best shows the use of analogy in a poem?

A. a description of a candle flame that can be compared to a life
B. a description of a storm using images that appeal to the senses
C. a description of a character who undergoes changes
D. a description of sights and sounds found in nature

Vocabulary: Roots and Prefixes

16. What is the meaning of *ingratitude* in the following sentence?

I was surprised by Sheila's ingratitude after we had all worked so hard to help her.

A. thankfulness
B. anger
C. great show of emotion
D. lack of appreciation

17. What is the meaning of the prefix *trans-* in the word *transformed*?

A. on or to the other side
B. more than enough
C. within
D. out of

18. Which word has the same root as the word *recede*?

A. prevail
B. conceit
C. succeed
D. sediment

Name ______________________________ Date ______________

19. Which of these best defines *inverted* in the following sentence?

The coin was extremely valuable because the year on it was inverted.

A. correct
B. upside down
C. missing
D. lacking color

20. Which word is the opposite of *inaccuracy* as it is used in the following sentence?

I apologize for my mistakes, and for the inaccuracy of my facts.

A. expression
B. extremity
C. correctness
D. humor

21. What is the meaning of *exceed* in the following sentence?

Jane was promoted because she always tried to exceed what was expected of her.

A. forget
B. explain
C. do less than
D. do more than

Grammar

22. What is the preposition in the following sentence?

The poet drew inspiration from nature.

A. poet
B. drew
C. from
D. nature

23. What is the prepositional phrase in the following sentence?

Each day, White created both humorous and touching poetry in his attic room.

A. in his attic room
B. both humorous and touching poetry
C. each day
D. his attic room

24. What does a prepositional phrase show?

A. action
B. possession
C. relationship
D. cause and effect

25. Which sentence contains an infinitive phrase?

A. To Jenny, the poem sounded false.
B. Eduardo recited the lines to me.
C. We hope to visit the poet's birthplace.
D. The writer paid tribute to his parents.

26. Which is the best way to vary the dull pattern in the following sentence?

The cyclists pedaled to the top of the hill.

A. The cyclists pedaled quickly to the top of the hill.
B. The three cyclists pedaled to the top of the steep hill.
C. Huffing and chuffing, the cyclists pedaled slowly up the steep hill.
D. Several cyclists rode slowly up the steep hill.

Name ______________________________ Date ______________

27. Which of these best defines an appositive phrase?
    A. a phrase that begins with a preposition and ends with a noun
    B. a noun phrase that defines other words in a sentence
    C. an infinitive with a modifier that acts as a single part of speech
    D. a form of verb that follows the word *to* and acts as a noun, adjective, or adverb

28. What statement about the following sentence is accurate?

    Looking under his bed, Derek finally found the belt he wanted to wear.

    A. It has neither a prepositional phrase nor an infinitive phrase.
    B. It has a prepositional phrase, but not an infinitive phrase.
    C. It has an infinitive phrase, but not a prepositional phrase.
    D. It has a prepositional phrase and an infinitive phrase.

Spelling

29. In which sentence is the underlined word spelled correctly?
    A. Phil's <u>absince</u> affected the project.
    B. Her argument seemed <u>ilogical</u>.
    C. We found an <u>affordable</u> vacation.
    D. There was <u>resistence</u> to my idea.

30. Which word would correctly complete the following sentence?

    An additional __________ of the play is scheduled for Sunday afternoon.

    A. performance
    B. performence
    C. performmence
    D. performince

ESSAY

Writing

31. Imagine that you want to write either a lyric or a narrative poem about a river. Decide whether you want to describe your impressions of the river or tell a story about it. Write the first line of a poem you might write. If you are writing a lyric poem, make sure to include at least two details about the river's qualities; if you are writing a narrative poem, include information about the setting and a character in the poem.

32. Choose one of the poems from this test and imagine that you have been asked to write a review of it. Write the headings "Word Choice" and "Imagery." Then, write an example of each from the poem and tell whether you think the poet uses the word or words and images effectively. Give reasons for your opinions.

33. You are planning a summer trip to another state, far away from your home state. Should you travel by plane or by car? Write a comparison-and-contrast essay in which you examine the similarities and differences between the two methods of travel.

Name ________________________ Date ____________

Vocabulary in Context

Identify the answer choice that best completes the statement.

1. I dreamed of a figure dressed in white with wings and a halo, who looked like an ______ .
   A. ninny
   B. nitwit
   C. angel
   D. eagle

2. If you need help, just ring the bell and a maid will appear ______ .
   A. strictly
   B. awkwardly
   C. rigidly
   D. instantly

3. After college, this is a city where I would like to ______ down.
   A. settle
   B. wander
   C. sprawl
   D. disturb

4. I would like to pay my bills and get up to date with my ______ .
   A. terms
   B. accounts
   C. impact
   D. privacy

5. He was rejected by the older kids and ______ by them.
   A. sensitive
   B. blunt
   C. bullied
   D. bearable

6. She carried the important papers under her arm in a ______ .
   A. postal
   B. blackmail
   C. bookcase
   D. satchel

7. The moon goes through several different ______ each month.
   A. restrictions
   B. phases
   C. performances
   D. successions

Name ______________________________ Date ________________

8. Our tent was destroyed, so we had to create this ______ shelter.
   A. exposed
   B. leisure
   C. rural
   D. makeshift

9. Pigs like to sit in mud and ______ in it.
   A. wallow
   B. lax
   C. reap
   D. menace

10. Do you know on what day the sanitation workers will pick up ______ ?
    A. discrepancies
    B. trimmings
    C. rubbish
    D. curtsies

11. My banker takes care of my money and handles other ______ matters.
    A. social
    B. ideal
    C. financial
    D. cultured

12. In times gone by, children of wealthy families were often taught at home by ______ .
    A. heirlooms
    B. governesses
    C. chambermaids
    D. poets

13. She and I like to visit each other; we have had so many pleasant ______ .
    A. intentions
    B. compassionate
    C. broadcasts
    D. conversations

14. Campers caused the forest fire through their ______ .
    A. realization
    B. carelessness
    C. indignation
    D. restrictions

Name ______________________________ Date ______________

15. My brother and sister seldom agree and are always fighting and______.
   A. bickering
   B. intimate
   C. undisturbed
   D. bewildered

16. Don't forget to turn on the outside lights in the______.
   A. holidays
   B. autumn
   C. evening
   D. interval

17. The actor shaved off his hair because the role called for him to be______.
   A. bald
   B. bearable
   C. lack
   D. spineless

18. I didn't want another pet after my dog died until I had time to______.
   A. apply
   B. grieve
   C. indicate
   D. distinguish

19. The fire in our garage was not costly to us because we were______.
   A. relieved
   B. gouged
   C. insured
   D. regulated

20. This building on the fairgrounds is devoted to farming and other______ exhibits.
   A. agricultural
   B. galactic
   C. psychological
   D. evading

Name ______________________________ Date ______________

Diagnostic Tests and Vocabulary in Context Use and Interpretation

The Diagnostic Tests and Vocabulary in Context were developed to assist teachers in making the most appropriate assignment of *Prentice Hall Literature* program selections to students. The purpose of these assessments is to indicate the degree of difficulty that students are likely to have in reading/comprehending the selections presented in the *following* unit of instruction. Tests are provided at six separate times in each in each grade level—a *Diagnostic Test* (to be used prior to beginning the year's instruction) and a *Vocabulary in Context*, the final segment of the Benchmark Test appearing at the end of each of the first five units of instruction. Note that the tests are intended for use not as summative assessments for the prior unit, but as guidance for assigning literature selections in the upcoming unit of instruction.

The structure of all Diagnostic Tests and Vocabulary in Context in this series is the same. All test items are four-option, multiple-choice items. The format is established to assess a student's ability to construct sufficient meaning from the context sentence to choose the only provided word that fits both the semantics (meaning) and syntax (structure) of the context sentence. All words in the context sentences are chosen to be "below-level" words that students reading at this grade level should know. All answer choices fit *either* the meaning or structure of the context sentence, but only the correct choice fits *both* semantics and syntax. All answer choices—both correct answers and incorrect options—are key words chosen from specifically taught words that will occur in the subsequent unit of program instruction. This careful restriction of the assessed words permits a sound diagnosis of students' current reading achievement and prediction of the most appropriate level of readings to assign in the upcoming unit of instruction.

The assessment of vocabulary in context skill has consistently been shown in reading research studies to correlate very highly with "reading comprehension." This is not surprising as the format essentially assesses comprehension, albeit in sentence-length "chunks." Decades of research demonstrate that vocabulary assessment provides a strong, reliable prediction of comprehension achievement—the purpose of these tests. Further, because this format demands very little testing time, these diagnoses can be made efficiently, permitting teachers to move forward with critical instructional tasks rather than devoting excessive time to assessment.

It is important to stress that while the Diagnostic and Vocabulary in Context were carefully developed and will yield sound assignment decisions, they were designed to *reinforce*, not supplant, teacher judgment as to the most appropriate instructional placement for individual students. Teacher judgment should always prevail in making placement—or indeed other important instructional—decisions concerning students.

Name ______________________________ Date ______________

Diagnostic Tests and Vocabulary in Context Branching Suggestions

These tests are designed to provide maximum flexibility for teachers. Your *Unit Resources* books contain the 40-question **Diagnostic Test** and 20-question **Vocabulary in Context** tests. At *PHLitOnline,* you can access the Diagnostic Test and complete 40-question Vocabulary in Context tests. Procedures for administering the tests are described below. Choose the procedure based on the time you wish to devote to the activity and your comfort with the assignment decisions relative to the individual students. Remember that your judgment of a student's reading level should always take precedence over the results of a single written test.

Feel free to use different procedures at different times of the year. For example, for early units, you may wish to be more confident in the assignments you make—thus, using the "two-stage" process below. Later, you may choose the quicker diagnosis, confirming the results with your observations of the students' performance built up throughout the year.

The **Diagnostic Test** is composed of a single 40-item assessment. Based on the results of this assessment, make the following assignment of students to the reading selections in Unit 1:

Diagnostic Test Score	Selection to Use
If the student's score is 0–25	more accessible
If the student's score is 26–40	more challenging

Outlined below are the three basic options for administering **Vocabulary in Context** and basing selection assignments on the results of these assessments.

1. For a one-stage, quicker diagnosis using the *20-item* test in the *Unit Resources:*

Vocabulary in Context Test Score	Selection to Use
If the student's score is 0–13	more accessible
If the student's score is 14–20	more challenging

2. If you wish to confirm your assignment decisions with a *two-stage* diagnosis:

Stage 1: Administer the 20-item test in the *Unit Resources*	
Vocabulary in Context Test Score	**Selection to Use**
If the student's score is 0–9	more accessible
If the student's score is 10–15	(Go to Stage 2.)
If the student's score is 16–20	more challenging

Stage 2: Administer items 21–40 from *PHLitOnline*	
Vocabulary in Context Test Score	**Selection to Use**
If the student's score is 0–12	more accessible
If the student's score is 13–20	more challenging

3. If you base your assignment decisions on the full 40-item **Vocabulary in Context** from *PHLitOnline:*

Vocabulary in Context Test Score	Selection to Use
If the student's score is 0–25	more accessible
If the student's score is 26–40	more challenging

Name ______________________ Date ______________

Grade 8—Benchmark Test 7
Interpretation Guide

For remediation of specific skills, you may assign students the relevant Reading Kit Practice and Assess pages indicated in the far-right column of this chart. You will find rubrics for evaluating writing samples in the last section of your Professional Development Guidebook.

Skill Objective	Test Items	Number Correct	Reading Kit
Reading Skill			
Context	1, 2, 3, 4, 5, 6		pp. 152, 153
Compare and Contrast Features of Consumer Materials	7, 8, 9, 10		pp. 154, 155
Literary Analysis			
Sound Devices	11, 12,13		pp. 156, 157
Figurative Language	14, 15, 16, 17		pp. 158, 159
Comparing Poetry and Prose	18, 19, 20		pp. 160, 161
Vocabulary			
Prefixes and Suffixes *im-, -ous, -ive*	21, 22, 23, 24, 25, 26		pp. 162, 163
Grammar			
Subject Complements	27, 28		pp. 164, 165
Direct and Indirect Objects	29, 30, 31		pp. 166, 167
Verb in Active Voice	32, 33		pp. 168, 169
Writing			
Introduction	34	Use rubric	pp. 170, 171
Study of a poem	35	Use rubric	pp. 172, 173
Problem-and-Solution Essay	36	Use rubric	pp. 174, 175

Name ______________________ Date ______________

Grade 8—Benchmark Test 8
Interpretation Guide

For remediation of specific skills, you may assign students the relevant Reading Kit Practice and Assess pages indicated in the far-right column of this chart. You will find rubrics for evaluating writing samples in the last section of your Professional Development Guidebook.

Skill Objective	Test Items	Number Correct	Reading Kit
Reading Skill			
Paraphrase	1, 2, 3		pp. 176, 177
Analyze Technical Directions	4, 5, 6		pp. 178, 179
Literary Analysis			
Poetic Forms	7, 8, 10		pp. 180, 181
Imagery	11, 12, 13		pp. 182, 183
Compare Types of Description	9, 14, 15		pp. 184, 185
Vocabulary			
Roots and Prefixes *in-*, *trans-*, *-cede-*, *-vert-*	16, 17, 18, 19, 20, 21		pp. 186, 187
Grammar			
Prepositions and Prepositional Phrases	22, 23, 24		pp. 188, 189
Infinitive Phrases	25, 28		pp. 190, 191
Revising to Vary Sentence Patterns	26, 27		pp. 192, 193
Spelling			
Words with Prefixes and Suffixes	29, 30		pp. 194, 195
Writing			
Lyric or narrative poem	31	Use rubric	pp. 196, 197
Review	32	Use rubric	pp. 198, 199
Comparison-and-Contrast Essay	33	Use rubric	pp. 200, 201

ANSWERS

Big Question Vocabulary—1, p. 1

Sample Answers

A. 1. feedback
2. cultural
3. meaningful
4. misunderstand
5. benefit

B. 1. cultural
2. meaningful
3. feedback
4. benefit
5. misunderstand

Big Question Vocabulary—2, p. 2

Sample Answers

Gail: Please help me. I want to *express* my feelings and really make a *connection* with my grandmother.

Hannah: Why not include *relevant* details about a wonderful *experience* you and she shared?

Maria: And make the poem really strong by using *sensory details* that bring that experience back to life for her.

Big Question Vocabulary—3, p. 3

Sample Answers

1. MSNBC; *The New York Times; Newsweek*
   My family watches the news on MSNBC almost every night before dinner.
2. my soccer skills; my red hair; my stamp collection
   I'm the only one in my class with red hair, so it is part of my individuality.
3. The capital is Austin. San Antonio has the Spurs. Houston is a big city.
   One valid fact about Texas is that San Antonio has a basketball team called the Spurs.
4. Milk builds bones. Carrots help eyesight. Green vegetables contain iron.
   The fact that milk, carrots, and green vegetables are good for you proves the significance of good nutrition.
5. The Red Sox play baseball. They play in Boston. They won the World Series.
   Do I need to inform you that the Red Sox won the World Series in 2004 and 2007?

Poetry by Jacqueline Woodson

Vocabulary Warm-up Exercises, p. 8

A. 1. upstate
2. awhile
3. dabbing
4. regular
5. squints
6. grins

B. Sample Answers

1. When *lava* and ash shoot out of a *volcano*, tourists are urged to stay far away from the dangerous site.
2. Planting a *maple* in the front yard of a house in Vermont is a wise choice.
3. The *preacher* addresses his congregation each Sunday to talk about religious ideas.
4. When creating *superheroes*, the artists try to make them look unusual and give them extraordinary powers.
5. The most amazing *moment* of the year was the stroke of midnight on New Year's Eve, when confetti poured down from the ceiling.

Reading Warm-up A, p. 9

Sample Answers

1. (everyday); My regular morning routine begins with waking up at 6:00 A.M., eating a quick breakfast, taking a fast shower, and running out the door.
2. a brief time; I played video games for awhile yesterday.
3. (farther south); Upstate is the area in the northern part of a state.
4. (frowns); smiles
5. (a tear away); someone might be dabbing spilled soda off of a table.
6. peers; When someone squints, they narrow their eyes to help them to see better.

Reading Warm-up B, p. 10

Sample Answers

1. Leaving her friends in Chicago would be the most horrible moment for Tonya.; A *moment* is "a particular point in time."
2. favorite climbing tree; A *maple* is a big tree of hard wood that has pretty leaves and produces sweet sap.
3. (Her ten-year-old brother); A *preacher* talks about religious ideas, and paradise is a place people associate with religion.
4. an island; A *volcano* is a mountain with a large hole in the top that can explode and send hot, melted rock called *lava* into the air.
5. (fairy-tale endings; the ease of change); One of my favorite *superheroes* was a woman who could fly through the air and see through walls.

Jacqueline Woodson

Listening and Viewing, p. 11

Segment 1. Jacqueline Woodson's interest in writing began when she learned to write her name and understood that letters made words and words made sentences. She then understood that the world is moved through words, and realized what great power words, therefore, hold. Students may suggest that because Woodson tries to begin from a place that is real to her, her stories are valid and appealing to her audience. Being honest in her writing enables her to develop realistic characters who deal with universal issues.

Segment 2. Jacqueline Woodson thinks the white space on the page surrounding a poem is important because it offers a break from stimuli or distraction; the white space around the poem is like air that allows the words to sink in.

Segment 3. Jacqueline Woodson first hears a voice in her head; the voice is usually a character telling her a story. She then develops details about the character. Students may suggest that they would not outline or envision the ending of a story, but would pull bits and pieces of the story together over time and might work on several different types of writing at once.

Segment 4. Jacqueline Woodson is rewarded when she knows that she has written a good, complete story that can impact the world somehow. Students may suggest that self-expression is so important that a writer should not fear the reaction from a reader but embrace it. Alternatively, students may say that a writer must consider readers in order to appeal to them.

Learning About Poetry, p. 12

1. C; **2.** B; **3.** B; **4.** B; **5.** B; **6.** C

The Poetry of Jacqueline Woodson

Model Selection: Poetry, p. 13

1. alliteration ("Ms. Marcus"); assonance ("little bit skinny")
2. simile; Eric's voice with an angel's voice
3. personification (Some students may say that *like* in the second line introduces a simile. Explain that the simile involves personification.)
4. assonance: "leaves . . . reaching"; alliteration: "like . . . like . . . leaves"

Open-Book Test, p. 14

Short Answer

1. When a poet uses sensory language, the speaker's experience really comes alive for the reader because the reader can see, feel, and hear the things the speaker is experiencing.
   Difficulty: *Average* **Objective:** *Literary Analysis*
2. It is called onomatopoeia, and it is the use of words that imitate sounds.
   Difficulty: *Easy* **Objective:** *Literary Analysis*
3. Both similes and metaphors compare unlike things, but a simile uses the word *like* or *as*, while a metaphor describes one thing as if it were something else.
   Difficulty: *Challenging* **Objective:** *Literary Analysis*
4. Free verse has no regular meter and no intentional rhyme.
   Difficulty: *Average* **Objective:** *Literary Analysis*
5. He is admiring but a little fearful. He praises Eric's singing voice, but he doesn't turn in the assignment because he fears Eric will be angry about it.
   Difficulty: *Average* **Objective:** *Interpretation*
6. It is a simile because it uses "like" to compare.
   Difficulty: *Average* **Objective:** *Literary Analysis*
7. He feels proud because a poet's heart, he says, is "a good thing to have. And I'm the one who has it."
   Difficulty: *Easy* **Objective:** *Interpretation*
8. Details such as "Rodney's arm around my shoulder," "Miss Edna's Sunday cooking," and "Can't imagine moving away/From/Home" show that the speaker is happy with his foster family and feels grateful to be with them.
   Difficulty: *Challenging* **Objective:** *Interpretation*
9. She is using personification, giving the trees human qualities such as hands and the power of speech.
   Difficulty: *Average* **Objective:** *Literary Analysis*
10. They both have the same speaker, are written in free verse, and feature Ms. Marcus as a character.
    Difficulty: *Challenging* **Objective:** *Interpretation*

Essay

11. Students should point out that Lonnie is warm, observant, positive, and appreciative. He can see the good in others, but he is also somewhat timid. Students should explain why they would like to know Lonnie personally or not.
    Difficulty: *Easy* **Objective:** *Essay*
12. Students should point out that the poem they chose expresses the thoughts and feelings of a single speaker. Students should provide examples of language that appeals to the senses, similes, metaphors, personification, or sound devices from the poem they chose.
    Difficulty: *Average* **Objective:** *Essay*
13. Students' choices of details will vary. They should point out that the details in "Describe Somebody" create a mood of pleasure and point to the central message that everyone has a skill and the ability to achieve. The details in "Almost a Summer Sky" create a mood of pleasure too and point to the overall message of harmony with one's surroundings.
    Difficulty: *Challenging* **Objective:** *Essay*
14. Students who choose "Describe Somebody" may note that Lonnie realizes the words he uses in his description can make people pleased, angry, or embarrassed. In "Almost a Summer Sky," Lonnie's conversation with his brother leads him to realize that Rodney's words have the power to explain, hurt, and comfort him all at once. Students should support their responses using lines from the poem they choose.
    Difficulty: *Average* **Objective:** *Essay*

Oral Response

15. Oral responses should be clear, well organized, and well supported by appropriate examples from the selections.
Difficulty: *Average* **Objective:** *Oral Interpretation*

Selection Test A, p. 17

Learning About Poetry

1. ANS: A	DIF: Easy	OBJ: Literary Analysis
2. ANS: D	DIF: Easy	OBJ: Literary Analysis
3. ANS: C	DIF: Easy	OBJ: Literary Analysis
4. ANS: D	DIF: Easy	OBJ: Literary Analysis
5. ANS: D	DIF: Easy	OBJ: Literary Analysis

Critical Reading

6. ANS: D	DIF: Easy	OBJ: Comprehension
7. ANS: C	DIF: Easy	OBJ: Comprehension
8. ANS: C	DIF: Easy	OBJ: Interpretation
9. ANS: C	DIF: Easy	OBJ: Comprehension
10. ANS: B	DIF: Easy	OBJ: Interpretation
11. ANS: C	DIF: Easy	OBJ: Comprehension
12. ANS: A	DIF: Easy	OBJ: Comprehension
13. ANS: B	DIF: Easy	OBJ: Literary Analysis
14. ANS: C	DIF: Easy	OBJ: Comprehension
15. ANS: C	DIF: Easy	OBJ: Interpretation

Essay

16. Students should point out that Lonnie is warm, observant, positive, and appreciative. Lonnie is quick to see the good in others, and he appreciates the support given him by figures such as Ms. Marcus, the teacher, and Rodney, Miss Edna's son, who fills the role of older foster brother and mentor to Lonnie. At the same time, Lonnie is portrayed as timid. For example, in "Describe Somebody," he fears Eric's anger, and in "Almost a Summer Sky," he claims he understands why Rodney had to live upstate with the trees for a while, even though he does *not* understand why. Students should explain whether or not they would like to know Lonnie personally, and why.
Difficulty: *Easy*
Objective: *Essay*

17. A possible theme statement for "Describe Somebody" might be "Everyone around us, including those who may appear mean or unlikable, possesses a talent or an ability." The theme is supported by the speaker's revelation that Eric is in a choir and sings beautifully and by the speaker's comments about Angel's ability at science and Lamont's talent for drawing. In "Almost a Summer Sky," the theme might be stated as follows: "Just as families offer their members protection, shelter, and comfort, nature offers shade and protection to those who live in harmony with their environment." This theme is supported by Rodney's description of the trees upstate as well as by Lonnie's comfort in living with Miss Edna and her family.
Difficulty: *Easy*
Objective: *Essay*

18. Students who choose "Describe Somebody" may note that Lonnie realizes the words he uses in his description can make people pleased, angry, or embarrassed. In "Almost a Summer Sky," Lonnie's conversation with his brother leads him to realize that Rodney's words have the power to explain, hurt, and comfort him all at once. Students should support their responses using lines from the poem they choose.
Difficulty: *Average*
Objective: *Essay*

Selection Test B, p. 20

Learning About Poetry

1. ANS: B	DIF: Average	OBJ: Literary Analysis
2. ANS: D	DIF: Average	OBJ: Literary Analysis
3. ANS: C	DIF: Average	OBJ: Literary Analysis
4. ANS: C	DIF: Challenging	OBJ: Literary Analysis
5. ANS: D	DIF: Average	OBJ: Literary Analysis
6. ANS: A	DIF: Average	OBJ: Literary Analysis
7. ANS: D	DIF: Average	OBJ: Literary Analysis

Critical Reading

8. ANS: B	DIF: Average	OBJ: Comprehension
9. ANS: B	DIF: Challenging	OBJ: Comprehension
10. ANS: C	DIF: Average	OBJ: Comprehension
11. ANS: A	DIF: Average	OBJ: Literary Analysis
12. ANS: A	DIF: Average	OBJ: Interpretation
13. ANS: B	DIF: Average	OBJ: Interpretation
14. ANS: C	DIF: Average	OBJ: Comprehension
15. ANS: B	DIF: Average	OBJ: Interpretation
16. ANS: B	DIF: Average	OBJ: Literary Analysis
17. ANS: B	DIF: Challenging	OBJ: Interpretation
18. ANS: D	DIF: Challenging	OBJ: Interpretation

Essay

19. Students' choice of details will vary. In "Describe Somebody," for example, they may cite Ms. Marcus's smile, Angel's volcano exhibit for science fair, and Eric's "angel voice." These details create a mood of pleasure and point to the central message: everyone has a strength and capacity for achievement. In "Almost a Summer Sky," students might single out the light, warm rain, the blue patch in the sky, the upstate trees as big as three men,

Lily's big smile, and Rodney's comparison of the leaves to hands that offer shade. These details also create a mood of pleasure, and they point to the overall message of harmony with one's surroundings.

Difficulty: *Average*

Objective: *Essay*

20. In their essays, students should point out that the poem they have chosen qualifies as a lyric poem because it expresses the thoughts and feelings of a single speaker, Lonnie. If students opt to offer an example of figurative language from the poem they have selected, they might cite the simile comparing Eric's voice to an angel's in "Describe Somebody" or the personification comparing the trees' leaves to hands reaching out in "Almost a Summer Sky." Sensory images abound in both poems—for example, Ms. Marcus's long, shiny, brown hair in "Describe Somebody" and the light, warm rain in "Almost a Summer Sky." Repetition includes the expression "real good" in "Describe Somebody" and "a poet's heart," "brother," and "trees" in "Almost a Summer Sky."

    Difficulty: *Average*

    Objective: *Essay*

21. Students who choose "Describe Somebody" may note that Lonnie realizes the words he uses in his description can make people pleased, angry, or embarrassed. In "Almost a Summer Sky," Lonnie's conversation with his brother leads him to realize that Rodney's words have the power to explain, hurt, and comfort him all at once. Students should support their responses using lines from the poem they choose.

    Difficulty: *Average*

    Objective: *Essay*

Poetry Collection: Eleanor Farjeon, Walter de la Mare, Georgia Douglas Johnson

Vocabulary Warm-up Exercises, p. 24

A.
1. gleam
2. horizon
3. peers
4. throbbed
5. scampering
6. scatter

B. Sample Answers
1. *Casements* allow windows to open by swinging out to the sides instead of having to be pulled up.
2. I'd rather sleep on a cotton mattress than on a *thatch* one because the straw would be hard and scratchy.
3. I think the state with the city at the *uttermost* point from an Alaskan city would be Florida.
4. If the coast were constantly *battered*, then waves and wind would be hitting the rocky shores.
5. Since everything appears huge to a small child, even a small lake would seem to have *immensity*.
6. I would describe gelatin as *slithery*.

Reading Warm-up A, p. 25

Sample Answers
1. the sun sinks slowly; The *horizon* is the place where land or water seems to meet the sky.
2. (into the growing gloom); Since *peers* is used to describe how a person looks hard at something that is difficult to see, it is a good word to use when talking about how someone can't see very well as darkness comes.
3. hustles home before nightfall; *Scampering* means "the act of running with short, quick steps."
4. (moon); Stars also *gleam* at night.
5. They are afraid of becoming the mighty bird's evening meal; *Scatter* means "to toss around or cause to go here and there."
6. (activity and excitement); *Throbbed* means "beat quickly, as a heart."

Reading Warm-up B, p. 26

Sample Answers
1. the tops of makeshift shelters; *Thatch* is dried straw used to make roofs.
2. (are thrown open); Every night across the planet, windows are opened wide so people can lean out of them and gaze up at the skies.
3. universe; If you were traveling in space and got lost, you might never find your way back to Earth because of its *immensity*.
4. (sticks together); *Slithery* surfaces, like wet floors, can cause people to fall, and that can be disastrous.
5. (smooth); Forces such as wind, meteors, and other flying objects might have *battered* space vehicles and space stations.
6. (universe); People want to explore *uttermost* places of our universe because they want to discover new things and have always been curious about the unknown.

Writing About the Big Question, p. 27

A.
1. relevant
2. misunderstand
3. sensory
4. individuality
5. feedback

B. Sample Answers
1. I have benefited greatly from the connection I have made with my classmate Jo. She listens to me express my feelings and thoughts.
2. One way to resolve a misunderstanding resulting from a cultural conflict is to take each culture's experience into consideration. Another is to recognize the significance of a person's culture in his or her actions.

C. Sample Answer

Poets use sounds and rhythms to make their work mimic noises we find in everyday life.

Reading: Preview to Determine Meanings From Context, p. 28

1. catch (line 13)
2. A. It is a tree.
   B. bark (line 26)
3. sees
4. "Where the sky-line encircled the sea"
5. A. It is a noun.
   B. distant corner; places that are hard to get to

Literary Analysis: Sound Devices, p. 29

"Cat!"

Rhythm—The poem captures the chase by using very short lines that open on a strong beat: good examples include lines 3, 11, and 13. *Rhyme*—While there is no real pattern of end rhyme, there is frequent use of the same few sounds—for instance, lines 1, 2, and 7 (*cat/scat/mat*) and lines 3–6 (*after her/flatterer/chatterer/scatter her*). *Alliteration*—The many *s* sounds, echoing the cat's hiss or scratch, include those in lines 4–6 (*sleeky, spitfire, scatter*) and the *sl* sounds in lines 15–16 (*slathery, slithery*). *Onomatopoeia*—Among the many examples (some of which are invented by the poet) are *wuff, scratcher, hisser, pffts,* and *scritching.*

"Silver"

Rhythm—The poem captures the steady movement of the moonlight in lines that contain four beats and often open on a beat; good examples include the first four lines. *Rhyme*—The end rhymes form a pattern in which each pair of lines rhyme (*moon/shoon* in lines 1–2, *sees/trees* in lines 3–4, and so on). *Alliteration*—Examples include the *th* in line 3 (*this, that*) and the *k* sounds in line 5 (*casements, catch*). *Onomatopoiea—scampering*

"Your World"

Rhythm—Each line has three beats, but the odd-numbered lines have an extra syllable at the end. Two unstressed syllables often precede a stressed syllable, as in line 5: "But I SIGHTed the DIStant hoRIzon." The steady da-da-DUM of the rhythm beats home the poem's advice. *Rhyme*—The even-numbered lines rhyme (*abide/side* in lines 2 and 4 and so on). *Alliteration*—Examples include the *n* sounds in line 3 *(narrowest, nest). Onomatopoeia—throbbed, battered,* perhaps *soared.*

Vocabulary Builder, p. 30

A. 1. F; 2. F; 3. T; 4. T; 5. F; 6. T; 7. T

B. Sample Answers

1. A flatterer lavishly praises someone else.
2. You might keep a pet dog in a kennel.
3. A person who is feeling absolutely wonderful might say he or she is in a state of rapture.

C. Sample Answers

1. Yes; "not proper" means that the action is socially unacceptable.
2. The person is likely to fidget, pace, or be grumpy because he does not have patience.

Enrichment: Phases of the Moon, p. 31

1. It takes about a month for the moon to complete its phases and orbit around Earth.
2. They traveled when the moon was full because the nights were the least dark then.
3. They probably tried to commit them during a new moon because the nights were darkest then, and it was easier to go unnoticed and escape capture.
4. *Wax* means "to grow in size"; *wane* means "to get smaller." *Sample sentence:* His interest in the film began to *wane* until finally he dozed off.

Open-Book Test, p. 32

Short Answer

1. It imitates the sound of scratching—the cat is scratching the bark of the sycamore tree.
   Difficulty: *Easy* **Objective:** *Literary Analysis*
2. The very short lines contain mostly strong beats. Wherever several of these short lines appear together, a pounding rhythm is created.
   Difficulty: *Challenging* **Objective:** *Literary Analysis*
3. The speaker seems to dislike the cat and wants to drive her away. He calls her a "whiskery spitter" and wants to "Scatter her, scatter her/Off her mat!"
   Difficulty: *Easy* **Objective:** *Interpretation*
4. He or she would be likely to say something nice or complimentary but insincere, because a flatterer speaks to win approval.
   Difficulty: *Average* **Objective:** *Vocabulary*
5. It means "looks" or "sees." The word *sees* hints at the meaning of *peers.*
   Difficulty: *Easy* **Objective:** *Reading*
6. The word *walks* is a hint that *shoon* means "shoes." Since the moon is wearing her shoon to walk, shoon must be something worn on the feet.
   Difficulty: *Average* **Objective:** *Reading*
7. He wants to emphasize that the moon casts a silvery glow on everything.
   Difficulty: *Average* **Objective:** *Interpretation*
8. These specific, descriptive words are a direct way of making the point that the world is big.
   Difficulty: *Challenging* **Objective:** *Interpretation*
9. The second and fourth lines in each stanza end in rhyming words. Lines 2 and 4 end in *abide* and *side*;

lines 6 and 8 end in *sea* and *immensity*; lines 10 and 12 end in *breeze* and *ease*.

Difficulty: *Average* **Objective:** *Literary Analysis*

10. Sample answers: Onomatopoeia—wuff ("Cat!"); alliteration—silver stream ("Silver"); rhyme—abide/side ("Your World")

The use of *wuff* helps the reader hear the scuffle between cat and dog. *Silver stream* and *abide/side* both add to the poems' musical qualities.

Difficulty: *Average* **Objective:** *Literary Analysis*

Essay

11. Students should choose one poem, state their opinion about it, and cite examples of at least two sound devices. For "Cat!" they could cite examples of onomatopoeia, rhythm, or rhyme; for "Silver" and "Your World," they could cite examples of rhythm, rhyme, alliteration, or onomatopoeia.

Difficulty: *Easy* **Objective:** *Essay*

12. Students should recognize that the poem describes a moonlit night with a peaceful, magical feeling. They should cite images and word choices that contribute to the mood. They should also recognize that the alliteration and regular rhyme and rhythm contribute to the slow music of the poem.

Difficulty: *Average* **Objective:** *Essay*

13. Students should recognize the poem's central message that our world, or life experience, can be as broad and open as we want to make it. They should cite details from the poem that express that view. Those who agree with the view will probably put the stress on individual experience and personal perceptions, while those who disagree may mention social, political, and economic factors or may stress the family or social responsibilities that have to be met.

Difficulty: *Challenging* **Objective:** *Essay*

14. Students should choose one poem and give examples of words and phrases that were particularly moving. Examples may include "Run till you're dithery" from "Cat!"; "doves in a silver-feathered sleep" from "Silver"; or "With rapture, with power, with ease!" from "Your World."

Difficulty: *Average* **Objective:** *Essay*

Oral Response

15. Oral responses should be clear, well organized, and well supported by appropriate examples from the selections.

Difficulty: *Average* **Objective:** *Oral Intepretation*

Selection Test A, p. 35

Critical Reading

1. **ANS:** A	**DIF:** Easy	**OBJ:** Comprehension
2. **ANS:** B	**DIF:** Easy	**OBJ:** Literary Analysis
3. **ANS:** C	**DIF:** Easy	**OBJ:** Interpretation
4. **ANS:** A	**DIF:** Easy	**OBJ:** Reading
5. **ANS:** D	**DIF:** Easy	**OBJ:** Comprehension
6. **ANS:** B	**DIF:** Easy	**OBJ:** Literary Analysis
7. **ANS:** B	**DIF:** Easy	**OBJ:** Reading
8. **ANS:** C	**DIF:** Easy	**OBJ:** Comprehension
9. **ANS:** B	**DIF:** Easy	**OBJ:** Interpretation
10. **ANS:** A	**DIF:** Easy	**OBJ:** Comprehension
11. **ANS:** C	**DIF:** Easy	**OBJ:** Reading
12. **ANS:** B	**DIF:** Easy	**OBJ:** Literary Analysis
13. **ANS:** A	**DIF:** Easy	**OBJ:** Literary Analysis

Vocabulary and Grammar

14. **ANS:** A	**DIF:** Easy	**OBJ:** Grammar
15. **ANS:** D	**DIF:** Easy	**OBJ:** Vocabulary

Essay

16. Students should recognize that the speaker is chasing the cat. The speaker does not seem to like the cat. Students should cite details to support their inferences. They may speculate that the speaker is a dog and should cite details to support that inference, including the "Wuff!" lines and/or the speaker's actions and negative remarks about the cat.

Difficulty: *Easy*

Objective: *Essay*

17. Students should choose one poem, state their opinion about it, and cite examples of at least two sound devices. For "Cat!" they could cite examples of onomatopoeia and rhythm and recognize that the poem also uses a great deal of rhyme, even though the end-of-line rhymes do not form a regular pattern. For "Silver" and "Your World," they could cite examples of rhythm, rhyme, alliteration, or onomatopoeia.

Difficulty: *Easy*

Objective: *Essay*

18. Students should choose one poem and give examples of words and phrases that were particularly moving. Examples may include "Run till you're dithery" from "Cat!", "doves in a silver-feathered sleep" from "Silver," or "With rapture, with power, with ease!" from "Your World."

Difficulty: *Average*

Objective: *Essay*

Selection Test B, p. 38

Critical Reading

1. **ANS:** B	**DIF:** Average	**OBJ:** Interpretation
2. **ANS:** D	**DIF:** Average	**OBJ:** Interpretation
3. **ANS:** A	**DIF:** Average	**OBJ:** Literary Analysis
4. **ANS:** A	**DIF:** Challenging	**OBJ:** Literary Analysis

5. **ANS:** A	**DIF:** Average	**OBJ:** Interpretation
6. **ANS:** B	**DIF:** Average	**OBJ:** Reading
7. **ANS:** A	**DIF:** Challenging	**OBJ:** Literary Analysis
8. **ANS:** D	**DIF:** Average	**OBJ:** Literary Analysis
9. **ANS:** C	**DIF:** Average	**OBJ:** Comprehension
10. **ANS:** D	**DIF:** Challenging	**OBJ:** Reading
11. **ANS:** C	**DIF:** Average	**OBJ:** Literary Analysis
12. **ANS:** C	**DIF:** Challenging	**OBJ:** Literary Analysis
13. **ANS:** A	**DIF:** Average	**OBJ:** Literary Analysis

Vocabulary and Grammar

14. **ANS:** D	**DIF:** Average	**OBJ:** Vocabulary
15. **ANS:** D	**DIF:** Average	**OBJ:** Vocabulary
16. **ANS:** B	**DIF:** Average	**OBJ:** Grammar
17. **ANS:** A	**DIF:** Average	**OBJ:** Grammar

Essay

18. Students should recognize that the poem describes a moonlit night with a peaceful, magical mood, or atmosphere. They should cite images and word choices as well as sound devices that contribute to the mood. Among the images they may mention are the opening image of the moon silently walking through the night in silver shoes, the moonbeams on the sleeping dog, and the fish gleaming in a silver stream of silver reeds. Among the word choices they may mention are the old-fashioned word *shoon* and the repetition of *silver*. In discussing the sound devices, they should mention that alliteration contributes to the poem's magical music, citing examples such as the *s* sounds in *slowly* and *silently* in line 1, the *b* sounds in *beams beneath* in line 6, as well as the *k* sounds in *casements catch* in line 5 and in *couched* and *kennel* in line 7. They should also recognize that each pair of lines rhymes and that the rhythm is also regular, contributing to the slow music of the poem.

    Difficulty: *Average*

    Objective: *Essay*

19. Students should recognize the poem's central message that our world, or life experience, can be as broad and open as we want to make it. They should cite details from the poem that express that view, literally (as in the first line) or figuratively (in the bird imagery, for example). They should then react to that view, giving reasons and examples why they agree or disagree. Those who agree will likely put the stress on individual experience and personal perceptions, while those who disagree may mention social, political, and economic factors or may criticize the worldview as self-indulgent for not taking into account family or social responsibilities that have to be met.

    Difficulty: *Challenging*

    Objective: *Essay*

20. Students should choose one poem and give examples of words and phrases that were particularly moving. Examples may include "Run till you're dithery" from "Cat!", "doves in a silver-feathered sleep" from "Silver," or "With rapture, with power, with ease!" from "Your World."

    Difficulty: *Average*

    Objective: *Essay*

Poetry Collection: Eve Merriam; Nikki Giovanni; Alfred, Lord Tennyson

Vocabulary Warm-up Exercises, p. 42

A.
1. ancient
2. funeral
3. captured
4. triumph
5. foul
6. interior

B. Sample Answers

1. Both my *signature* and the *whorls* on my fingertips are unique only to me.
2. Since an *atom* is so small, you would need a powerful microscope to see it.
3. I would like to *imprint* on people's minds that every human being deserves to be loved.
4. People take others to court for *slander* because a bad reputation can ruin your life.
5. When I read about earthquakes and other natural disasters, I feel *mournful* for the victims.

Reading Warm-up A, p. 43

Sample Answers

1. actions; One example of *foul* behavior prompted by violence would be physically hurting someone else.
2. gaining equal rights; I felt *triumph* when I finally made the honor roll.
3. he staged boycotts and marches to speak out against injustices in America; *Captured* means "taken by force."
4. (extraordinary); A very smart person would have an interesting *interior* life because his or her mind would always be full of new and thoughtful ideas.
5. modern; *Ancient* times are days of long ago. The days of the Egyptians and Romans are *ancient* times.
6. (at his home church in Atlanta, at his college); I think King's *funeral* service in Atlanta included many political figures and many, many tearful African Americans.

Reading Warm-up B, p. 44

Sample Answers

1. handwriting; A *signature* is the unique way you write your own name.

2. on the pads of your fingers; The *whorls* on my fingers are different from everyone else's.
3. (others' faces); I would like to *imprint* on others' minds that using violence is not the way to go about bringing change.
4. these new developments; Many people are *unhappy* about these new developments.
5. Imagine accusing the true cardholder of a crime committed by the identity thief!; If you wrongly accuse someone of something, you are damaging his or her reputation, and that is *slander.*
6. (split); Since an *atom* is so tiny, splitting it would have been really hard.

Writing About the Big Question, p. 45

A. 1. inform
2. media
3. benefit
4. significance
5. valid

B. Sample Answers
1. The cold metal of the desk legs was sheetrock gray. The wood of the desktop was smooth to the touch.
2. People can often benefit from a misunderstanding if they discuss the experience, express their feelings, and come to a meaningful resolution.

C. Sample Answer

Poetry and songs touch people in ways that are surprising.

Reading: Preview to Determine Meanings From Context, p. 46

unique: context clues—"mine alone"; likely meaning—one and only; dictionary meaning—having no equal

kettles: context clues—"big bass drums," "roar," "resounding against the wood"; likely meaning—large drums; dictionary meaning—drums made of copper or brass with thin material (parchment) stretched over the top

slander: context clues—"spite"; "love of truth and right" (contrast); likely meaning—dishonest insult; spiteful lies; dictionary meaning—false statement that is damaging to another's character or reputation

Literary Analysis: Sound Devices, p. 47

1. Examples include the aspirated *w* sounds in line 2 *(whorls, whirls, wheels)* and the repeated *m* sounds in line 19 *(my mark).*
2. Examples include *Pa-Rum* and *rat-tat-tat.* The two words imitate the sound of a drum.
3. Examples of alliteration: *Ring-rich-redress* (lines 11–12), *modes-manners* (lines 15–16), *care-coldness* (lines 17–18), *mournful-minstrel* (lines 19–20). An example of onomatopoeia is the word *ring,* used throughout the poem. *Ring* imitates the sound of a bell.
4. "Ring Out, Wild Bells" follows an *abba* pattern of rhymes in which the first and fourth lines of each stanza rhyme with each other and the second and third lines rhyme with each other.
5. The poet is trying to imitate the rhythm of drumbeats.
6. It is about ringing bells, which are musical.

Vocabulary Builder, p. 48

A. Sample Answers
1. Yes, the twentieth century saw a lot of strife.
2. An independent person might display singularity in his or her personality or interests.
3. At a loud concert you might hear resounding music.
4. He might feel spite for his enemy.
5. They place an imprint on the book.
6. They can be called modes of learning.

B. Sample Answers
1. Teeth can be *implanted,* or placed in the mouth.
2. No; a person who is *imperiled* is in danger.

Enrichment: Fingerprints, p. 49

A. Sample Answers
1. The same fingerprints at different crime scenes would prove that the same criminal is responsible for each of the crimes.
2. Smooth, clean surfaces would probably provide the clearest fingerprints.
3. Rain or snow might spoil fingerprints left at crime scenes. Any disturbance to the fingerprints, such as touching them, would also destroy prints.
4. He or she might wear gloves.
5. They might be used to identify people for other reasons—to make sure people do not vote twice, for example.

B. Students' descriptions will vary.

Poetry Collections: Eleanor Farjeon, Walter de la Mare, Georgia Douglas Johnson; Eve Merriam; Nikki Giovanni; Alfred, Lord Tennyson

Integrated Language Skills: Grammar, p. 50

Subject Complements

A. 1. musical, PA; 2. example, PN; 3. I, PP; 4. familiar, PA; 5. none (*Sounded* in this sentence is not a linking verb.)

B. Sample Sentences
1. The cat is a good hunter. PN
2. Martin Luther King, Jr., was a very influential person. PN
3. The fingerprint seemed unclear to me. PA
4. The bravest person is she. PP
5. The bells are very melodious. PA

Open-Book Test, p. 53

Short Answer

1. It means "leave," because the speaker is saying she can use her thumbprint to leave a mark on the world.
   Difficulty: *Easy* **Objective:** *Reading*
2. Both are expressions of her individuality, as indicated by the words "unique design" and "singularity."
   Difficulty: *Average* **Objective:** *Interpretation*
3. *Base* means "lowly." The word *grand* is an antonym of *base* and helps define it.
   Difficulty: *Average* **Objective:** *Reading*
4. The poet wants to emphasize how drums affect people and how people use drums. All of these people used or spoke about drums.
   Difficulty: *Easy* **Objective:** *Interpretation*
5. *Rat-tat-tat* and *Pa-Rum Pa-Rum* are onomatopoeic words that mimic the sound of drumbeats.
   Difficulty: *Average* **Objective:** *Literary Analysis*
6. All three poems—"Thumbprint" ("whorls, whirls, wheels"), "The Drum" ("big," "bass") and "Ring Out, Wild Bells" ("Ring in redress")—use alliteration.
   Difficulty: *Easy* **Objective:** *Literary Analysis*
7. Sample answer:
   (col 2, row 2) Righting wrongs
   (col 2, row 3) Better singers
   Yes, it is possible to right many of the wrongs committed against certain parts of society, and doing so might help make rich and poor more equal. Better singers are realistic, but they might not help much with worry and sadness.
   Difficulty: *Average* **Objective:** *Interpretation*
8. He means that people should not be proud of themselves just because of their social position or birth.
   Difficulty: *Challenging* **Objective:** *Interpretation*
9. In each stanza, the last words in the first and fourth lines rhyme, and the last words in the middle two lines rhyme. Example: Stanza 1: *sky/die* and *light/night.* Stanza 2: *new/true*; *snow/go.*
   Difficulty: *Average* **Objective:** *Literary Analysis*
10. He wants to replace strife, or conflict, with good manners and good laws.
    Difficulty: *Challenging* **Objective:** *Vocabulary*

Essay

11. Students should recognize that the speaker values her thumbprint and sees it as a sign of her individuality. They should cite details from the poem to support their observations about the thumbprint.
    Difficulty: *Easy* **Objective:** *Essay*
12. Students may cite the strong rhythm created by the pauses in each line and the onomatopoeia in which *Pa-Rum* and *rat-tat-tat* are repeated throughout the poem. They might recognize that these devices capture the sound of a beating drum. Some students may mention examples of alliteration, such as *big* and *bass*, and suggest that the alliteration contributes to the poem's steady music.
    Difficulty: *Average* **Objective:** *Essay*
13. Students should note that the speaker envisions a world filled with truth, good manners, good laws, a love of right and good, and peace, and without grief, rich and poor, want, hardship, sin, false pride, greed, disease, and war. Students' opinions will vary, but many may believe that it would be impossible to achieve such a perfect world.
    Difficulty: *Challenging* **Objective:** *Essay*
14. Students who choose "Thumbprint" may point out the words "impress," "implant," and "imprint," which stress the speaker's individuality. Those who choose "The Drum" should mention words such as "Pa-Rum" and "rat-tat-tat," which signal the poet's reference to icons of freedom. Those who choose "Ring Out, Wild Bells" should note that the poet repeats the words "Ring out" and "Ring in" to stress the idea that the evils of the world should be replaced by good.
    Difficulty: *Average* **Objective:** *Essay*

Oral Response

15. Oral responses should be clear, well organized, and well supported by appropriate examples from the selections.
    Difficulty: *Average* **Objective:** *Oral Interpretation*

Poetry Collections: Eve Merriam; Nikki Giovanni; Alfred, Lord Tennyson

Selection Test A, p. 56

Critical Reading

1. **ANS:** D	**DIF:** Easy	**OBJ:** Interpretation
2. **ANS:** A	**DIF:** Easy	**OBJ:** Comprehension
3. **ANS:** A	**DIF:** Easy	**OBJ:** Literary Analysis
4. **ANS:** B	**DIF:** Easy	**OBJ:** Reading
5. **ANS:** D	**DIF:** Easy	**OBJ:** Comprehension
6. **ANS:** D	**DIF:** Easy	**OBJ:** Comprehension
7. **ANS:** A	**DIF:** Easy	**OBJ:** Literary Analysis
8. **ANS:** B	**DIF:** Easy	**OBJ:** Interpretation
9. **ANS:** C	**DIF:** Easy	**OBJ:** Comprehension
10. **ANS:** D	**DIF:** Easy	**OBJ:** Reading
11. **ANS:** B	**DIF:** Easy	**OBJ:** Reading
12. **ANS:** A	**DIF:** Easy	**OBJ:** Literary Analysis
13. **ANS:** C	**DIF:** Easy	**OBJ:** Literary Analysis

Vocabulary and Grammar

14. **ANS:** A	**DIF:** Easy	**OBJ:** Vocabulary
15. **ANS:** C	**DIF:** Easy	**OBJ:** Grammar

Essay

16. Students should recognize that the speaker values her thumbprint and sees it as a sign of her individuality, or uniqueness. They should cite details—such as "mine alone," "What a treasure," and "my universe key"—from the poem to support their observations about the thumbprint.
    Difficulty: *Easy*
    Objective: *Essay*

17. Students should choose one poem, state their opinion about it, and illustrate its musicality by citing examples of sound devices. For "The Drum," they should cite the strong rhythm and onomatopoeia, and recognize that these devices help capture the sound a drum beating. For "Ring Out, Wild Bells," they should cite rhythm and rhyme, recognizing that these form a regular pattern; and onomatopoeia, mentioning the word *ring* and recognizing how the repetition of this word helps captures the sound of the bells. Students also may include examples of alliteration from the poem, such as *mind* and *more*, *ring* and *redress*, *mournful* and *minstrel*. In the unlikely event students name "Thumbprint!" as the most musical of the three poems, they should cite the poem's rhythm and also may mention the occasional instances of alliteration (as in *whorls*, *whirls*, *wheels*) and onomatopoeia (as in *whirls* and *wheels*).
    Difficulty: *Easy*
    Objective: *Essay*

18. Students who choose "Thumbprint" may point out the words "impress," "implant," and "imprint," which give meaning about the speaker as an individual. Those who choose "The Drum" should mention words such as "Pa-Rum" and "rat-tat-tat," which refer to the idea of freedom. Those who choose "Ring Out, Wild Bells" might note that the poet repeats the words "Ring out" and "Ring in" to stress the idea that the evils of the world should be replaced by good.
    Difficulty: *Average*
    Objective: *Essay*

Selection Test B, p. 59

Critical Reading

1. **ANS:** D	**DIF:** Average	**OBJ:** Interpretation
2. **ANS:** A	**DIF:** Challenging	**OBJ:** Literary Analysis
3. **ANS:** A	**DIF:** Average	**OBJ:** Interpretation
4. **ANS:** B	**DIF:** Challenging	**OBJ:** Reading
5. **ANS:** B	**DIF:** Average	**OBJ:** Reading
6. **ANS:** C	**DIF:** Average	**OBJ:** Literary Analysis
7. **ANS:** D	**DIF:** Average	**OBJ:** Reading
8. **ANS:** A	**DIF:** Average	**OBJ:** Interpretation
9. **ANS:** A	**DIF:** Average	**OBJ:** Interpretation
10. **ANS:** D	**DIF:** Average	**OBJ:** Interpretation
11. **ANS:** A	**DIF:** Challenging	**OBJ:** Comprehension
12. **ANS:** A	**DIF:** Average	**OBJ:** Literary Analysis
13. **ANS:** D	**DIF:** Challenging	**OBJ:** Literary Analysis

Vocabulary and Grammar

14. **ANS:** A	**DIF:** Average	**OBJ:** Vocabulary
15. **ANS:** C	**DIF:** Average	**OBJ:** Vocabulary
16. **ANS:** B	**DIF:** Average	**OBJ:** Grammar
17. **ANS:** A	**DIF:** Average	**OBJ:** Grammar

Essay

18. Students may cite the strong rhythm created by the pauses in each line and the onomatopoeia in which *pa-rum* and *rat-tat-tat* are repeated periodically throughout the poem. They might recognize that the rhythm and onomatopoeia capture the sound of a beating drum. Some students may mention examples of alliteration, such as *big* and *bass* in the second stanza and *different drum* in the third, and suggest that the alliteration contributes to the poem's steady music.
    Difficulty: *Average*
    Objective: *Essay*

19. Students should recognize that the poem describes the poet's hope that the new year will bring a better world. They should point to the many unjust or unpleasant details that the poet hopes the New Year's bells will ring out and the many good things he hopes the bells will ring in. Students should recognize that the strong pattern of rhythm and rhyme, as well as the repetition of the onomatopoeic word *ring*, not only stresses the ringing that the poem describes but also underscores the theme of change and hope.
    Difficulty: *Challenging*
    Objective: *Essay*

20. Students who choose "Thumbprint" may point out the words "impress," "implant," and "imprint," which stress the speaker's individuality. Those who choose "The Drum" should mention words such as "Pa-Rum" and "rat-tat-tat," which signal the poet's reference to icons of freedom. Those who choose "Ring Out, Wild Bells" should note that the poet repeats the words "Ring out" and "Ring in" to stress the idea that the evils of the world should be replaced by good.
    Difficulty: *Average*
    Objective: *Essay*

Poetry Collection: Patricia Hubbell, Richard García, Langston Hughes

Vocabulary Warm-up Exercises, p. 63

A.
1. dew
2. bulging
3. hose
4. perch

4. perch
5. muck
6. direct

B. Sample Answers

1. The *elevator* doors closed and we began to move up and up, from the shoe department to sporting goods.
2. We mixed cement in the *trough* while the vegetables drained in the sink.
3. The coal *tenders* did not let the supply of fuel run out.
4. *Urban* shopping centers are always in cities.
5. The farmer is *raising* the barn with the help of his neighbors, and it will take a week or so.
6. A floor of *concrete* is much less likely to catch fire than one made of wood.

Reading Warm-up A, p. 64

Sample Answers

1. (The sun has risen just enough for us to walk safely without a flashlight.); *Dew* is small drops of liquid that are sometimes on things outdoors in the early morning.
2. <u>on a high branch</u>; I like to *perch* on top of the car and watch the fireworks on the Fourth of July.
3. (bucket, brush, shampoo bottle); I fell in a big mud puddle in the park and got covered in *muck*.
4. (the stream of water); He attempts to *aim* the stream of water at Terry.
5. <u>(garden hose, turns on the faucet, stream of water)</u>; It's probably best not to try to *hose* down things indoors because the water will spread all over the floor and ruin everything in the house.
6. <u>pocket</u>; I think some big, delicious doggie treats were in the *bulging* pocket.

Reading Warm-up B, p. 65

Sample Answers

1. <u>big, city</u>; I live in Chicago, which is a big *urban* area where lots of people live and work.
2. (tall buildings); Workers are *raising* a new high-rise apartment building in my town.
3. <u>cement, water, and other things</u>; Sidewalks are made of *concrete*.
4. (mixing cement, water, and other things); A *trough* might also be used to mix large amounts of dough or to feed and water animals.
5. (watch over bulldozers, cement mixers, cranes, and other heavy machinery); I was a *tender* when my dad asked me to watch the pot of soup that was cooking on the stove.
6. <u>rise to new heights</u>; I once rode in an *elevator* to the observation deck of the Empire State Building. I thought we would never get to the top.

Writing About the Big Question, p. 66

A.
1. experience
2. express
3. meaningful
4. connection
5. sensory

B. Sample Answers

1. The media plays a large role in the information we receive. It is important to evaluate the reliability of the news as the media presents it.
2. I express my individuality by the way I dress, the connections I make with others, and through sharing my perspective of different experiences.

C. Sample Answer

The sounds of languages influence meaning in literature, giving us impressions of the world around us.

Reading: Reread and Read Ahead to Determine Meanings From Context, p. 67

1. Likely meaning of <u>hose</u> in line 2: water (something) by training a hose on it
   Clue: "drivers are washing"
2. Likely meaning of <u>muck</u> in line 5: a wet and sticky substance; goop
   Clue: "standing in"
3. Likely meaning of <u>perch</u> in line 7: sitting on top
   Clue: "on their backs"
4. Likely meaning of <u>bellow</u> in line 14: cry out, scream
   Clue: none
5. Likely meaning of <u>urban</u> in line 16: relating to a city
   Clue: "raising a city"

Literary Analysis: Figurative Language, p. 68

1. Similes in "Concrete Mixers": lines 1–2, drivers of concrete mixers and elephant tenders; lines 4–6, rows of concrete mixers and rows of elephants; line 7, drivers and mahouts (Asian elephant drivers, or keepers); line 9, trough on concrete mixer and elephant trunk; lines 14–16, concrete mixers and elephants,
2. Metaphor in "Concrete Mixers": line 3, concrete mixers and monsters
3. Personification in "Concrete Mixers": line 16, concrete mixers and urban elephants raising a city

4. Personification in "The City Is So Big": line 2, bridges and human beings quaking with fear; line 7, machines and people eating; line 8, stairways (escalators) and people walking

Vocabulary Builder, p. 69

A. Sample Answers

1. The owner of a suitcase with lots of travel labels probably likes to roam around the world.
2. A ponderous suitcase would be hard to carry.
3. You might call it a bellow.
4. Dew might cover flowers' petals.
5. You might describe it as an urban landscape.

B. Sample Answers

1. No, something *instantaneous* takes only an instant, so it is quick.
2. No, something *frivolous* is characterized by frivolity, which is not necessary.

Enrichment: Concrete, p. 70

A.
1. *concrete:* a substance used in construction; made from a mixture of cement, water, and inert materials
2. *inert:* not participating in a chemical reaction
3. *aggregate:* any of the substances, such as gravel or sand, mixed with water and cement to form concrete
4. *hydration:* a chemical reaction in which a substance mixes with water
5. *water/cement ratio:* the amount of water compared with the amount of cement in concrete
6. *portland cement:* a type of cement developed in 1824 and used in making concrete today

B. Sample Questions

1. What sort of aggregate should I use?
2. What water/cement ratio should I use?
3. At what temperature should the concrete be mixed?

Open-Book Test, p. 71

Short Answer

1. It compares the machines to elephants, using phrases such as "gray-skinned monsters," "elephant-bellied," and "like rows of elephants."
   Difficulty: *Easy* **Objective:** *Literary Analysis*
2. It would move slowly and carefully because it is so heavy.
   Difficulty: *Average* **Objective:** *Vocabulary*
3. It means "having to do with the city." The word "city" gives its meaning in context.
   Difficulty: *Average* **Objective:** *Reading*
4. Details such as "quake with fear" and "people disappear" indicate that the speaker finds the city frightening.
   Difficulty: *Average* **Objective:** *Interpretation*
5. It probably means "shake," because that's what people do when they are afraid.
   Difficulty: *Easy* **Objective:** *Reading*
6. Bridges, trains, and stairways are personified. Bridges show fear, trains smile, and stairways walk.
   Difficulty: *Challenging* **Objective:** *Literary Analysis*
7. He enjoys Harlem and finds it vibrant and interesting. Details such as "singing," "Moon is shining," and "A band is playing" are all positive and create a feeling of joy.
   Difficulty: *Challenging* **Objective:** *Interpretation*
8. Sample answer: The speaker's mood is romantic. He repeats "I love you" twice, and urges his beloved to "roam the night" with him, "singing."
   Difficulty: *Average* **Objective:** *Interpretation*
9. Sample answers: "Concrete Mixers"—concrete mixers; elephants. "Harlem Night Song"—stars; drops of golden dew.
   Comparisions help the reader imagine the subject more clearly.
   Difficulty: *Average* **Objective:** *Literary Analysis*
10. He uses *roam* to stress the slow and meandering nature of the walk he wants to take with his loved one.
    Difficulty: *Challenging* **Objective:** *Vocabulary*

Essay

11. Students may note that the poet's childlike descriptions of the city as "big" and of "machines eating buildings" reflect the theme that the city is overwhelming and frightening to many people, just as it may be to a small child.
    Difficulty: *Easy* **Objective:** *Essay*
12. Students should recognize that the poem compares concrete mixers to elephants and their drivers to elephant tenders. They should give examples of the way in which the metaphor is extended to include parts, sounds, and movements of mixers and elephants.
    Difficulty: *Average* **Objective:** *Essay*
13. Students should recognize that the three poems celebrate cities as vibrant, poetic places. They should cite examples that illustrate the poets' views. The impressions differ in that Hubbell focuses on the playfulness of the city, Hughes on the romance of the city, and García on the mystery and danger of the city. Students should give and defend their own views of city life.
    Difficulty: *Challenging* **Objective:** *Essay*
14. Students may choose to consider the figurative language of the poem they choose, as well as the details they find compelling and vivid. Students' essays should include words and phrases that support their opinion of the poem they chose.
    Difficulty: *Average* **Objective:** *Essay*

Oral Response

15. Oral responses should be clear, well organized, and well supported by appropriate examples from the selections.
    Difficulty: *Average* **Objective:** *Oral Interpretation*

Selection Test A, p. 74

Critical Reading

1. **ANS:** C	**DIF:** Easy	**OBJ:** Comprehension
2. **ANS:** B	**DIF:** Easy	**OBJ:** Literary Analysis
3. **ANS:** A	**DIF:** Easy	**OBJ:** Literary Analysis
4. **ANS:** D	**DIF:** Easy	**OBJ:** Reading
5. **ANS:** B	**DIF:** Easy	**OBJ:** Comprehension
6. **ANS:** D	**DIF:** Easy	**OBJ:** Interpretation
7. **ANS:** B	**DIF:** Easy	**OBJ:** Literary Analysis
8. **ANS:** C	**DIF:** Easy	**OBJ:** Reading
9. **ANS:** D	**DIF:** Easy	**OBJ:** Interpretation
10. **ANS:** A	**DIF:** Easy	**OBJ:** Comprehension
11. **ANS:** B	**DIF:** Easy	**OBJ:** Reading
12. **ANS:** C	**DIF:** Easy	**OBJ:** Literary Analysis
13. **ANS:** A	**DIF:** Easy	**OBJ:** Literary Analysis

Vocabulary and Grammar

14. **ANS:** A	**DIF:** Easy	**OBJ:** Vocabulary
15. **ANS:** B	**DIF:** Easy	**OBJ:** Grammar

Essay

16. Students should recognize that all three poets make cities seem like vibrant, poetic places, although some students may feel that García also makes cities seem a little scary. Some students may have the poets discuss the use of figurative language, especially in "Concrete Mixers" and "The City Is So Big."

    Difficulty: *Easy*

    Objective: *Essay*

17. Students should choose one poem, state their opinion about it, and cite examples from the poem to explain their opinions. They should consider figurative language as well as other aspects of the poem, such as whether they can relate to it or whether they find it musical.

    Difficulty: *Easy*

    Objective: *Essay*

18. Students may want to consider the figurative language of the poem they choose, as well as the details they find compelling and vivid. Students' essays should include words and phrases that support their opinion of the poem they chose.

    Difficulty: *Average*

    Objective: *Essay*

Selection Test B, p. 77

Critical Reading

1. **ANS:** A	**DIF:** Challenging	**OBJ:** Literary Analysis
2. **ANS:** B	**DIF:** Average	**OBJ:** Interpretation
3. **ANS:** C	**DIF:** Average	**OBJ:** Literary Analysis
4. **ANS:** D	**DIF:** Average	**OBJ:** Reading
5. **ANS:** D	**DIF:** Challenging	**OBJ:** Reading
6. **ANS:** B	**DIF:** Average	**OBJ:** Comprehension
7. **ANS:** C	**DIF:** Average	**OBJ:** Interpretation
8. **ANS:** A	**DIF:** Average	**OBJ:** Interpretation
9. **ANS:** D	**DIF:** Average	**OBJ:** Literary Analysis
10. **ANS:** D	**DIF:** Average	**OBJ:** Interpretation
11. **ANS:** B	**DIF:** Challenging	**OBJ:** Literary Analysis
12. **ANS:** C	**DIF:** Average	**OBJ:** Interpretation
13. **ANS:** B	**DIF:** Average	**OBJ:** Comprehension
14. **ANS:** D	**DIF:** Challenging	**OBJ:** Literary Analysis

Vocabulary and Grammar

15. **ANS:** A	**DIF:** Average	**OBJ:** Vocabulary
16. **ANS:** B	**DIF:** Average	**OBJ:** Grammar
17. **ANS:** D	**DIF:** Average	**OBJ:** Grammar

Essay

18. Students should recognize that the poem compares concrete mixers to elephants and their drivers to elephant tenders, or mahouts. They should also recognize that the comparison is extended with more specific details, such as the rows of mixers compared to elephants lined up tail to trunk, the movement of the mixers to the movement of elephants, the sound of the mixers to the bellow of elephants, and the spray of the mixers to the spray of elephants.

    Difficulty: *Average*

    Objective: *Essay*

19. Students should recognize that the three poems celebrate cities as vibrant, poetic places and should cite examples from the poems that illustrate the poets' views. The three impressions contrast in that Hubbell focuses on the playfulness of the city, Hughes on the romance and music of the city, and García on the mystery of the city. Students should then give their own views, defending them with sufficient examples and other details.

    Difficulty: *Challenging*

    Objective: *Essay*

20. Students may consider the figurative language of the poem they chose, as well as the details they find compelling and vivid. Students' essays should include words and phrases that support their opinion of the poem they chose.

    Difficulty: *Average*

    Objective: *Essay*

Poetry Collection: Pablo Neruda, Elizabeth Bishop, Emily Dickinson

Vocabulary Warm-up Exercises, p. 81

A.
1. limp
2. cicada
3. sawing
4. drifting

5. relieved
6. rut

B. Sample Answers

1. F. A *boulevard* is a wide street.
2. T. A farmer would be unlikely to own a crown, or *diadem*, because it would take a lot of money to buy one.
3. F. The *mangrove* tree grows along the shore.
4. F. *Keys* are small, low islands.
5. F. In *latticework*, half the strips run in one direction and half in the other.
6. F. The *heron* is a bird that lives near the shore and wades in water.

Reading Warm-up A, p. 82

Sample Answers

1. (wind); I might see a balloon *drifting* with the wind.
2. in every road was filled with water or mud; A deep *rut* in a road can damage the underside of a car or its tires if you drive through it too fast.
3. (insect; loud sawing noise); Katydids make a loud *sawing* noise on summer nights.
4. the weather grew hot and muggy; A *limp* handshake would be one in which someone did not grasp your hand very firmly.
5. (cool breeze); I had a bad scrape on my leg and I was *relieved* from the pain once I put on antibiotic cream and a bandage.

Reading Warm-up B, p. 83

Sample Answers

1. an unusual kind of tree; A *mangrove* would not grow where I live because it is too cold and there is no coast.
2. (twisted stilts); A pie's *latticework* top crust would be strips of dough that crisscross.
3. low-lying islands; We took a boat ride around several of the *keys* and saw lots of birds and other wildlife.
4. watery; The *boulevard* near my house is six lanes wide and has a grassy center strip with trees and benches.
5. (wading birds); Since a *heron* must dip its beak in water to get its dinner, a heron most likely eats fish.
6. (crown); I saw the winner of Miss Teen America wearing a *diadem*.

Writing About the Big Question, p. 84

A.
1. significance
2. benefit
3. valid
4. experience
5. feedback

B. Sample Answers

1. I have to learn to express my thoughts and feelings clearly. I know that I will benefit from the experience.
2. To express my anger, I shouted loudly. However, my friend misunderstood what I was saying and started to cry.

C. Sample Answer

Writers often respond to nature in poetry because they are amazed by its beauty and simplicity. Natural settings such as forests or beaches are often quiet compared to urban life. They offer a space for reflection. At the same time, when writers use images found in nature, their readers can often visualize and relate to these images easily—imagery that evokes the sun or moon or clouds has a universal quality. This is part of the secret to reaching someone with words.

Reading: Reread and Read Ahead to Determine Meanings From Context, p. 85

latticework: context clues—"Under the trees light / has dropped," "light / like a green / latticework of branches"; likely meaning—crossing; dictionary meaning: a lacy cross pattern

heron: context clues—"the mangrove keys . . . / where occasionally a heron may undo his head, / shake up his feathers"; likely meaning—a type of bird; dictionary meaning: wading bird with a long neck, long legs, and a long, tapered bill, living along marshes and river banks

uninjured: context clue—"someone sleeping . . . barely disturbed"; likely meaning—safe; dictionary meaning: not harmed

Literary Analysis: Figurative Language, p. 86

1. "like a green / latticework of branches," (line 4–5) "like clean / white sand" (line 8–9)
2. Students' opinions will vary, but many students are likely to say that "like clean / white sand" captures some of the beauty and enchantment the poet wants to convey.
3. The cicada is said to be creating a song, a human activity.
4. "The world is / a glass overflowing / with water." (line 13–15)
5. It helps convey a sense of wonder, beauty, abundance, and satisfaction.

Vocabulary Builder, p. 87

A. 1. T; 2. T; 3. F; 4. F; 5. F; 6. T

1. A nightmare disrupts sleep as one wakes up in fear.
2. They might not hear your question if they are thinking about something else.
3. A rut would be inconvenient to fix for a homeowner.
4. An impulsive person would be likely to make quick, thoughtless decisions.
5. Cicadas are in fact very noisy.
6. Boulevards typically have trees on either side of the street.

B.

1. A person who is *indecisive* has trouble taking action because he is weighing his options carefully.
2. An *impulsive* person might act quickly, without thinking beforehand.

Enrichment: Wind Force, p. 88

Students' descriptions should show a convincing progression from calm air to the conditions present anywhere along the Beaufort scale from "moderate gale" to "hurricane."

Poetry Collections: Patricia Hubbell, Richard García, Langston Hughes; Pablo Neruda, Elizabeth Bishop, Emily Dickinson

Integrated Language Skills: Grammar, p. 89

Direct and Indirect Objects

A. 1. direct object; role
2. indirect object: us; direct object: advice
3. direct object: Nancy and me(corrected from *Nancy and I*);
4. indirect object: readers; direct object: feelings
5. none

B. Sample Sentences (4 and 5 include indirect objects)

1. The heavy machinerytore holes in the ground.
2. Great poets enrich our lives.
3. My thoughts scared me to death.
4. The glowing light showed us the way home.
5. The islanders taught me songs.

Poetry Collection: Pablo Neruda, Elizabeth Bishop, Emily Dickinson

Open-Book Test, p. 92

Short Answer

1. It means a crisscrossing. The word "branches" is a context clue that provides a hint to the meaning.
Difficulty: *Average* **Objective:** *Reading*
2. With imagery such as "light/has dropped from the top of the sky" and "drifting down like clean/white sand," he gives the impression that nature is beautiful and peaceful.
Difficulty: *Average* **Objective:** *Interpretation*
3. It compares the world to a glass overflowing with water.
Difficulty: *Easy* **Objective:** *Literary Analysis*
4. Since storms can be scary, a person might be made nervous and restless by an approaching storm.
Difficulty: *Average* **Objective:** *Vocabulary*
5. A heron is a bird. The word "feathers" helps define *heron.*
Difficulty: *Easy* **Objective:** *Reading*
6. A flash of lightning is probably lighting up the palm trees. Lightning is mentioned earlier in the poem, and the word "suddenly" is used. Also, the trees appear as "fistfuls of limp fish-skeletons" because the lightning is so bright against the dark sky.
Difficulty: *Challenging* **Objective:** *Interpretation*
7. She wants to show how the storm moves dramatically from place to place. These stage directions create the sense that the speaker is watching the storm much as someone would watch a play.
Difficulty: *Challenging* **Objective:** *Interpretation*
8. Sample answer: "Little Exercise"—boulevard is "relieved" or storm is "like a dog." "Ode to Enchanted Light"—The world is an overflowing glass of water.
Giving the street the human quality of feeling relief makes the storm's rains seem refreshing.
Difficulty: *Average* **Objective:** *Literary Analysis*
9. Sample answer: We are probably having an argument, because someone who debates is having trouble deciding.
Difficulty: *Average* **Objective:** *Vocabulary*
10. She gives the wind the human quality of being dissatisfied or unhappy. The wind is said to be "complaining" about how someone else has treated "him."
Difficulty: *Challenging* **Objective:** *Literary Analysis*

Essay

11. Students should relate that a storm hits a coastal area where mangrove trees grow. One boulevard with rows of palm trees is hit. The rain pours down; the storm finally goes away. Someone sleeps through the storm at the bottom of a rowboat.
Difficulty: *Easy* **Objective:** *Essay*
12. Students should discuss the sense of wonder that the poem conveys about nature and might point out the relationship of the word "enchanted" with magic and things magical. Students should point out the poem's figurative language and note how it helps convey that sense of wonder and enchantment.
Difficulty: *Average* **Objective:** *Essay*
13. Students should realize that the final two lines of the poem state the theme figuratively: Nature, like humans, sometimes has bad days. They should explain that the personification in the poem reinforces the central idea of nature's similarity to human beings.
Difficulty: *Challenging* **Objective:** *Essay*
14. Students should choose one poem and support their opinion with words and phrases from the poem. Those who choose "Ode to Enchanted Light" may cite "The world is a glass overflowing with water." Those who choose "Little Exercise" may cite the storm roaming "uneasily." Those who choose "The Sky Is Low . . ." may refer to "a narrow wind complains all day."
Difficulty: *Average* **Objective:** *Essay*

Oral Response

15. Oral responses should be clear, well organized, and well supported by appropriate examples from the selections.
Difficulty: *Average* **Objective:** *Oral Interpretation*

Selection Test A, p. 95

Critical Reading

1. ANS: A	DIF: Easy	OBJ: Comprehension
2. ANS: B	DIF: Easy	OBJ: Interpretation

3. **ANS:** C	**DIF:** Easy	**OBJ:** Literary Analysis
4. **ANS:** C	**DIF:** Easy	**OBJ:** Literary Analysis
5. **ANS:** B	**DIF:** Easy	**OBJ:** Comprehension
6. **ANS:** A	**DIF:** Easy	**OBJ:** Literary Analysis
7. **ANS:** D	**DIF:** Easy	**OBJ:** Reading
8. **ANS:** D	**DIF:** Easy	**OBJ:** Comprehension
9. **ANS:** B	**DIF:** Easy	**OBJ:** Comprehension
10. **ANS:** C	**DIF:** Easy	**OBJ:** Literary Analysis
11. **ANS:** C	**DIF:** Easy	**OBJ:** Reading
12. **ANS:** A	**DIF:** Easy	**OBJ:** Literary Analysis

Vocabulary and Grammar

13. **ANS:** A	**DIF:** Easy	**OBJ:** Vocabulary
14. **ANS:** B	**DIF:** Easy	**OBJ:** Grammar
15. **ANS:** A	**DIF:** Easy	**OBJ:** Vocabulary

Essay

16. Students should explain that "Ode to Enchanted Light" describes a peaceful, wonderful scene and that "The Sky Is Low, the Clouds Are Mean" describes an unpleasant, uncomfortable scene. Students should cite figures of speech and other details that contribute to the scene they describe—for example, the comparison to "clean white sand" or the cicadas singing in "Ode to Enchanted Light," or the mean clouds and complaining wind in "The Sky Is Low, the Clouds Are Mean."
    Difficulty: *Easy*
    Objective: *Essay*
17. Students should relate that a storm hits a coastal area on or near mangrove keys (little islands where tropical trees called mangroves grow). One little boulevard with rows of palm trees is hit. The rain pours. Then, the storm goes away. One person has slept through it in the bottom of his rowboat.
    Difficulty: *Easy*
    Objective: *Essay*
18. Students should choose one poem and support their opinion with words and phrases from the poem. Those who choose "Ode to Enchanted Light" may cite "The world is a glass overflowing with water." Those who choose "Little Exercise" may cite the storm roaming "uneasily." Those who choose "The Sky Is Low . . ." may refer to "a narrow wind complains all day."
    Difficulty: *Average*
    Objective: *Essay*

Selection Test B, p. 98

Critical Reading

1. **ANS:** A	**DIF:** Average	**OBJ:** Comprehension
2. **ANS:** C	**DIF:** Average	**OBJ:** Interpretation
3. **ANS:** D	**DIF:** Average	**OBJ:** Literary Analysis
4. **ANS:** C	**DIF:** Average	**OBJ:** Reading
5. **ANS:** A	**DIF:** Average	**OBJ:** Interpretation
6. **ANS:** C	**DIF:** Challenging	**OBJ:** Literary Analysis
7. **ANS:** A	**DIF:** Average	**OBJ:** Comprehension
8. **ANS:** D	**DIF:** Average	**OBJ:** Literary Analysis
9. **ANS:** B	**DIF:** Average	**OBJ:** Reading
10. **ANS:** A	**DIF:** Average	**OBJ:** Literary Analysis
11. **ANS:** B	**DIF:** Average	**OBJ:** Literary Analysis
12. **ANS:** B	**DIF:** Challenging	**OBJ:** Literary Analysis

Vocabulary and Grammar

13. **ANS:** A	**DIF:** Average	**OBJ:** Vocabulary
14. **ANS:** B	**DIF:** Average	**OBJ:** Vocabulary
15. **ANS:** B	**DIF:** Average	**OBJ:** Grammar
16. **ANS:** C	**DIF:** Average	**OBJ:** Grammar
17. **ANS:** D	**DIF:** Average	**OBJ:** Grammar

Essay

18. Students should discuss the sense of wonder that the poem conveys about nature and should indicate that the word *enchanted* helps convey that sense of wonder. A good essay might provide a definition of *enchanted* that recognizes its association with magic. Students should then discuss how the poem's figurative language and other imagery, particularly the final metaphor of the overlowing glass, convey that sense of wonder or enchantment.
    Difficulty: *Average*
    Objective: *Essay*
19. Students should note that the final two lines of the poem state the central theme figuratively, and they should restate it literally: Nature, like people, sometimes has its bad days. They may expand this idea to a recognition that Dickinson uses the poem to try to help us understand nature and that she attributes no malice to nature for the cold, nasty day but instead implies that we should forgive nature as we do a friend or relative having a bad day. Students should explain that all the personification in the poem reinforces the central idea of nature's similarity to human beings. Among the examples of personification they may mention are the clouds being mean, the flake of snow debating whether it will cross the barn or go through a rut, the narrow wind complaining about maltreatment, and the idea of nature being capable of wearing a diadem, or crown.
    Difficulty: *Challenging*
    Objective: *Essay*
20. Students should choose one poem and support their opinion with words and phrases from the poem. Those who choose "Ode to Enchanted Light" may cite "The world is a glass overflowing with water." Those who

choose "Little Exercise" may cite the storm roaming "uneasily." Those who choose "The Sky Is Low . . ." may refer to "a narrow wind complains all day."

Difficulty: *Average*

Objective: *Essay*

"Snake on the Etowah" by David Bottoms
"Vanishing Species" by Bailey White

Vocabulary Warm-up Exercises, p. 102

A.
1. majestic
2. eased
3. shudder
4. draped
5. slumped
6. smear

B. Sample Answers
1. If a person is *spooked*, he is frightened, so a man who is sitting calmly with tea and a book is not *spooked*.
2. If a weather report says that conditions are *hazy*, you would expect to see some fog, mist, or smoke clouding the air when you opened your front door.
3. If an animal is *bellowing*, it is making a loud roaring sound, therefore it would be using its voice.
4. A tiger is almost always considered an extremely dangerous animal, so it would be natural to *flinch*, or move backward suddenly, in response to this danger.
5. If a person's backpack becomes snagged on a doorknob, he should untangle the part of the pack that has caught on the knob.
6. If a light has a *flicker*, it means that the light makes a quick, sparkling movement, so a strong, steady lighthouse beam does not have a *flicker*.

Reading Warm-up A, p. 103

Sample Answers
1. rope, over a high tree branch: The curtains in my bedroom are pieces of cloth *draped* over a rod.
2. (involuntary shivering movement): A person who is afraid of heights might *shudder* while standing at the edge of a cliff.
3. their legs from their sleeping bags: *Yanked* is a word that means the opposite of *eased* as it is used in this sentence.
4. (grand and impressive): The giant, stately redwood trees of California are *majestic*.
5. (peanut butter): A *smear* is made when one substance rubs against another and leaves a spot or a mark.
6. (relief): Shana felt so comfortable and relaxed at her friend Amy's house that she *slumped* on the couch when they watched a movie.

Reading Warm-up B, p. 104

Sample Answers
1. a pair of lions: Walruses, bulls, howler monkeys, and alligators are some of the other kinds of animals that make sounds that could be described as bellowing.
2. (wobbly): A candle flame can have a *flicker* when air disturbs it or when the burning wick makes sparks.
3. (a bush): During the hike up the mountain trail, a tree root snagged Bill's right foot.
4. (the dark): Last night, Jamie felt *spooked* by the scary sound of the howling wind.
5. the sound of a nighttime screech: *Flinch* means to cringe, wince, or shrink back from something you hear, see, taste, or touch.
6. foggy or misty: On a hot, summer day when there was a lot of air pollution, the air above my city looked *hazy*.

Writing About the Big Question, p. 105

A.
1. express
2. meaningful
3. experience

B. Sample Answers
1. I like to write about the significant things I observe. I also like to paint or sketch these things.
2. One experience I had was finding a stray dog alongside the road, which my mom let me pick up. When he looked into my eyes, I could not misunderstand—I knew I had made a friend forever.

C. Sample Answer

Sensory details can help make an experience real by showing us how things look and feel.

Literary Analysis: Comparing Poetry and Prose, p. 106

"Snake on the Etowah"

form: poetry

literary technique/language: imagery, figurative language

setting/mood: rural Georgia/reflective

events: encounters with various snakes

"Vanishing Species"

form: prose

literary technique/language: dialogue, humor, plot, characters

Setting/mood: rural Georgia/humorous

events: visitor comes to tape alligator and is foiled

Students should construct a comparison and contrast paragraph that identifies "Snake on the Etowah" as poetry and "Vanishing Species" as prose. The settings of these selections are the same—a rural Georgia landscape. The topics are also similar in that they address nature, especially dangerous elements of nature. However, they differ in their mood and language. "Snake on the Etowah" is reflective and expressive, whereas "Vanishing Species" is humorous. The poem uses precise imagery to elicit an emotional response, whereas the essay includes a plot, dialogue, and narration to convey a story.

Vocabulary Builder, p. 107

A. Sample Answers

1. It is likely to die out and no longer exist.
2. The fashion comes into style again.
3. You take possession of it.
4. holidays, religious ceremonies, weddings, funerals, etc.
5. It is creeping toward you.
6. I might witness the undulation of waves in the ocean.

B. 1. F; 2. T; 3. T; 4. F; 5. F

Open-Book Test, p. 109

Short Answer

1. The phrase "kicking through woods and fields" tells you that the speaker spends a lot of time in the wilderness.
   Difficulty: *Average* **Objective:** *Interpretation*
2. He means that sometimes the most dangerous, fearsome things are the most beautiful.
   Difficulty: *Challenging* **Objective:** *Interpretation*
3. Sample answers: "bronze spoon of a copperhead"; "wide undulation of tail"; "buff and copper swish"; "spiny, cool, just below/the surface"
   Difficulty: *Easy* **Objective:** *Interpretation*
4. At first the narrator doesn't think much of Mr. Linley. She says they were not impressed with him and that he just seemed like a nervous little man. However, when she sees how good he is at his work and how brave he is as he approaches the alligator, she realizes he is impressive after all.
   Difficulty: *Average* **Objective:** *Interpretation*
5. Sample answer: She means that they realized that Mr. Linley's nervous eyes and hands indicated speed and quick reflexes.
   Difficulty: *Challenging* **Objective:** *Interpretation*
6. Sample answer: The alligator is being defiant. He knows they want him to bellow (Aunt Belle has "trained" him to do so "on command"), but he just lies in the mud and "glare[s] at Mr. Linley." Maybe he is mad because he couldn't catch Mr. Linley the first time.
   Difficulty: *Average* **Objective:** *Interpretation*
7. They are both potentially dangerous to humans.
   Difficulty: *Easy* **Objective:** *Literary Analysis*
8. Sample answer: Mr. Linley—seeks out the alligator; Both—encounter a wild creature; Speaker—runs into the snake accidentally. Accept all reasonable responses. Both respect and appreciate wild animals.
   Difficulty: *Average* **Objective:** *Literary Analysis*
9. Sample answer: Like the poem, it paints a descriptive picture of an encounter between a human being and a wild creature. Unlike the poem, it is comical.
   Difficulty: *Average* **Objective:** *Literary Analysis*
10. The works would help people remember what those creatures had been like when they existed.
    Difficulty: *Average* **Objective:** *Vocabulary*

Essay

11. Students who choose "Snake on the Etowah" may appreciate the poet's use of vivid details and the suspense and danger associated with an encounter with a deadly snake. Students who choose "Vanishing Species" may enjoy the author's comic descriptions and her memorable depiction of Mr. Linley. Evaluate students' responses for discussion of at least two of the listed elements, and for clarity of thought.
    Difficulty: *Easy* **Objective:** *Essay*
12. Students may respond that the theme of "Snake on the Etowah" is *The copperhead is both beautiful and dangerous*, and that the theme of "Vanishing Species" is *Some wild creatures are as smart as—or smarter than—humans*. Explanations of the authors' delineations of theme should refer specifically to each text and should relate directly to the themes students have identified. Evaluate essays for clarity, reasonableness, and completion of all three parts of the question.
    Difficulty: *Average* **Objective:** *Essay*
13. Students may respond that the tone of "Snake on the Etowah" is both tense and awestruck; and that the tone of "Vanishing Species" is casual and comical. Students may also suggest that the form of the poem allows Bottoms to capture the episode in few words, which in turn helps him recreate his brief moment of tension—and connection to the snake's beauty—for the reader. They may also say that the form of the narrative essay allows White to create a detailed portrait of Mr. Linley, and also to offer comical commentary (through the narrator) on the day's events. Evaluate essays for logic, clarity, and consistency.
    Difficulty: *Challenging* **Objective:** *Essay*
14. Students should explain how the selection reached them by citing the words and phrases they found most powerful. Those who choose "Snake on the Etowah" might point out how the vivid language describing the snake, such as "little tongue reaching in two directions" and "a wide undulation of tail," makes the reader think about appreciating the beauty of all wildlife. In "Vanishing Species," the descriptions of Mr. Linley's enthusiasm communicate a similar message about appreciating wildlife. Students might mention the passage in which Mr. Linley plays the recordings of all the animals, and the repetition the author uses there.
    Difficulty: *Average* **Objective:** *Essay*

Oral Response

15. Oral responses should be clear, well organized, and well supported by appropriate examples from the selections.
Difficulty: *Average* **Objective:** *Oral Interpretation*

Selection Test A, p. 112

Critical Reading

1. ANS: B	DIF: Easy	OBJ: Comprehension
2. ANS: A	DIF: Average	OBJ: Literary Analysis
3. ANS: B	DIF: Average	OBJ: Literary Analysis
4. ANS: C	DIF: Easy	OBJ: Interpretation
5. ANS: A	DIF: Average	OBJ: Literary Analysis
6. ANS: D	DIF: Easy	OBJ: Comprehension
7. ANS: C	DIF: Easy	OBJ: Interpretation
8. ANS: A	DIF: Easy	OBJ: Reading Skill
9. ANS: A	DIF: Easy	OBJ: Comprehension
10. ANS: B	DIF: Average	OBJ: Interpretation
11. ANS: D	DIF: Average	OBJ: Literary Analysis
12. ANS: C	DIF: Average	OBJ: Interpretation

Vocabulary

13. ANS: C	DIF: Average	OBJ: Vocabulary
14. ANS: B	DIF: Average	OBJ: Vocabulary
15. ANS: D	DIF: Average	OBJ: Vocabulary

Essay

16. The author of "Snake on the Etowah" presents the setting using sensory details and precise language to create a picture of the environment. The feeling he creates is one of respect and awe. The author of "Vanishing Species" uses informal language and humorous description to bring the setting to life. She attempts to create a sense of "being there" with her descriptions.
Difficulty: *Easy*
Objective: *Essay*

17. These two works share the theme of appreciation of nature. The poet presents the theme through select word choice and imagery that brings nature to life. He shows his respect for and love of nature through his images. White, on the other hand, tells the story of her experience with her aunt's alligator and Mr. Linley's trying to preserve its memory. She comments directly on the survival of the alligator and implicitly on her faith in nature.
Difficulty: *Average*
Objective: *Essay*

18. Students should explain how the selection reached them by citing the words and phrases they found more powerful. Those who choose "Snake on the Etowah" might point out how the vivid language describing the snake (such as "little tongue reaching in two directions" and "a wide undulation of tail") makes the reader think about the beauty of all wildlife. In "Vanishing Species," the descriptions of Mr. Linley's feelings get across a similar message about appreciating wildlife. Students might mention the passage in which Mr. Linley plays the recordings of all the animals.
Difficulty: *Average*
Objective: *Essay*

Selection Test B, p. 115

Critical Reading

1. ANS: C	DIF: Challenging	OBJ: Interpretation
2. ANS: C	DIF: Challenging	OBJ: Literary Analysis
3. ANS: A	DIF: Challenging	OBJ: Literary Analysis
4. ANS: D	DIF: Average	OBJ: Comprehension
5. ANS: C	DIF: Average	OBJ: Literary Analysis
6. ANS: B	DIF: Average	OBJ: Interpretation
7. ANS: A	DIF: Average	OBJ: Reading Skills
8. ANS: D	DIF: Challenging	OBJ: Literary Analysis
9. ANS: B	DIF: Challenging	OBJ: Interpretation
10. ANS: C	DIF: Average	OBJ: Comprehension
11. ANS: A	DIF: Average	OBJ: Literary Analysis
12. ANS: B	DIF: Challenging	OBJ: Comprehension
13. ANS: A	DIF: Average	OBJ: Literary Analysis
14. ANS: D	DIF: Challenging	OBJ: Interpretation

Vocabulary

15. ANS: A	DIF: Average	OBJ: Vocabulary
16. ANS: B	DIF: Average	OBJ: Vocabulary
17. ANS: C	DIF: Average	OBJ: Vocabulary

Essay

18. The poem uses figurative language, such as "like a bow" and "like a bootlace" to compare the snakes to benign objects. The poet also incorporates precise adjectives and verbs to bring the scene to life, including words like *kicking, curled, hazy bank, drifted, quivering, shudder,* and *sidling.* White also uses precise adjectives and verbs, such as *bellow, majestic, slung, vaulted, crawling, ragged jaws,* and so on. Bottoms uses these techniques to paint a serious and respectful picture of nature, whereas White portrays an experience of nature in a humorous light.
Difficulty: *Average*
Objective: *Essay*

19. In "Snake on the Etowah," the speaker has pleasant observations of snakes and considers them beautiful. He then encounters a poisonous copperhead and feels awe, fear, and respect for its beauty. The attitude the speaker takes toward nature is, overall, one of respect for its power and beauty. In "Vanishing Species," the author also shows her respect for nature but through humor. She tells about the power of the alligator and how they do stay away from it, unlike the visitor. She

also explains that the alligators survive, though she wonders about Mr. Linley.

Difficulty: *Challenging*

Objective: *Essay*

20. Students should explain how the selection reached them by citing the words and phrases they found more powerful. Those who choose "Snake on the Etowah" might point out how the vivid language describing the snake, such as ""little tongue reaching in two directions" and "a wide undulation of tail," makes the reader think about appreciating the beauty of all wildlife. In "Vanishing Species," the descriptions of Mr. Linley's enthusiasm communicate a similar message about appreciating wildlife. Students might mention the passage in which Mr. Linley plays the recordings of all the animals, and the repetition the author uses there.

Difficulty: *Average*

Objective: *Essay*

Writing Workshop

Writing for Assessment: Integrating Grammar Skills, p. 119

A 1. active; 2. passive; 3. active; 4. passive

B 1. A flash of lightning releases energy.

2. Rapid heating of the air produces thunder.
3. Owners of buildings use lightning rods.
4. The metal in umbrellas attracts lightning.

Benchmark Test 7, p. 120

MULTIPLE CHOICE

1. **ANS:** D
2. **ANS:** D
3. **ANS:** A
4. **ANS:** A
5. **ANS:** C
6. **ANS:** A
7. **ANS:** D
8. **ANS:** A
9. **ANS:** B
10. **ANS:** D
11. **ANS:** A
12. **ANS:** B
13. **ANS:** C
14. **ANS:** B
15. **ANS:** D
16. **ANS:** A
17. **ANS:** C
18. **ANS:** D
19. **ANS:** A
20. **ANS:** C
21. **ANS:** C
22. **ANS:** B
23. **ANS:** A
24. **ANS:** D
25. **ANS:** B
26. **ANS:** C
27. **ANS:** B
28. **ANS:** C
29. **ANS:** D
30. **ANS:** B
31. **ANS:** A
32. **ANS:** C
33. **ANS:** A

ESSAY

34. Students' ideas should clearly give supporting reasons why the song is important and should cite one or more examples of the use of sound devices in the song.
35. Students' notes should include things that appeal to the senses. For three of the items on the list, students should show examples of comparisons using figurative languages, demonstrating an understanding of the distinctions among simile, metaphor, and personification.
36. Students should list three ways that poetry helps us connect with others, such as by expressing feelings that we might share about the power of nature, about the difficulties of growing up, or about the satisfaction of doing a job well.

Poetry Collection: Robert Hayden, William Shakespeare, Ricardo Sánchez

Vocabulary Warm-up Exercises, p. 128

A. 1. resolution

2. familial
3. benefits
4. thicketed
5. aromas
6. brethren

B. Sample Answers

1. The *bonanza* find produced a lot of gold.
2. If it begins to rain at the party, you can *dart* underneath the canopy.
3. In modern times, believing that the earth is flat is sheer *folly*.
4. Wearing *shackles*, the animals could hardly move at all across the field.
5. The awards assembly began with the *summoning* of all winners to the stage.
6. Pick peaches from *yonder* tree, the one on this side of the hill.

Reading Warm-up A, p. 129

Sample Answers

1. (all of us were related); A synonym for *brethren* is brothers.
2. low shrubs and berry bushes; There is a thicketed area of forsythia bushes behind my house where the rabbits hide.
3. (they were relatives); Everyone in my family has the same shape of nose.
4. grilling meats and vegetables; My favorite aromas are roses and baking brownies.
5. advantage; To me, the benefits of being on the swim team are making good friends and getting lots of exercise.
6. (determination); I studied for my midterm exams with complete resolution, and I got all As.

Reading Warm-up B, p. 130

Sample Answers

1. freed from, slavery, better lives; *Shackles* means "metal rings and chains around a person's wrists or ankles" and "the lack of freedom caused by slavery."
2. (gold, rich); *Bonanza* means "relating to suddenly finding a lot of money or having a lot of good luck."
3. (hundreds of miles away); While I wait in the car, would you go into *yonder* convenience store and get me a quart of milk?
4. Some freed slaves heeded the army's calling of soldiers to fight Indians on the Great Plains.; I heeded the coach's *summoning* of all students interested in playing soccer.
5. this way and that, trying to avoid being caught; The fish in my dentist's aquarium *dart* in and out of the rocks and plants.
6. She was always ready with her fists; I think it is *folly* to make children play a musical instrument that they are not at all interested in.

Writing About the Big Question, p. 131

A. 1. inform
2. cultural
3. individuality

B. Sample Answers

1. If I express the benefits of meaningful experiences, I can share with others relevant events from my life to help them through their own difficulties.
2. I received feedback on a presentation from a peer group. It seemed horribly critical. They misunderstood my intentions and my main point.

C. Sample Answer

Reading about other people's feelings and experiences may benefit people and help them see the world from a different point of view.

Reading: Reread to Paraphrase, p. 132

Sample paraphrase of "Blow, Blow, Thou Winter Wind": (Winter wind, go ahead and blow.) Your cold is not as harsh as that of humans who don't give thanks. Your bite isn't as sharp even though you make the air rough. Under the holly, sing that most friends are false and most love is foolish. Life is jolly nevertheless. Make us cold, winter sky. You don't pain as much as people who forget favors we do for them. Although you freeze waters, your sting is not as sharp as the pain someone feels when forgotten by a friend.

Sample paraphrase of "Old Man": The old man (the speaker's grandfather) was wise. He had a face of wrinkles from the life he'd lived. Long ago, during nights at family get-togethers in Albuquerque, he told me, "You are of Indian blood, among other things." The old man, loved and respected, used to talk about Indian villages, where the family came from. That blood predates the arrival of Spaniards, from whom our blood also comes. The mixed blood was rich but caused a lot of pain. The old man was in touch with the earth and is now gone in body but alive in spirit.

Literary Analysis: Lyric and Narrative Poetry, p. 133

A. *Lyric poem title:* "Blow . . ." or "Old Man"

1. It has one speaker who expresses his or her feelings and thoughts.
2. Among the emotions students may identify for "Blow . . ." are anger toward humans, hostile challenge to the wind. Among the emotions for "Old Man" are love, respect, honor, the pang of memory.
3. *Images in "Blow . . .":* keen tooth, rude breath to express negatives in man; *Images in "Old Man":* running rivulets . . . rich furrows to express marks life left on him; "who felt the heated sweetness of chile verde" to express old man's closeness to the basic things in life.
4. *Main impression of "Blow . . .":* Disappointment in humans; *Main impression of "Old Man":* love for grandfather

B. *Narrative poem title:* "Runagate Runagate"

1. It's a narrative poem because it tells a series of events—a story.
2. The first stanza tells about a general uprising of slaves—how they could not turn back—and indicates how slave owners identified people as their property. The second stanza introduces Harriet Tubman and her role in leading slaves to freedom.
3. The main conflict is between escaping slaves and slave owners. In the end, the slaves maintain their commitment to escape.
4. The main setting is the woods that the slaves traveled through on their way to freedom.
5. In the first stanza, unnamed slaves are the main characters. The second stanza focuses on Harriet Tubman, leader of the escaped slaves. The slave owners, although intimidating, might be considered minor characters.

Vocabulary Builder, p. 134

A. 1. A rich relative might leave someone a *legacy* when he or she dies.

2. A person who fails to give thanks to those who help him or her shows *ingratitude*.

3. A light in the darkness would be *beckoning*, drawing me toward it.

4. You might call them *aromas*.

5. You could use *shackles*.

6. You might describe it as *supple*.

B. Sample Answers

1. He might ask a student or teacher for help because he is not able to solve the problem on his own.

2. No; if plans are indefinite, they are not definite or fixed.

Enrichment: Old Age and Harriet Tubman, p. 135

A. Responses will vary, depending on the ads students find.

B. Tubman's achievements later in life include assisting the writer of Tubman's biography, speaking out for the rights of women and African Americans, helping to organize the African Methodist Episcopal (AME) Church, and setting up a home for elderly African Americans.

Open-Book Test, p. 136

Short Answer

1. It is set on a dark night sometime during the later years of slavery in the United States. Details such as "darkness into darkness" and "blackness ahead" reveal that it is night. Since slaves are trying to escape, slavery must still be legal.

Difficulty: *Easy* **Objective:** *Literary Analysis*

2. I would rather die than continue in slavery.

Difficulty: *Easy* **Objective:** *Reading*

3. It represents freedom; the speaker says, "North star and bonanza gold/I'm bound for the freedom."

Difficulty: *Average* **Objective:** *Interpretation*

4. The speaker expresses disappointment in human relationships when he says, for example, "Most friendship is feigning, most loving mere folly."

Difficulty: *Average* **Objective:** *Literary Analysis*

5. The speaker says winter is harsh, but humans are even harsher. The point is that people are not very nice at all. Some details used for the comparison are "Thou art not so unkind" and "Thy sting is not so sharp."

Difficulty: *Challenging* **Objective:** *Interpretation*

6. I would feel upset or annoyed if someone was not thankful for something I had done or a gift I had given.

Difficulty: *Average* **Objective:** *Vocabulary*

7. Sample answers:

(col 2, row 1) Your bite is not so sharp.

(col 2, row 2) Friendships usually aren't genuine.

(col 2, row 3) Life is enjoyable.

When I can put the lines in my own words, I know I understand what they mean.

Difficulty: *Average* **Objective:** *Reading*

8. He learned pride in his heritage by hearing the stories his grandfather told about their Native American and Spanish ancestors.

Difficulty: *Easy* **Objective:** *Interpretation*

9. He expresses admiration and respect when he lovingly describes the way the old man looked, the stories he told, and the way others regarded him.

Difficulty: *Challenging* **Objective:** *Literary Analysis*

10. What the grandfather (an ancestor) leaves, or hands down to, the speaker is a sense of his own history.

Difficulty: *Average* **Objective:** *Vocabulary*

Essay

11. Students should recognize that the grandfather is a proud old man who lived a traditional life. They should note that he teaches the speaker about his dual Native American and Spanish heritage and the speaker admires and respects him very much.

Difficulty: *Easy* **Objective:** *Essay*

12. Students should point out that a lyric poem is one in which the speaker expresses thoughts and feelings to create a certain impression of a subject. Students should cite lines from the poem that express the speaker's dissatisfaction with human relationships and that give an overall impression of disappointment.

Difficulty: *Average* **Objective:** *Essay*

13. Students should note details that contribute to suspense, such as the darkness, the shapes of terror, the hounds, and the conductor's threats. Some students may also discuss the rhythm as a tool adding to the suspense, noting that in the opening lines the poet captures the rhythm of fearful running.

Difficulty: *Challenging* **Objective:** *Essay*

14. Students should note that the speaker of "Runagate Runagate" is expressing his fear and desire to be free, as when he says, "Never make it,/we'll never make it." The speaker of "Blow, Blow, Thou Winter Wind" is trying to say that friends can betray and that betrayal is very painful. Students may note the words "Thou art not so unkind/As man's ingratitude," for example. The speaker of "Old Man" is expressing his love for his grandfather when he refers to "a mindsoul touched by you."

Difficulty: *Average* **Objective:** *Essay*

Oral Response

15. Oral responses should be clear, well organized, and well supported by appropriate examples from the selections.

Difficulty: *Average* **Objective:** *Oral Interpretation*

Selection Test A, p. 139

Critical Reading

1. ANS: C	DIF: Easy	OBJ: Comprehension
2. ANS: A	DIF: Easy	OBJ: Reading
3. ANS: D	DIF: Easy	OBJ: Literary Analysis
4. ANS: D	DIF: Easy	OBJ: Interpretation
5. ANS: B	DIF: Easy	OBJ: Comprehension
6. ANS: C	DIF: Easy	OBJ: Literary Analysis
7. ANS: A	DIF: Easy	OBJ: Interpretation
8. ANS: B	DIF: Easy	OBJ: Reading
9. ANS: C	DIF: Easy	OBJ: Literary Analysis
10. ANS: A	DIF: Easy	OBJ: Interpretation
11. ANS: D	DIF: Easy	OBJ: Comprehension
12. ANS: B	DIF: Easy	OBJ: Reading

Vocabulary and Grammar

13. ANS: D	DIF: Easy	OBJ: Vocabulary
14. ANS: D	DIF: Easy	OBJ: Vocabulary
15. ANS: B	DIF: Easy	OBJ: Grammar

Essay

16. *Sample paraphrase of first stanza of "Blow, Blow, Thou Winter Wind":* Blow, winter wind. You are not as mean as people who do not show gratitude when they should. Even though you are harsh and unseen, your bite is not as sharp as that of those unkind, ungrateful people. Sing heigh-ho under the green holly. Most friendship is false, and most love is foolishness. Still, life is happy.

    Difficulty: *Easy*

    Objective: *Essay*

17. Students should recognize that the grandfather is a proud old man who lived a traditional life close to the earth. They should recognize that he teaches the speaker about his dual Indian (or Native American) and Spanish heritage and that the speaker admires and respects him very much.

    Difficulty: *Easy*

    Objective: *Essay*

18. Students might note that the speaker of "Runagate Runagate" is expressing his fear and desire to be free, as when he says, "Never make it,/we'll never make it." The speaker of "Blow, Blow, Thou Winter Wind" is trying to say that friends can betray and that betrayal is very painful. Students may note the words "Thou art not so unkind/As man's ingratitude," for example. The speaker of "Old Man" is expressing his love for his grandfather when he refers to "a mindsoul touched by you."

    Difficulty: *Average*

    Objective: *Essay*

Selection Test B, p. 142

Critical Reading

1. ANS: B	DIF: Average	OBJ: Interpretation
2. ANS: A	DIF: Average	OBJ: Interpretation
3. ANS: A	DIF: Average	OBJ: Reading
4. ANS: D	DIF: Average	OBJ: Literary Analysis
5. ANS: C	DIF: Average	OBJ: Literary Analysis
6. ANS: B	DIF: Challenging	OBJ: Comprehension
7. ANS: A	DIF: Average	OBJ: Interpretation
8. ANS: C	DIF: Average	OBJ: Reading
9. ANS: C	DIF: Average	OBJ: Literary Analysis
10. ANS: B	DIF: Average	OBJ: Literary Analysis
11. ANS: B	DIF: Challenging	OBJ: Interpretation
12. ANS: C	DIF: Average	OBJ: Comprehension
13. ANS: B	DIF: Challenging	OBJ: Reading

Vocabulary and Grammar

14. ANS: D	DIF: Average	OBJ: Vocabulary
15. ANS: D	DIF: Average	OBJ: Vocabulary
16. ANS: A	DIF: Average	OBJ: Grammar
17. ANS: B	DIF: Average	OBJ: Grammar

Essay

18. Students' definitions should recognize that a lyric poem is one in which the speaker expresses his or her thoughts and feelings. Students should then prove that either poem is a lyric poem by citing examples of thoughts and feelings expressed by the poem's speaker.

    Difficulty: *Average*

    Objective: *Essay*

19. Students should note details in the poem that contribute to the suspense, such as the darkness, the shapes of terror in the opening lines, the description of "no place to hide" (line 45), the hounds in the opening lines and in the second part of the poem (line 47), the escaping slaves' expressions of doubt and the conductor's leveled pistol and threats in response, the quotations from "wanted" posters, and the details about hoot owls, ghosted air, "hants," scary leaves, and the ghost-story train. Some students may also discuss the rhythm as a tool adding to the suspense, noting particularly that in the opening lines the poet captures the sound of fearful running.

    Difficulty: *Challenging*

    Objective: *Essay*

20. Students should note that the speaker of "Runagate Runagate" is expressing his fear and desire to be free, as when he says, "Never make it,/we'll never make it." The speaker of "Blow, Blow, Thou Winter Wind" is trying to say that friends can betray and that betrayal is very painful. Students may note the words "Thou art not so

unkind/As man's ingratitude," for example. The speaker of "Old Man" is expressing his love for his grandfather when he refers to "a mindsoul touched by you."

Difficulty: *Average*

Objective: *Essay*

Poetry Collection: Emma Lazarus, Henry Wadsworth Longfellow, Paul Laurence Dunbar

Vocabulary Warm-up Exercises, p. 146

A. 1. defiance
2. hovel
3. huddled
4. cruelties
5. refuse
6. peril

B. Sample Answers

1. Going to the dentist doesn't fill me with *dread* because he uses a painless drill.
2. I would not buy a *steed* for a young child learning to ride because the horse would not be gentle enough for a learner.
3. Some people who have long vacations look *transfigured* because they are relaxed and rested.
4. I would want to avoid *teeming* highways during rush hours, when a lot of cars are on the road.
5. It is important for the *masses* to vote in elections so they have a say in the government.
6. When people don't listen to their *consciences*, they often regret their actions.

Reading Warm-up A, p. 147

Sample Answers

1. Americans were not going to stand for any laws being forced on them!; I was once in *defiance* of my older sister when she blamed me for breaking something, and I said I did not do it and, therefore, would not pay for it.
2. (together); During rush hour, I had to stand *huddled* in the corner of a bus because there was not much room.
3. (beat, sold); Some *cruelties* that take place today include torturing prisoners of war and harming innocent animals for no reason.
4. fine home; A *hovel* might be one small room with a dirt floor and only mats to sleep on.
5. a cruel ruler's soldiers who knocked down your door and attacked you; My uncle was in a bad car accident and he was in *peril* of dying, but he pulled through.
6. (garbage); Please place all *refuse* in the trashcan.

Reading Warm-up B, p. 148

Sample Answers

1. sitting atop, ride; His *steed* might have been strong and fast, and it might have been all white with a black diamond on its forehead.
2. (leaders); Egyptian pharaohs made the *masses* build huge pyramids for them.
3. (much stronger British army); I had a feeling of *dread* when I had to give a speech in front of the school assembly.
4. New buildings began rising up everywhere. Docks for ships stretched out into the sea.; Our basement was *transfigured* into a family room and playroom after the renovation.
5. (people, industry); In a *teeming* city, lots of people would be going into and coming out of buildings, jamming the sidewalks, and crowding into the buses and subways.
6. freedom should extend to all; My friends and I followed our *consciences* when we decided not to join some other groups making mischief after the football game.

Writing About the Big Question, p. 149

A. 1. cultural
2. experience
3. significance
4. connection

B. Sample Answers

1. I include meaningful information and valid details that express the essence of the experience.
2. Longfellow makes the connection between history and romance in "Paul Revere's Ride." He elaborates on the experience and shows the benefit of cooperation and patriotism.

C. Sample Answer

Someone who has contributed greatly to our country is Walt Whitman.

Reading: Reread to Paraphrase, p. 150

Sample paraphrase of "The New Colossus": (Unlike the giant bronze statue on the Greek island of Rhodes, with its image of conquest,) the statue on our shores is a mighty but motherly woman. As she looks out at the harbor between two cities, she holds a torch that welcomes immigrants. She seems to tell the nations of the Old World to keep their stuffy ceremony. This statue instead asks for poor outcasts who yearn to live more freely.

Sample paraphrase of "Harriet Beecher Stowe": Stowe's courageous book *Uncle Tom's Cabin* helped many people emotionally understand the cruelty of slavery. With her book, she awakened their consciences. The book's message of freedom affected both black and white Americans at all economic levels. Her book told people what to do and foretold events. The conflict between blacks and whites changed both. Blessed be this daring woman. She brought both freedom to African Americans and fame to herself.

Literary Analysis: Lyric and Narrative Poetry, p. 151

A. Lyric Poem Title: "Harriet Beecher Stowe" or "The New Colossus"

1. It has one speaker who expresses his or her feelings and thoughts.
2. Among the emotions students may identify for "The New Colossus" are patriotism, sympathy for the oppressed, admiration for the statue, and contempt for Old World pomp and snobbery; for "Harriet Beecher Stowe," admiration for Stowe, love of freedom, sympathy for the oppressed, and brotherhood toward people of all races.
3. *Images in "The New Colossus" and their ideas:* conquering limbs astride from land to land to describe the Colossus of Rhodes as pompous; golden door as an image of America as a welcoming place; *Images in "Harriet Beecher Stowe" and their ideas:* freedom's clear reveille sweeping from hovels to thrones to summarize the book's effects on the powerful and powerless alike; justice depicted as a sword coming from its sheath to conquer injustice; two peoples in the fiery wave to describe the book's effects on both white and black Americans.
4. *Main impression of "The New Colossus":* The Statue of Liberty represents America's welcome to those who must leave their homelands; *Main impression of "Harriet Beecher Stowe":* In writing *Uncle Tom's Cabin,* Stowe had a revolutionary effect on American history.

B. Narrative Poem Title: "Paul Revere's Ride"

1. It tells a story.
2. Paul Revere learns when and where the British troops are coming and rides through the night to warn the colonists in the villages and farms of Massachusetts.
3. The conflict is Revere's efforts in fighting the British (during the American Revolution). He succeeds in warning the colonists before the British advance.
4. the Massachusetts colony on the night of April 18, 1775
5. Paul Revere is the main character. Minor characters include his friend, the people he warns, and the British troops.

Vocabulary Builder, p. 152

A.
1. The mood at a funeral is usually *somber.*
2. The adjective *yearning* describes a person who craves a piece of candy.
3. It can be described as *peril.*
4. They are called *exiles.*
5. It could be described as *defiance.*
6. It is said to be *transfigured.*

B. Sample Answers
1. A translator's job is to change information from one language to another.
2. A person will likely have to move, or change locations.

Enrichment: American Heroes, p. 153

A.
1. Among the many possible traits students may name are perseverance, self-reliance, ambition, desire to help others, and patriotism.
2. Students should recognize that in times past, women had fewer opportunities outside the home.
3. Students should support their opinions with concrete examples.
4. Students are likely to feel that it is important to have heroes to knit together a society, instill pride, serve as role models for youngsters, and embody the values and achievements of that society.
5. Students who think our idea of heroism will change may suggest that valued achievements do change over time as science advances and new needs or dangers are faced. Students who think our idea of heroism will not change are likely to focus on the enduring values that heroes embody rather than on the specific achievements they attain.

B. Responses will vary, but students should offer support for calling the person heroic.

Poetry Collections: Robert Hayden, William Shakespeare, Ricardo Sánchez; Emma Lazarus, Henry Wadsworth Longfellow, Paul Laurence Dunbar

Integrated Language Skills: Grammar, p. 154

Prepositions and Prepositional Phrases

A.
1. preposition: of; object: poetry; phrase: of poetry; modifies *study;* adjective
2. preposition: between; object: lines; phrase: between the lines; modifies *read;* adverb
3. preposition: by; object: poet; phrase: by an African American poet; modifies *poem;* adjective
4. preposition: after; object: Civil War; phrase: after the Civil War; modifies *wrote;* adverb
5. preposition: with; object: me; phrase: with me; modifies *read;* adverb

B. Sample expanded sentences:
1. The dog with black spots barked all night.
2. The moonlight streamed through the garden.
3. We sat together on an old stone bench.

Poetry Collection: Emma Lazarus, Henry Wadsworth Longfellow, Paul Laurence Dunbar

Open-Book Test, p. 157

Short Answer

1. She is saying welcome to needy immigrants who are in search of a new home. She tells other countries

("ancient lands") to send her their "tired," "poor," and "homeless."

Difficulty: *Easy* **Objective:** *Interpretation*

2. Using images such as "a mighty woman" and details such as "glows world-wide welcome," the poem creates a single impression of the opportunity that the Statue of Liberty represents.

   Difficulty: *Challenging* **Objective:** *Literary Analysis*

3. They are desperately wanting to be free because they come from countries where their freedom is limited or denied.

   Difficulty: *Average* **Objective:** *Vocabulary*

4. It is New York Harbor, the doorway to America. The statue calls it "golden" because the freedom it represents is so valuable.

   Difficulty: *Challenging* **Objective:** *Interpretation*

5. It is set at the start of the American Revolution. The speaker says it takes place on April 18th, in "seventy-five," and the reader infers this is 1775. Also, the British are marching.

   Difficulty: *Easy* **Objective:** *Literary Analysis*

6. Put a small glass lamp high up in the church tower.

   Difficulty: *Average* **Objective:** *Reading*

7. Sample answers:

   (col 2, row 2) Paul Revere, a Revolutionary War hero

   (col 2, row 3) "Paul Revere," "a cry of defiance and not of fear"

   (col 3, row 2) British soldiers against American freedom fighters

   (col 3, row 3) "the British Regulars fired and fled"

   (col 4, row 2) Paul Revere rides to alert people that the British have arrived.

   (col 4, row 3) "Ready to ride and spread the alarm"

   The plot is most important because his ride is dramatic and signals the start of a war.

   Difficulty: *Average* **Objective:** *Literary Analysis*

8. She made people think about a moral question they had been ignoring.

   Difficulty: *Average* **Objective:** *Reading*

9. The speaker expresses admiration for Harriet Beacher Stowe, calling her a "fearless woman" and a "prophet and priestess."

   Difficulty: *Average* **Objective:** *Literary Analysis*

10. They are African Americans and white Americans, and they were changed by the ending of slavery and the Civil War.

    Difficulty: *Challenging* **Objective:** *Interpretation*

Essay

11. Students should explain that "Paul Revere's Ride" is a narrative poem because it has a setting, a conflict, characters, and a plot. Students should point out that the events in the poem take place in New England one night at the start of the American Revolution. They should identify Paul Revere as the main character and explain that the war is the conflict. They should explain why Revere took his famous ride and summarize the events.

    Difficulty: *Easy* **Objective:** *Essay*

12. Students' essays should note that a lyric poem is one in which the speaker expresses his or her thoughts and feelings and creates a unified impression of a subject. They should then use examples from the poems to prove that either "The New Colossus" or "Harriet Beecher Stowe" is a lyric poem.

    Difficulty: *Average* **Objective:** *Essay*

13. Students who discuss the Statue of Liberty should recognize the statue as a symbol of freedom as well as a welcome to newcomers to America. Those who discuss Revere should point out that his courage in warning fellow colonists of the approaching British troops helped get the American Revolution off to a successful start. Those who discuss Stowe should recognize that her book *Uncle Tom's Cabin* helped sway public opinion against slavery at the time of the Civil War. Students should cite specific details from the poems to support their ideas.

    Difficulty: *Challenging* **Objective:** *Essay*

14. Students who choose "The New Colossus" should point out that the poet states the idea that America is a place of freedom to immigrants. Those who choose "Paul Revere's Ride" should note that the poet is using Revere's ride to illustrate the role of ordinary people in America's freedom. Those who choose "Harriet Beecher Stowe" should point out that the poet is saying that a writer was responsible for turning people's sympathies to the cause of freedom for the enslaved. Students should use examples from the poem they choose to support their response.

    Difficulty: *Average* **Objective:** *Essay*

Oral Response

15. Oral responses should be clear, well organized, and well supported by appropriate examples from the selections.

    Difficulty: *Average* **Objective:** *Oral Interpretation*

Selection Test A, p. 160

Critical Reading

1. ANS: B	**DIF:** Easy	**OBJ:** Comprehension
2. ANS: A	**DIF:** Easy	**OBJ:** Reading
3. ANS: B	**DIF:** Easy	**OBJ:** Interpretation
4. ANS: D	**DIF:** Easy	**OBJ:** Literary Analysis
5. ANS: C	**DIF:** Easy	**OBJ:** Interpretation
6. ANS: B	**DIF:** Easy	**OBJ:** Reading
7. ANS: B	**DIF:** Easy	**OBJ:** Comprehension
8. ANS: A	**DIF:** Easy	**OBJ:** Literary Analysis
9. ANS: A	**DIF:** Easy	**OBJ:** Literary Analysis
10. ANS: D	**DIF:** Easy	**OBJ:** Comprehension

11. **ANS:** B	**DIF:** Easy	**OBJ:** Interpretation
12. **ANS:** C	**DIF:** Easy	**OBJ:** Reading

Vocabulary and Grammar

13. **ANS:** A	**DIF:** Easy	**OBJ:** Vocabulary
14. **ANS:** A	**DIF:** Easy	**OBJ:** Vocabulary
15. **ANS:** B	**DIF:** Easy	**OBJ:** Grammar

Essay

16. Students should explain that "Paul Revere's Ride" takes place in New England one night at the start of the American Revolution. They should identify Paul Revere as the main character. They should explain the reason Revere makes his famous ride and sum up the route he took.
Difficulty: *Easy*
Objective: *Essay*

17. Students who discuss Revere should recognize that Revere's courage in warning his fellow colonists of the approaching British troops helped get the American Revolution off to a successful start. Those who discuss Stowe should recognize that her book *Uncle Tom's Cabin* helped sway public sympathy against slavery at the time of the Civil War. Students should cite specific details from the poems to support their ideas about the figure they discuss.
Difficulty: *Easy*
Objective: *Essay*

18. Students who choose "The New Colossus" might point out that the poet states the idea that America is a place of freedom for immigrants. Those who choose "Paul Revere's Ride" might note that the poet is using Revere's ride to illustrate the role of ordinary people in battling for America's freedom. Those who choose "Harriet Beecher Stowe" might point out that the poet is saying that a writer was able to create sympathy for the idea of freeing the slaves. Students should use examples from the poem they choose to support their response.
Difficulty: *Average*
Objective: *Essay*

Selection Test B, p. 163

Critical Reading

1. **ANS:** D	**DIF:** Average	**OBJ:** Interpretation
2. **ANS:** C	**DIF:** Average	**OBJ:** Comprehension
3. **ANS:** A	**DIF:** Challenging	**OBJ:** Reading
4. **ANS:** A	**DIF:** Average	**OBJ:** Literary Analysis
5. **ANS:** B	**DIF:** Challenging	**OBJ:** Reading
6. **ANS:** A	**DIF:** Average	**OBJ:** Interpretation
7. **ANS:** C	**DIF:** Challenging	**OBJ:** Comprehension
8. **ANS:** A	**DIF:** Average	**OBJ:** Literary Analysis
9. **ANS:** D	**DIF:** Challenging	**OBJ:** Literary Analysis
10. **ANS:** A	**DIF:** Average	**OBJ:** Literary Analysis
11. **ANS:** D	**DIF:** Average	**OBJ:** Comprehension
12. **ANS:** D	**DIF:** Average	**OBJ:** Reading
13. **ANS:** C	**DIF:** Average	**OBJ:** Literary Analysis

Vocabulary and Grammar

14. **ANS:** C	**DIF:** Average	**OBJ:** Vocabulary
15. **ANS:** B	**DIF:** Average	**OBJ:** Grammar
16. **ANS:** A	**DIF:** Average	**OBJ:** Vocabulary
17. **ANS:** D	**DIF:** Average	**OBJ:** Grammar

Essay

18. Students' essays should recognize that a lyric poem is one in which the speaker expresses his or her thoughts and feelings. They should then prove that either "The New Colossus" or "Harriet Beecher Stowe" is a lyric poem by citing examples of thoughts and feelings expressed by the poem's speaker.
Difficulty: *Average*
Objective: *Essay*

19. Students who discuss Revere should recognize that his courage in warning his fellow colonists of the approaching British troops helped get the American Revolution off to a successful start. Those who discuss Stowe should recognize that her book *Uncle Tom's Cabin* helped sway public sympathy against slavery at the time of the Civil War. Those who discuss the Statue of Liberty should recognize the statue as a symbol of liberty as well as a welcome for newcomers to America's shores. Students should cite specific details from the poems to support their ideas about the two figures they discuss.
Difficulty: *Challenging*
Objective: *Essay*

20. Students who choose "The New Colossus" should point out that the poet states the idea that America is a place of freedom to immigrants. Those who choose "Paul Revere's Ride" should note that the poet is using Revere's ride to illustrate the role of ordinary people in America's freedom. Those who choose "Harriet Beecher Stowe" should point out that the poet is saying that a writer was responsible for turning people's sympathies to the cause of freedom for the enslaved. Students should use examples from the poem they choose to support their response.
Difficulty: *Average*
Objective: *Essay*

Poetry Collection: John Updike, N. Scott Momaday, Alice Walker

Vocabulary Warm-up Exercises, p. 167

A.
1. continent
2. swarm
3. shimmer
4. dusk

5. withdraw
6. planes

B. Sample Answers

1. I would not use a *radiator* in a place that averaged ninety-degree temperatures because I would certainly not need to heat a room.
2. I think that a person might *stiffen* when feeling very afraid.
3. Athletes might wear *parkas* when snow skiing or doing any other sports outside in cold weather.
4. I would only use the word *behold* when I wanted to point out something very special.
5. I can recognize the *accents* of people from Boston, South Carolina, Brooklyn, and Minnesota.
6. Since *cedars* have sweet-smelling wood, it would be good for clothes chests because it would scent the stored clothes.

Reading Warm-up A, p. 168

Sample Answers

1. American; The names of each *continent* are as follows: Africa, Antarctica, Asia, Australia, Europe, North America, South America. (*Note:* some geographers call Europe and Asia, which are joined, Eurasia.)
2. (flashy jewelry); *Shimmer* means "to shine softly with a light that seems to shake."
3. good-looking; Cheekbones can look like *planes* because they can appear to be like flat surfaces.
4. (bees); I saw a *swarm* of people at the opening of last year's biggest movie.
5. as they aged; I had to *withdraw* from the library because I was laughing uncontrollably.
6. (on any summer day); *Dusk* is the beginning of nighttime, so people are usually home from work, young children are inside, and listening to music is relaxing in the evening.

Reading Warm-up B, p. 169

Sample Answers

1. historical places; *Behold* means "to look at or observe."
2. (frozen); A person who would *stiffen* would stop moving or move as if it were very difficult to take a step.
3. in the woods behind our house; *Cedars* are tall evergreens with needles and red-colored wood.
4. (snowshoes); They would wear *parkas*, which are thick, warm coats with hoods, so that they would stay warm in the cold, winter weather.
5. heated the room; I like to put my hands on the *radiator* to warm them.
6. (Bostonians); I have heard these three *accents:* German, Texan, and Brooklyn.

Writing About the Big Question, p. 170

A. 1. sensory
2. meaningful
3. connection

B. Sample Answers

1. By observing nature, I can understand the significance of my existence in relation to the rest of the world. Observation increases my awareness and allows me to form a connection with things outside me.
2. Last summer I had a meaningful encounter at the lake. In the heat of the afternoon, I experienced the beginning of a true friendship.

C. Sample Answer

Poetry written about nature helps us discover parts of the environment we overlook in our everyday lives.

Reading: Read According to Punctuation to Paraphrase, p. 171

Lines 3–5: The earth shines with leaves.

Lines 6–8: The sky shines with rain.

Lines 9–15: Winds that moan as they blow on the mountains carry pollen in the air.

Lines 16–19: Cedars blacken the slopes, as do pines.

Lines 20–28: At dawn, eagles fly above the flat land where light gathers in patches.

Lines 29–31: Grasses shine with a waving light.

Lines 32–36: Shadows shrink and move away like smoke.

Literary Analysis: Imagery, p. 172

Sample imagery for "January": Sight—sun a spark hung thin between the dark and dark; fat snowy footsteps tracked on the floor; parkas piled up near the door; still, frozen river beneath the trees' black lace; low sky; gray air; radiator; *Sound*—radiator purring all day; *Touch*—fat footsteps tracked on the floor; frozen river held still; *Smell*—none; *Taste*—none

Sample imagery for "New World": Sight—earth glitters with leaves; sky glistens with rain; cedars blacken the slope; light gathers in pools; grasses shimmer and shine; *Sound*—winds that low; *Touch*—Pollen is borne on winds; winds that lean upon mountains; eagles hie and hover; shadows withdraw and lie away like smoke; *Smell*—shadows lie away like smoke; *Taste*—none

Sample imagery for "For My Sister Molly . . .": Sight—fairy rooster. . . ; on nights the fire was burning low; as bright [as flowers]; *Sound*—And coached me in my songs of Africa; spoke in accents never heard; *Touch*—a fairy rooster from Mashed potatoes; when the sun was hot; the children's questions . . . Pouring; braided Hair; Frowned on wasp bites; *Smell*—And smelled as good as [flowers]; *Taste*—a fairy rooster from Mashed potatoes; green onions were his tail; waking up the story buds Like fruit

Vocabulary Builder, p. 173

A. 1. T; 2. F; 3. F; 4. T; 5. T; 6. T

Sample Answers

1. Recede means to go back; like the wave going back to the sea.

2. A remote land would be distant; not close by.
3. A wearisome task is long and difficult.
4. Pollen is used by flowers to reproduce.
5. An extinguished fire has been put out; and is no longer a threat.
6. An inexpressible emotion is difficult to put into words.

B. Sample Answers

1. The line goes forward quickly.
2. The person will likely get a raise or praise because she has gone past expectations.

C. 1. C; 2. A; 3. C; 4. B

Enrichment: The Pulitzer Prize, p. 174

1. Since he left money to make a positive impact, he must have felt grateful, proud, and patriotic.
2. He probably thought journalism was important and wanted to do something for the field in which he worked most of his life.
3. Winning a Pulitzer Prize would get a writer more attention and respect, which in turn would help sell his or her books.
4. No, Pulitzer Prizes are for American journalism, arts, and letters.

Open-Book Test, p. 175

Short Answer

1. Snow from people's boots is on the floor, and warm jackets form a heap near the door.

   Difficulty: *Easy* **Objective:** *Reading*
2. The "trees' black lace" is the shadow of the bare branches of the trees, which cross over one another to form a design. The branches must be bare since it is winter. The poet is probably talking about shadows, because he says the river is "Held still beneath" this black lace.

   Difficulty: *Challenging* **Objective:** *Literary Analysis*
3. From inside a house; he mentions the footprints on the floor and the sound of the radiator.

   Difficulty: *Challenging* **Objective:** *Interpretation*
4. Sample answer: The water in a lake under sunshine glistens when it sparkles in the sun.

   Difficulty: *Average* **Objective:** *Vocabulary*
5. Flower powder is carried on winds that moan and press on the mountains.

   Difficulty: *Average* **Objective:** *Reading*
6. The imagery appeals to sight (the turtles can be seen moving slowly) and to touch (the loam is described as warm).

   Difficulty: *Easy* **Objective:** *Literary Analysis*
7. He follows the progression of time, starting with "First Man" and moving through dawn, noon, and dusk. This progression creates a sense of a completed cycle.

   Difficulty: *Challenging* **Objective:** *Interpretation*
8. Sample answer:

   (col 2, row 2) purring radiator

   (col 2, row 3) sound

   (col 3, row 2) shimmering grasses

   (col 3, row 3) sight

   (col 4, row 2) bright and blinding light

   (col 4, row 3) sight

   Describing the sister as a bright light is very powerful since it is such a personal image with strong feeling behind it.

   Difficulty: *Average* **Objective:** *Literary Analysis*
9. She loves and admires her sister. She describes all the nice things Molly did (reading to her and sending her money) and the courage with which she "went exploring."

   Difficulty: *Easy* **Objective:** *Interpretation*
10. She teaches her about literature, creativity, and their heritage. The speaker describes what Molly read to her, the stories about Africa she told, and the creative tales she made up.

    Difficulty: *Average* **Objective:** *Interpretation*

Essay

11. Students should recognize that Updike's description features cold temperatures, short days, and snow. Those who live in warmer areas might find their January has less in common with Updike's than those who live in colder places. Students should include details that compare and contrast with Updike's images.

    Difficulty: *Easy* **Objective:** *Essay*
12. Students should note that the images in "New World" change from the first stanza through the last by starting out very bright and becoming darker as the day goes on. The images are also softer in the beginning and become harsher by the end.

    Difficulty: *Average* **Objective:** *Essay*
13. Students who choose "January" should explain how particular images help convey the speaker's appreciation of the beauty of winter and the cozy warmth inside. Those who choose "New World" should explain how particular images help convey the speaker's admiration for the landscape. Those who choose "For My Sister Molly . . ." should explain how particular images help convey the gratitude and admiration that the speaker feels for Molly.

    Difficulty: *Challenging* **Objective:** *Essay*
14. Students who choose the cozy, warm world of "January" may cite the radiator that "Purrs all day." Those who choose the awe-inspiring "New World" may refer to "the plain/where light/gathers/in pools." Those who choose the family-centered, realistic world of "For My Sister Molly . . ." might refer to Molly's "love burning/ Inexpressible."

    Difficulty: *Average* **Objective:** *Essay*

Oral Response

15. Oral responses should be clear, well organized, and well supported by appropriate examples from the selections.
    Difficulty: *Average* **Objective:** *Oral Presentation*

Selection Test A, p. 178

Critical Reading

1. ANS: A	DIF: Easy	OBJ: Comprehension
2. ANS: A	DIF: Easy	OBJ: Literary Analysis
3. ANS: C	DIF: Easy	OBJ: Reading
4. ANS: C	DIF: Easy	OBJ: Interpretation
5. ANS: B	DIF: Easy	OBJ: Comprehension
6. ANS: A	DIF: Easy	OBJ: Reading
7. ANS: B	DIF: Easy	OBJ: Literary Analysis
8. ANS: D	DIF: Easy	OBJ: Reading
9. ANS: C	DIF: Easy	OBJ: Interpretation
10. ANS: A	DIF: Easy	OBJ: Literary Analysis

Vocabulary and Grammar

11. ANS: C	DIF: Easy	OBJ: Vocabulary
12. ANS: D	DIF: Easy	OBJ: Vocabulary
13. ANS: B	DIF: Easy	OBJ: Grammar

Essay

14. Students will probably write a sentence or separate paragraph for each stanza of the poem they choose—for "New World," four sentences or paragraphs; for "For My Sister Molly Who . . . ," three. They should restate the basic content of the poem using simpler language and sentence structures. They should add words to elliptical structures and clarify figurative language—for example, adding *She* before "Knew all the written things" and restating "waking up the story buds" as something such as "interesting us in stories." They should also eliminate repetition, such as the repetition of *moon* in the final sentence of "New World."
    Difficulty: *Easy*
    Objective: *Essay*
15. Students should recognize that Updike's description features not only cold temperatures but also short days and a cessation of the growing season. Those who live in more northerly climate zones are likely to find more in common with Updike's description, but even those in warmer, more southerly areas should recognize that days are shorter in winter.
    Difficulty: *Easy*
    Objective: *Essay*
16. Students who choose the cozy, warm world of "January" may cite the radiator that "Purrs all day." Those who choose "New World" may refer to "the plain/where light/gathers/in pools." Those who choose the family-centered, realistic world of "For My Sister Molly . . ." might refer to Molly's "love burning/Inexpressible."
    Difficulty: *Average*
    Objective: *Essay*

Selection Test B, p. 181

Critical Reading

1. ANS: A	DIF: Average	OBJ: Comprehension
2. ANS: D	DIF: Average	OBJ: Interpretation
3. ANS: A	DIF: Challenging	OBJ: Literary Analysis
4. ANS: C	DIF: Average	OBJ: Literary Analysis
5. ANS: B	DIF: Average	OBJ: Reading
6. ANS: B	DIF: Average	OBJ: Interpretation
7. ANS: D	DIF: Average	OBJ: Comprehension
8. ANS: C	DIF: Average	OBJ: Literary Analysis
9. ANS: D	DIF: Average	OBJ: Reading
10. ANS: B	DIF: Average	OBJ: Interpretation
11. ANS: A	DIF: Average	OBJ: Reading
12. ANS: D	DIF: Average	OBJ: Interpretation
13. ANS: D	DIF: Challenging	OBJ: Reading

Vocabulary and Grammar

14. ANS: A	DIF: Average	OBJ: Vocabulary
15. ANS: C	DIF: Average	OBJ: Vocabulary
16. ANS: B	DIF: Average	OBJ: Grammar
17. ANS: D	DIF: Average	OBJ: Grammar

Essay

18. Students should recognize that Molly is a creative, kind, and entertaining older sister with a strong interest in literature and culture. They should cite details to support their conclusions, such as Molly's making the fairy rooster, Molly's never refusing to answer the speaker's many questions, Molly's knowing Hamlet well and loving to read "Sam McGee from Tennessee," and Molly's telling stories.
    Difficulty: *Average*
    Objective: *Essay*
19. Students who choose "January" should explain how particular images help convey the speaker's appreciation of the cold winter beauty and the cozy warmth inside. Those who choose "New World" should explain how particular images help convey the speaker's admiration for the lush landscape. Those who choose "For My Sister Molly . . ." should explain how particular images help convey the gratitude and admiration that the speaker feels for Molly.
    Difficulty: *Average*
    Objective: *Essay*
20. Students who choose the cozy, warm world of "January" may cite the radiator that "Purrs all day." Those who choose the awe-inspiring "New World" may refer to "the plain/where light/gathers/in pools." Those who choose the family-centered, realistic world of

"For My Sister Molly . . ." might refer to Molly's "love burning/Inexpressible."

Difficulty: *Average*

Objective: *Essay*

Poetry Collection: Amy Ling, Wendy Rose, E. E. Cummings

Vocabulary Warm-up Exercises, p. 185

A.
1. century
2. eldest
3. delicious
4. image
5. perch
6. twinkling

B. Sample Answers
1. F. A *woodpecker* will live only in areas with trees, since that is how it gets its food.
2. T. Because most people are at work or school on weekday mornings, you aren't as likely to experience *jostling* then.
3. F. *Slippered* feet are not appropriate for a hike, or even the outdoors, because feet in slippers would be wearing soft, light shoes instead of sturdy, hard-soled shoes.
4. F. Mother Nature does give us *exquisite* gifts, but earthquakes are not among them because they are disastrous, not enjoyable and delightful.
5. T. Since these things can all be bluish-green, you could use *aqua* to describe them.
6. T. A *humorous* line would be a funny line, which could make you laugh aloud.

Reading Warm-up A, p. 186

Sample Answers
1. to be so admired just for doing what a giant sea turtle does best; What is *delicious* to me is a long, hot shower.
2. (size); An *image* is a representation of something; in this case, it's what the people see when they look at the turtle.
3. flying; A good place for a bird to *perch* would be on a limb that is high off the ground.
4. (more than eighty years); The *eldest* member of our family is my ninety-year-old grandmother, who is still very active in her retirement home.
5. fireworks; I have seen the lights of airplanes that have been *twinkling* in the dark sky.
6. (year); The turtle saw the beginning of the twenty-first *century* (the year 2000).

Reading Warm-up B, p. 187

Sample Answers
1. smile; The most *exquisite* nonverbal communication I have seen was a father hugging his baby with a lot of tenderness.
2. (serious); I heard a very *humorous* opening act during a late-night television show last weekend.
3. ocean; *Aqua* means "bluish-green in color."
4. (mimes try to avoid creating any sounds); My *slippered* feet are covered in thick, black socks with fur trim.
5. (a scene); Since *jostling* involves pushing and shoving, you can imagine that people might be speaking angrily. Also, you could hear things like backpacks and purses bumping around.
6. watching a mime perform; The work of a *woodpecker* is noisily drilling holes into trees with its beak to get its food (insects).

Writing About the Big Question, p. 188

A.
1. benefit
2. significance
3. relevant

B. Sample Answers
1. The school recently informed students that extra-curricular activities were to be cut. I think the benefit of sports and other clubs should be appreciated and funded.
2. In "your little voice," Cummings writes about the excitement of receiving a phone call from a girl the speaker loves. I know how excited I am to make a connection over the phone or in person with someone I care about. He captures the feeling in the poem.

C. Sample Answer

Stimulating the senses can stir up memories of childhood.

Reading: Read According to Punctuation to Paraphrase, p. 189

Lines 3–4: I suddenly felt dizzy.

Lines 5–10: Colorful flowers were moving before my eyes or twinkling as they moved toward my side and seemed like pushy but gorgeous faces looking up at me.

Line 11: They seemed like floating hands touching me.

Lines 12–17: The experience made me feel as if I were dancing and seemed to send me up to the sky with the stars and the moon.

Lines 18–19: Dear girl, how crazy I felt when I heard you.

Lines 19–24: How I cried when I heard your sweet voice on the phone, seeming to overcome the laws of time and nature.

Literary Analysis: Imagery, p. 190

Sample imagery for "Grandma Ling": Sight—deep hole; aqua paper-covered door; *Sound*—I heard her slippered foot softly measure the tatami floor with even step; *Touch*—not strong enough to dig that hole; stretched her arms; I could hug her; *Smell*—none; *Taste*—none

Sample imagery for "Drum Song": Sight—flat round feet of four claws each; red head; a line of mountains with blankets on their hips; *Sound*—a shake of gourds; *Touch*—go slow, so steady; lift your red head; a shake of gourds; *Smell*—none; *Taste*—none

Sample imagery for "your little voice": Sight—wee skipping high-heeled flames; twinkling; pale important stars; *Sound*—little voice over the wires came leaping; shouting of merry flowers; *Touch*—jostling of merry flowers; floating hands were laid upon me; whirled and tossed; delicious dancing; *Smell*—none; *Taste*—delicious dancing

Vocabulary Builder, p. 191

A. 1. T; 2. F; 3. F; 4. T; 5. T

1. A burrow is a home underground.
2. If you speak impertinently; you are being rude.
3. A jostling ride is bouncy and uncomfortable.
4. To hold your tongue means to restrain yourself from speaking.
5. An exquisite diamond is precious and is pricey.

B. Sample Answers

1. He would suffer from dizziness because he perceives things turning.
2. Vertebrae function as joints that allow us to bend and turn.

C. 1. B; 2. A; 3. C

Enrichment: The Telegraph and the Telephone, p. 192

A. 1. It allowed communications over great distances in a short time.

2. It lets the communicating parties hear each other in real time; it also lets many people use the wires at the same time.
3. Some people probably were delighted by them.
4. the speaker's excitement on hearing a beloved on the phone

B. Answers will vary.

Poetry Collections: John Updike, N. Scott Momaday, Alice Walker; Amy Ling, Wendy Rose, E. E. Cummings

Integrated Language Skills: Grammar, p. 193

Infinitives and Infinitive Phrases

A. 1. to read poetry aloud; noun, serves as direct object (of *like*).

2. to recite poetry with a strong rhythm; adverb, modifies *easiest*
3. to do a poetry reading; adjective, modifies *assignment*
4. to set the poem to music; noun, serves as subject
5. to rehearse twice; adverb, modifies *able*

B. Sample Answers

1. I really want to get more exercise.
2. It is fun to go for long walks in good weather.
3. My cousin gave me tips to improve my stamina.

Open-Book Test, p. 196

Short Answer

1. The words "slippered feet softly measure" and "even step" create an image that gives a feeling of comfort and peacefulness.
   Difficulty: *Average* **Objective:** *Literary Analysis*
2. I saw someone who looked like me but was fifty years older.
   Difficulty: *Challenging* **Objective:** *Reading*
3. She feels warmly toward her grandmother; she gives her a hug.
   Difficulty: *Easy* **Objective:** *Interpretation*
4. Word such as "flat round feet" and "rock to water" appeal to the sense of sight.
   Difficulty: *Easy* **Objective:** *Literary Analysis*
5. Sample answer: A fox, a groundhog, or a badger might have a burrow, because they all live in underground holes.
   Difficulty: *Average* **Objective:** *Vocabulary*
6. Details such as "you lift your red head" and "your whiskers dance" show that the speaker has closely observed the animals in the wild. She knows a lot about their behavior and appearance and seems to share a close relationship with them.
   Difficulty: *Average* **Objective:** *Interpretation*
7. The first three stanzas are about animals, and the last is about humans (women). By including women with the animals and addressing them in the same way (for example, "your belly drags" for the snowhare and "your tongues melt" for women), the writer implies that human beings are part of nature.
   Difficulty: *Challenging* **Objective:** *Interpretation*
8. Your small, soft voice came over the phone.
   Difficulty: *Average* **Objective:** *Reading*
9. (col 2, row 2) checkmark
   (col 2, row 3) checkmark
   (col 3, row 2) blank
   (col 3, row 3) checkmark
   (col 4, row 2) checkmark
   (col 4, row 3) blank
   Sample answer: The first example creates a joyful feeling.
   Difficulty: *Average* **Objective:** *Literary Analysis*
10. He feels very loving toward the person. Her voice makes him dizzy, and he thinks of flowers and cries.
    Difficulty: *Challenging* **Objective:** *Interpretation*

Essay

11. Students who discuss "Grandma Ling" should recognize that the speaker loves her grandmother and feels connected to her, even without language. Those who discuss "your little voice" should recognize that the

speaker is probably addressing a loved one and is amazed and delighted by the telephone's ability to carry the voice over the wires.

Difficulty: *Easy* **Objective:** *Essay*

12. Students should recognize the positive view of nature presented in the poem and the central idea that all animals, including human beings, are part of nature and follow nature's rhythms. They should cite details that show the actions of the animals and then point out the similarities of human beings in the final stanza.

Difficulty: *Average* **Objective:** *Essay*

13. Regardless of their choice of poem, students should recognize that the poem uses strong images, and should cite examples. They should point out that the poem uses images to convey the speaker's positive attitude toward the subject. "Grandma Ling" presents the speaker's feelings more directly, while "your little voice" requires more interpretation from the reader.

Difficulty: *Challenging* **Objective:** *Essay*

14. Students should explain why the poem they choose has the greatest effect on them and should point out words from the poem that make the woman or women seem interesting. Students who choose "Grandma Ling" may cite "her slippered feet." Those who choose "Drum Song" may refer to the women's tongues melting or to the "blankets/on their/hips." Those who choose "your little voice" may cite "leaping/Sweetly/your voice."

Difficulty: *Average* **Objective:** *Essay*

Oral Response

15. Oral responses should be clear, well organized, and well supported by appropriate examples from the selections.

Difficulty: *Average* **Objective:** *Oral Interpretation*

Poetry Collection: Amy Ling, Wendy Rose, E. E. Cummings

Selection Test A, p. 199

Critical Reading

1. **ANS:** B	**DIF:** Easy	**OBJ:** Comprehension
2. **ANS:** C	**DIF:** Easy	**OBJ:** Interpretation
3. **ANS:** A	**DIF:** Easy	**OBJ:** Literary Analysis
4. **ANS:** A	**DIF:** Easy	**OBJ:** Reading
5. **ANS:** D	**DIF:** Easy	**OBJ:** Comprehension
6. **ANS:** D	**DIF:** Easy	**OBJ:** Literary Analysis
7. **ANS:** B	**DIF:** Easy	**OBJ:** Reading
8. **ANS:** A	**DIF:** Easy	**OBJ:** Interpretation
9. **ANS:** D	**DIF:** Easy	**OBJ:** Comprehension
10. **ANS:** B	**DIF:** Easy	**OBJ:** Interpretation
11. **ANS:** A	**DIF:** Easy	**OBJ:** Reading
12. **ANS:** B	**DIF:** Easy	**OBJ:** Literary Analysis

Vocabulary and Grammar

13. **ANS:** A	**DIF:** Easy	**OBJ:** Vocabulary
14. **ANS:** C	**DIF:** Easy	**OBJ:** Vocabulary
15. **ANS:** D	**DIF:** Easy	**OBJ:** Grammar

Essay

16. Students will probably write four sentences or short paragraphs, one for each stanza of the poem. They should restate the basic content of each stanza, using simpler language and sentence structures—for example, using "tree" for "vertical earth / of tree bark and / branch." They should add words that are implied but not stated, such as "your whiskers dance *from the* bush to *the* burrow."

Difficulty: *Easy*

Objective: *Essay*

17. Students who discuss "Grandma Ling" should recognize that the speaker loves her grandmother and feels connected to her even though they cannot use language to communicate. Those who discuss "your little voice" should recognize that the speaker is probably addressing a beloved and is amazed and delighted by the telephone's ability to carry the voice over the wires.

Difficulty: *Easy*

Objective: *Essay*

18. Students should explain why the poem they choose has the greatest effect on them and should point out words from the poem that make the woman or women seem interesting. Students who choose "Grandma Ling" may cite "her slippered feet." Those who choose "Drum Song" may refer to the women's tongues melting or to the "blankets/on their/hips." Those who choose "your little voice" may cite "leaping/Sweetly/your voice."

Difficulty: *Average*

Objective: *Essay*

Selection Test B, p. 202

Critical Reading

1. **ANS:** B	**DIF:** Average	**OBJ:** Comprehension
2. **ANS:** C	**DIF:** Average	**OBJ:** Reading
3. **ANS:** D	**DIF:** Average	**OBJ:** Interpretation
4. **ANS:** B	**DIF:** Challenging	**OBJ:** Literary Analysis
5. **ANS:** A	**DIF:** Challenging	**OBJ:** Literary Analysis
6. **ANS:** A	**DIF:** Average	**OBJ:** Interpretation
7. **ANS:** C	**DIF:** Average	**OBJ:** Reading
8. **ANS:** D	**DIF:** Challenging	**OBJ:** Literary Analysis
9. **ANS:** A	**DIF:** Average	**OBJ:** Interpretation
10. **ANS:** B	**DIF:** Average	**OBJ:** Interpretation
11. **ANS:** D	**DIF:** Challenging	**OBJ:** Literary Analysis
12. **ANS:** D	**DIF:** Average	**OBJ:** Literary Analysis
13. **ANS:** B	**DIF:** Average	**OBJ:** Reading

Vocabulary and Grammar

14. ANS: B	DIF: Average	OBJ: Vocabulary
15. ANS: A	DIF: Average	OBJ: Vocabulary
16. ANS: A	DIF: Average	OBJ: Grammar
17. ANS: D	DIF: Average	OBJ: Grammar

Essay

18. Students should recognize the positive view of nature presented in the poem and the central idea that all animals, including human beings, are part of nature and follow nature's rhythm in order to survive and prosper. They should cite details from the first three stanzas that show the actions of the turtle, the woodpecker, and the snowhare, respectively, and should then point out the similarity of human beings implied by making the final stanza parallel to the other three.

    Difficulty: *Average*

    Objective: *Essay*

19. Students should note that both poems use strong images and should cite examples. They should recognize that both poems use images to convey a positive attitude toward their subject—Grandma Ling in one case, the person addressed and the telephone in the other. "Grandma Ling" is more direct in conveying its speaker's emotions and attitude, while "your little voice" relies on images that require more interpretation by the reader.

    Difficulty: *Challenging*

    Objective: *Essay*

20. Students should explain why the poem they choose has the greatest effect on them and should point out words from the poem that make the woman or women seem interesting. Students who choose "Grandma Ling" may cite "her slippered feet." Those who choose "Drum Song" may refer to the women's tongues melting or to the "blankets/on their/hips." Those who choose "your little voice" may cite "leaping/Sweetly/your voice."

    Difficulty: *Average*

    Objective: *Essay*

"The Road Not Taken" by Robert Frost
"O Captain! My Captain" by Walt Whitman

Vocabulary Warm-up Exercises, p. 206

A.
1. flung
2. grim
3. fearful
4. trodden
5. swaying
6. victor

B. Sample Answers

1. T. People often send bunches of flowers, or *bouquets*, to loved ones.
2. T. If a bird *trills* loudly enough, it could wake you if were asleep at five in the morning.
3. F. A desert has no trees, so there can be no *undergrowth*, or bushes and plants growing underneath them.
4. F. *Mournful* music would make you sad or sadder.
5. T. If your eleven o'clock curfew starts today, *hence* you should be home before eleven.
6. F. Both children have a *claim* on your attention.

Reading Warm-up A, p. 207

Sample Answers

1. (harsh, gloomy); After the hurricane, the scenes of the beach looked *grim*.
2. The snow had been coming down for hours, and now the winds had reached blizzard speed.; Last summer, we escaped a *fearful* tornado when we were visiting family in Iowa.
3. (wrapped); A glass bowl that was *flung* would break into pieces.
4. (walked); Doreen walked along the shoulder of the road through snow that no one else had *trampled*.
5. (the wind); The little girl laughed as she sat on the *swaying* swing.
6. saved the most travelers stranded in the blizzard; I was a *victor* last season when our softball team won all our games.

Reading Warm-up B, p. 208

Sample Answers

1. (the country, death); My friends and softball practice both have a *claim* on my afternoons.
2. death, funeral; An event where crowds would be joyous or happy—the opposite of *mournful*—is a Fourth of July parade.
3. (beneath towering trees); Some things you might find in the *undergrowth* are shrubs, reeds, flowers, weeds, and grass.
4. spring flowers; People might bring *bouquets* to someone's house when they are invited to dinner.
5. (bugle, notes, tune); A bird *trills* when it sings its song.
6. (time); However, it would be a long time *from this point* before that healing would begin.

Writing About the Big Question, p. 209

A.
1. connection
2. significance
3. meaningful

B. Sample Answers

1. I have used information and personal experience to inform my choices. I understand that some situations have more than one valid response.
2. My grandmother has reached me with her meaningful stories of life in a war-torn country. Her cultural background benefits me by giving me knowledge and appreciation for the life I have.

C. Sample Answer

Choosing words carefully when we write helps us to distinguish our individual experience and clarify events in our mind.

Literary Analysis: Comparing Types of Description, p. 210

Sample Answers

2. grassy and wanted wear = the less popular route through life
3. Captain = Lincoln; trip = Civil War; ship = United States; rack = hard times; prize = peace and union
4. My Captain . . . my father—Lincoln; does not answer; no pulse = death

Vocabulary Builder, p. 211

A. Sample Answers

1. synonym—divided; antonym—converged; sentence—The road I was traveling on diverged and I was not sure which way to go.
2. synonym—rejoicing; antonym—mourning; sentence—Exulting over my *A* on the final exam, I reminded myself how smart it was of me to study hard.

B. 1. B; 2. C

Open-Book Test, p. 213

Short Answer

1. If the roads had not branched off, he would not have had to make a choice, so every choice and action based on that choice would have been different.
   Difficulty: *Average* **Objective:** *Vocabulary*
2. He means he wishes he could go down both roads at the same time, but he can't because he is only one man.
   Difficulty: *Easy* **Objective:** *Interpretation*
3. Neither road had been walked on yet that morning.
   Difficulty: *Average* **Objective:** *Interpretation*
4. They represent the important decisions made in life—they diverge, and the one chosen makes all the difference.
   Difficulty: *Easy* **Objective:** *Literary Analysis*
5. Sample answer: He may be regretful—he says he may one day tell the story "with a sigh." On the other hand, the line "and that has made all the difference" might imply that the speaker is pleased with his choice.
   Difficulty: *Challenging* **Objective:** *Interpretation*
6. The Captain is compared with President Lincoln. The poem refers to his leading the nation through the Civil War and to his assassination.
   Difficulty: *Challenging* **Objective:** *Literary Analysis*
7. It represents the Civil War, a journey the U.S. took that was fearful and destructive.
   Difficulty: *Average* **Objective:** *Literary Analysis*
8. The Union has survived great difficulties and won the Civil War.
   Difficulty: *Challenging* **Objective:** *Interpretation*
9. The ship is the United States; it sails through the Civil War and lands "safe and sound."
   Difficulty: *Average* **Objective:** *Literary Analysis*
10. (col 2, row 2) I chose a road in the woods.
    (col 2, row 3) I chose a path in life.
    (col 3, row 2) The ship's journey is done, but the captain is dead.
    (col 3, row 3) The Civil War is over, but the president is dead.
    If you didn't understand the figurative meaning, the poems would just be about a walk in the woods and a ship.
    Difficulty: *Average* **Objective:** *Literary Analysis*

Essay

11. Students should note that literal meaning is the actual meaning of words. They should explain the literal meanings of "The Road Not Taken" and "O Captain! My Captain!" In the first, a person reflects on the road he took, choosing to take the one less traveled. In the second, a ship's captain dies after he brings the ship safely back from the dangerous journey.
    Difficulty: *Easy* **Objective:** *Essay*
12. Students should note that the speaker in "The Road Not Taken" tells of a decision represented by two roads dividing in the woods. They may say that the speaker feels curiosity or regret about the path he did not choose. The speaker in "O Captain! My Captain!" compares Lincoln to the captain of a ship, seeing Lincoln as a great leader who preserved the Union.
    Difficulty: *Average* **Objective:** *Essay*
13. Students should describe Frost's analogy, in which he uses choosing between two roads to represent making life choices. They should describe Whitman's analogy, in which he uses a ship and its captain to represent America during the Civil War and President Lincoln. Students' choice of which poem is more effective should be supported with examples from the poem. Students should note that both poets create literal images that successfully lead to the deeper meanings found in each poem. They should draw a conclusion as to why the poems have become so famous. Students might point to the inspiring, passionate tone of "O Captain! My Captain!" or the simplicity and accessibility of both works.
    Difficulty: *Challenging* **Objective:** *Essay*
14. Students should point out that the message of "The Road Not Taken" is that all choices lead one to wonder about the choice not made, while the message of "O Captain! My Captain!" is that the nation suffered a great loss with the death of President Lincoln. Students should choose one poem and cite words and phrases that struck them strongly.
    Difficulty: *Average* **Objective:** *Essay*

Oral Response

15. Oral responses should be clear, well organized, and well supported by appropriate examples from the selections.
Difficulty: *Average* **Objective:** *Oral Interpretation*

Selection Test A, p. 216

Critical Reading

1. **ANS:** A	**DIF:** Easy	**OBJ:** Comprehension
2. **ANS:** B	**DIF:** Easy	**OBJ:** Interpretation
3. **ANS:** C	**DIF:** Easy	**OBJ:** Comprehension
4. **ANS:** D	**DIF:** Easy	**OBJ:** Interpretation
5. **ANS:** B	**DIF:** Easy	**OBJ:** Literary Analysis
6. **ANS:** D	**DIF:** Easy	**OBJ:** Literary Analysis
7. **ANS:** C	**DIF:** Easy	**OBJ:** Literary Analysis
8. **ANS:** D	**DIF:** Easy	**OBJ:** Comprehension
9. **ANS:** C	**DIF:** Easy	**OBJ:** Comprehension
10. **ANS:** A	**DIF:** Easy	**OBJ:** Literary Analysis
11. **ANS:** B	**DIF:** Easy	**OBJ:** Interpretation
12. **ANS:** A	**DIF:** Easy	**OBJ:** Interpretation
13. **ANS:** A	**DIF:** Easy	**OBJ:** Literary Analysis

Vocabulary

14. **ANS:** A	**DIF:** Easy	**OBJ:** Vocabulary
15. **ANS:** D	**DIF:** Easy	**OBJ:** Vocabulary

Essay

16. Literal meaning is the actual, everyday meaning of words. The literal meaning in "The Road Not Taken" is a person reflecting on the road he took when the roads diverged in the woods. The person chose to take the road that was less traveled. The literal meaning in "O Captain! My Captain!" is the death of a ship's captain after he brought the ship safely back from a dangerous journey. The speaker of this poem is mourning the death of his beloved Captain.
Difficulty: *Easy*
Objective: *Essay*

17. The figurative meaning of an image relies on figures of speech and the symbolic nature of language. In "The Road Not Taken" the two roads symbolize making important decisions, the traveler is the person making the decision, and the road less traveled represents his choice. In "O Captain! My Captain!" the Captain is Abraham Lincoln, the ship is the United States, the voyage is the Civil War, and the port is peace after the war.
Difficulty: *Easy*
Objective: *Essay*

18. Students should point out that the message of "The Road Not Taken" is that all decisions lead one to wonder about the choice not made. The message of "O Captain! My Captain!" is that the nation suffered a great loss with the death of President Lincoln. Students should choose one poem and cite words and phrases that struck them strongly.
Difficulty: *Average*
Objective: *Essay*

Selection Test B, p. 219

Critical Reading

1. **ANS:** B	**DIF:** Average	**OBJ:** Literary Analysis
2. **ANS:** D	**DIF:** Average	**OBJ:** Literary Analysis
3. **ANS:** A	**DIF:** Average	**OBJ:** Comprehension
4. **ANS:** D	**DIF:** Average	**OBJ:** Interpretation
5. **ANS:** C	**DIF:** Average	**OBJ:** Interpretation
6. **ANS:** C	**DIF:** Average	**OBJ:** Literary Analysis
7. **ANS:** C	**DIF:** Average	**OBJ:** Comprehension
8. **ANS:** D	**DIF:** Average	**OBJ:** Literary Analysis
9. **ANS:** A	**DIF:** Average	**OBJ:** Literary Analysis
10. **ANS:** B	**DIF:** Challenging	**OBJ:** Interpretation
11. **ANS:** B	**DIF:** Challenging	**OBJ:** Comprehension
12. **ANS:** A	**DIF:** Average	**OBJ:** Interpretation
13. **ANS:** C	**DIF:** Challenging	**OBJ:** Literary Analysis

Vocabulary

14. **ANS:** B	**DIF:** Average	**OBJ:** Vocabulary
15. **ANS:** C	**DIF:** Average	**OBJ:** Vocabulary
16. **ANS:** A	**DIF:** Average	**OBJ:** Vocabulary

Essay

17. The speaker in "The Road Not Taken" tells of a decision that is represented by two roads dividing in the woods. Students may say that the speaker in "The Road Not Taken" may feel curiosity but not regret about the path he did not choose. The speaker in "O Captain! My Captain!" writes a eulogy comparing Lincoln to the captain of a ship. The speaker saw Lincoln as a great leader who preserved the union.
Difficulty: *Average*
Objective: *Essay*

18. Analogy is a type of figurative description that compares two or more things that are similar in some ways but otherwise unalike. In "The Road Not Taken," Frost creates an analogy between choosing between two roads in a wood and making important decisions in the course of one's life. The traveler is a person with a decision to make, the roads are the choices, and the less traveled path is the less conventional path that the speaker chose. In "O Captain! My Captain!" Whitman uses analogy to mourn the death of President Lincoln. Lincoln is the captain of a ship, the ship is America, the voyage is the Civil War, and the port is the peace that comes after war. Both authors create believable literal pictures that successfully lead to the deeper meanings found in each poem. Students should give reasons for why the poems are so famous, such as the inspiring tone of both poems, their accessible language, and universel themes.

Difficulty: *Average*

Objective: *Essay*

19. Students should point out that the message of "The Road Not Taken" is that all choices lead one to wonder about the choice not made, while the message of "O Captain! My Captain!" is that the nation suffered a great loss with the death of President Lincoln. Students should choose one poem and cite words and phrases that struck them strongly.

Difficulty: *Average*

Objective: *Essay*

Writing Workshop

Comparison-and-Contrast Essay: Integrating Grammar Skills, p. 223

A. In ancient Egypt, pharaohs built pyramids. The pyramids, tombs of the pharaohs, held immense treasures. Enormous and grand, the pyramids are exciting for archaeologists. During an expedition, archaeologists found a sealed door within a pyramid. Excited, they entered a room filled with ancient treasure.

B. Sample Answers

The mummy of King Tutankhamen, an Egyptian ruler, was in the tomb. Preserved by Egypt's dry climate, the body was in excellent condition. Wearing a mask of solid gold, King Tut looked magnificent! In King Tut's tomb, Archaeologists found many objects to study.

Vocabulary Workshop—I, p. 224

Sample Answers

1b	o	i	l	2s					
a				o					
b				u					
e				n					
	3d	e	a	d					
	e								
	e								
	4p	i	5e						
			y						
			e						
			l			7f	a	c	e
			i			e			
			6d	o	z	e	n		
						t			

Vocabulary Workshop—2, p. 225

Students should use the middle callouts to write or draw the literal image given by the idiom. The first one would be a line drawn; the second one would be a person biting a hand that is offering food. Then, they should explain each saying as follows:

1. When you draw a line, you set a limit of what is acceptable.
2. To bite the hand that feeds you means to do something mean to someone whom you depend on—never a good idea.

Benchmark Test 8, p. 227

MULTIPLE CHOICE

1. ANS: C
2. ANS: B
3. ANS: B
4. ANS: C
5. ANS: D
6. ANS: B
7. ANS: A
8. ANS: B
9. ANS: B
10. ANS: B
11. ANS: D
12. ANS: C
13. ANS: A
14. ANS: D
15. ANS: A
16. ANS: D
17. ANS: A
18. ANS: C
19. ANS: B
20. ANS: C
21. ANS: D
22. ANS: C
23. ANS: A
24. ANS: C
25. ANS: C
26. ANS: C
27. ANS: B
28. ANS: C
29. ANS: C
30. ANS: A

ESSAY

31. Students' first lines should clearly show whether the poem is to be a lyric or a narrative poem. The first line for a lyric poem should create an impression of the river by describing at least two details about it; the first line for a narrative poem should describe the setting and a main character.
32. Students should identify one example each of specific words and imagery from one of the poems in this test. They should clearly state whether they think the poet uses these effectively in the poem and should give supporting reasons for their opinions.
33. Students should list details that clearly address the writing prompt. They should include at least two similarities and two differences for each mode of travel. The similarities might include that both modes of travel can be exciting and that both afford interesting perspectives; differences might include that travel by car is slower and less convenient than travel by plane and that travel by car affords a better sense of the changing country than does travel by plane.

Vocabulary in Context 4, p. 232

MULTIPLE CHOICE

1. ANS: C
2. ANS: D
3. ANS: A
4. ANS: B
5. ANS: C
6. ANS: D
7. ANS: B
8. ANS: D
9. ANS: A
10. ANS: C
11. ANS: C
12. ANS: B
13. ANS: D
14. ANS: B
15. ANS: A
16. ANS: C
17. ANS: A
18. ANS: B
19. ANS: C
20. ANS: A